Climate change and global sustainability

Climate change and global
  sustainability

Sustainability Science Series

This book forms part of a series on sustainability science. The other titles in this series are:

Sustainability science: A multidisciplinary approach, edited by Hiroshi Komiyama, Kazuhiko Takeuchi, Hideaki Shiroyama and Takashi Mino, ISBN 978-82-808-1180-3

Establishing a resource-circulating society in Asia: Challenges and opportunities, edited by Tohru Morioka, Keisuke Hanaki and Yuichi Moriguchi, ISBN 978-92-808-1182-7

Designing our future: Local perspectives on bioproduction, ecosystems and humanity, edited by Mitsuru Osaki, Ademola K. Braimoh and Ken'ichi Nakagami, ISBN 978-92-808-1183-4

Achieving global sustainability: Policy recommendations, edited by Takamitsu Sawa, Susumu Iai and Seiji Ikkatai, ISBN 978-92-808-1184-1

Climate change and global sustainability: A holistic approach

Edited by Akimasa Sumi, Nobuo Mimura
and Toshihiko Masui

**United Nations
University Press**

TOKYO · NEW YORK · PARIS

2/12

United Nations University Press
United Nations University, 53-70, Jingumae 5-chome,
Shibuya-ku, Tokyo 150-8925, Japan
Tel: +81-3-5467-1212   Fax: +81-3-3406-7345
E-mail: sales@unu.edu   general enquiries: press@unu.edu
http://www.unu.edu

United Nations University Office at the United Nations, New York
2 United Nations Plaza, Room DC2-2062, New York, NY 10017, USA
Tel: +1-212-963-6387   Fax: +1-212-371-9454
E-mail: unuony@unu.edu

United Nations University Press is the publishing division of the United Nations University.

Cover design by Mori Design Inc., Tokyo

Printed in Hong Kong

ISBN 978-92-808-1181-0

Library of Congress Cataloging-in-Publication Data

Climate change and global sustainability : a holistic approach / edited by Akimasa Sumi, Nobuo Mimura and Toshihiko Masui.
    p.   cm. — (Sustainability science)
  Includes bibliographical references and index.
  ISBN 978-9280811810 (pbk.)
  1. Climatic changes—Environmental aspects. 2. Climatic changes—Social aspects. 3. Global warming—Social aspects. 4. Sustainable development. I. Sumi, Akimasa. II. Mimura, Nobuo, 1949– III. Masui, Toshihiko.
  QC903.C546   2011
  304.2'5—dc22   2010030724

Contents

Figures viii

Tables xii

Contributors xiv

Preface xvii

Abbreviations xix

1 Introduction: From climate change to global sustainability 1
   Akimasa Sumi and Nobuo Mimura

2 Structuring knowledge of climate change 10
   Ai Hiramatsu

3 Climate change risk communication 30
   Seita Emori

4 Climate change impacts and responses 45

   4-1 Overview of climate change impacts 46
      Nobuo Mimura

4-2 Climate change impacts in Japan 58
     Yasuaki Hijioka

4-3 Water resource problems due to climate change 72
     So Kazama

4-4 Climate change and world food production in the twenty-
     first century 83
     Hiroyuki Kawashima

4-5 Effects of climate change and global warming on marine
     ecosystems and fishery resources 95
     Yasuhiro Yamanaka and Masahiko Fujii

4-6 Vulnerability of coastal zones in the twenty-first century ... 111
     Hisamichi Nobuoka and Satoshi Murakami

4-7 Adaptation and mitigation strategies in response to climate
     change 133
     Makoto Tamura and Nobuo Mimura

5 Designing climate policy 151

5-1 New international framework beyond the Kyoto Protocol .. 152
     Hiroshi Hamasaki and Tatsuyoshi Saijo

5-2 Emission reductions policy mix: Industrial sector
     greenhouse gas emission reductions 164
     Seiji Ikkatai

5-3 Shell energy scenarios to 2050. 178
     Shell International BV

5-4 Climate policy and international development cooperation . 193
     Shunji Matsuoka

6 Transformation of social systems and lifestyles 207

6-1 Induction to a low-carbon city – Innovation of urban form
     and human activities 208
     Keisuke Hanaki

6-2 The process of political decision-making on climate change
      and journalism in Japan   217
      Tokuhisa Yoshida

6-3 The conceptions of "environment" and eco-philosophy   241
      Hideo Kawamoto

**7 Integration of a low-carbon society with a resource-circulating
   and nature-harmonious society**   258
      Toshihiko Masui

8 Future vision towards a sustainable society   278
      Akimasa Sumi

Index   284

Figures

1.1   Relationship between three systems   2

1.2   Integration of three societies.   3

2.1   Map of the seven phases with keywords   14

2.2   The mapping of scientific findings listed in IPCC AR4....   18

2.3   Number of scientific findings listed in IPCC AR4 for each phase..   19

2.4   Certainty rankings for answers to the key questions in each phase   20

2.5   Number and budget of research on climate change in Grants-in-Aid for Scientific Research (bottom-up research).......................................   24

2.6   Number and budget of research on climate change in research programmes of Japanese government (top-down research), 2006....................................   25

2.7   Budget of US governmental climate research, 2006   26

4.1.1   Illustrative map of combined mean change of annual runoff (%) between the present (1981–2000) and 2081–2100 for the SRES A1B emissions scenario   48

4.1.2   Examples of impacts associated with projected global average surface warming   53

4.2.1   Structure of AIM/Impact[Policy]   60

4.2.2   Impacts of climate change through the twenty-first century in Japan by sector...........................   66

4.3.1	Distribution of increase in potential damage cost from rainfall with 50- to 100-year return periods.	74
4.3.2	Landslide hazard probability maps for extreme precipitation in various return periods	77
4.3.3	Percentage difference in SWE between light and heavy snow years to maximum SWE on 15 March	78
4.3.4	SS load change ratio for 10- and 50-year return periods of drought.	81
4.3.5	BOD change ratio for 10- and 50-year return periods of drought.	81
4.4.1	Population growth, ratio to 1950.	85
4.4.2	Cereal production.	85
4.4.3	Cereal yield	86
4.4.4	Relationship between nitrogen fertilizer input and cereal yield	87
4.4.5	Meat production	87
4.4.6	Cereal feed.	88
4.4.7	Soybean production	89
4.4.8	Annual cereal supply per person	90
4.4.9	Annual meat supply per person	90
4.5.1	Components of natural marine environments	96
4.5.2	Time series of (a) Aleutian Low Pressure Index (ALPI); and (b) sardine and anchovy catches in seas close to Japan.	97
4.5.3	Schematic view of NEMURO.FISH.	99
4.5.4	Inter-annual variation of primary production and biomass, 1948–2002.	101
4.5.5	Time of maximum chlorophyll concentration in the spring bloom in Julian days.	103
4.5.6	Modelled histogram of weight of four-months-old Japanese sardines and averaged temperature in present and global warming simulations in the current main spawning region	104
4.5.7	Anticipated effects of global warming on corals in seas close to Japan.	106
4.6.1a	Storm surge deviation	115
4.6.1b	Potential flooded area	116
4.6.2	Increase in submergence area, 2000–2100	117
4.6.3	Increase in flooded area, 2000–2100.	118
4.6.4	Increase in submergence population, 2000–2100	118
4.6.5	Increase in flooded population, 2000–2100	119
4.6.6	Relative increase in submergence population in each region	120

4.6.7   Relative increase in flooded population in each region ...   121
4.6.8   Relative increase in flooded population and GDP per
         capita, 2000–2100.   123
4.6.9   Observation locations of land subsidence in the Chao
         Phraya delta.   127
4.6.10   Land subsidence map (1996–2003).   128
4.6.11   Comparisons of observed settlements with predicted
         results.   129
4.6.12   Future land subsidence map (2001–2100)   130
4.6.13   Inundation area caused by sea-level rise and land
         subsidence   131
4.7.1   Response strategies to climate change.   134
4.7.2   Stabilization scenario categories.   136
4.7.3   Adaptation planning.   142
4.7.4   Vulnerability and adaptive capacity   145
4.7.5   Adaptation and mitigation towards sustainability   147
5.1.1   Standard GTAP-E production structure   153
5.1.2   Production structure for electricity sector.   154
5.1.3   Global emissions.   156
5.1.4   Global emissions.   156
5.1.5   Global emission targets and paths, 2002–2020 (million
         tonnes of carbon)   158
5.1.6   Macroeconomic impact (GDP).   159
5.1.7   India's actual emissions and emission rights.   160
5.2.1   Trend of CO_2 emissions by sectors.   165
5.2.2   Nature of GHG reduction measures undertaken in fiscal
         year 2005   167
5.2.3   Scatter diagram showing GHG reduction cost.   171
5.3.1   Final energy consumption by region in Scramble   182
5.3.2   Primary energy by source in Scramble   183
5.3.3   Final energy consumption of biomass in Scramble   184
5.3.4   Final energy consumption of electricity in Blueprints.   188
5.3.5   Final energy consumption by sector in Blueprints.   190
5.3.6   Primary energy by source in Blueprints   191
6.1.1   Per capita CO_2 emissions in large cities in the UK, Japan
         and China.   210
6.1.2   Strategies for low-carbon cities of various sizes.   212
6.1.3   Per capita CO_2 emissions versus per capita GDP for
         various countries in 2006.   213
6.1.4   Trends of per capita CO_2 emissions in relation to per
         capita GDP for some developed countries   214
6.1.5   Energy consumption and standard of living in 34 large
         Chinese cities in 2006.   215

6.2.1   Three-way conflict in climate change policy and recent
         policy implementation under the leadership of the prime
         minister.   219
6.2.2   Chronological changes in GHG emissions, 1990–2007.   228
6.2.3   Increase or decrease in CO_2 emissions by sector and CO_2
         emission factors of electricity generation, 1990–2007   229
6.2.4   Results of public comments and the opinion poll on the
         medium-term goal.   234
6.3.1   The process of eutrophication with historicity in a lake . . .   251
6.3.2   The hypercycle.   254
6.3.3   Bioscleave house, 2008.   256
7.1   2050 changes in indicators from 2000 in the "Very Long-
         term Vision"   260
7.2   List of countermeasures for achieving a 70 per cent
         reduction in CO_2 emissions.   268
7.3   Factors for assessing the LCS, RCS and NHS.   270
7.4   The economic activity and commodity flow in the model. .   272
7.5   Changes in land productivity in regions in the model.   273
7.6 CO_2 emissions   274
7.7   Steel production   275
7.8   Paper production   275
7.9   Changes in forest area   276
8.1   Estimated economic mitigation potential by sector in 2030
         from bottom-up studies, compared to the respective
         baselines assumed in sector assessments   280

Tables

2.1	Phase classification	13
2.2	Key questions for each phase.............................	15
2.3	Keywords to extract research on climate change	23
2.4	Research on climate change in Grants-in-Aid for Scientific Research	23
4.2.1	Sectoral impact assessment using an integrated assessment model	63
4.3.1	Annual expected damage costs and return periods	74
4.3.2	Comparison of snow-water resources, snow-water resource amount per paddy-field area and its ratio to water demand during the irrigation period in three typical basins	79
4.6.1	Countries with the 10 largest increases in flooded population	122
4.6.2	Countries with the 10 largest increases in the relative flooded population	122
4.7.1	Adaptation in natural and human systems..................	137
4.7.2	Adaptation by sectors....................................	138
4.7.3	Characteristics of mitigation and adaptation................	143
4.7.4	Examples of possible synergies between mitigation and adaptation..	144
5.1.1	Categorizations of regions and sectors	155
5.1.2	International transfers under GETS (US$ million)...........	159
5.1.3	Comparison between Kyoto and GETS (%)	160
5.1.4	International transfers under GETS (US$ million)...........	161

5.1.5   GDP change (%)   161

5.2.1   Correlation between reduction activities and reduction
          motives   169

6.2.1   Six alternatives of the medium-term goal proposed by the
          government...   224

6.2.2   Comparison of editorials on setting the medium-term goal in
          four leading newspapers   236

7.1   Goals of MDGs and indicators for Goal 7   259

7.2   Ecosystem services examined by the Millennium Ecosystem
          Assessment...   263

7.3   Future environmental changes identified in the OECD
          outlook   266

7.4   Scenarios in Japan for 2050 under the LCS project..........   267

7.5   Regional definitions for the global model   271

7.6   Sectoral classifications for the global model   271

Contributors

Seita Emori is chief of the Climate Risk Assessment Research Section at the Center for Global Environmental Research of the National Institute for Environmental Studies. He also serves as an associate professor at the Atmosphere Ocean Research Institute at The University of Tokyo.

Masahiko Fujii is an associate professor at the Graduate School of Environmental Science, Hokkaido University. He engages in education and study for sustainable development, especially focusing on achieving a low-carbon society in Hokkaido and balancing the marine ecosystem and human activities, such as fisheries and marine tourism, in coastal regions including coral reefs in Asia.

Hiroshi Hamasaki is a research fellow in the Energy and Environmental Policy Group, Economic Research Center, Fujitsu Research Institute, Tokyo, Japan, and a visiting fellow at the Center for International Public Policy Studies in Tokyo.

Keisuke Hanaki is a professor in the Department of Urban Engineering as well as an adjunct professor of the Integrated Research System for Sustainability Science at The University of Tokyo. After obtaining his PhD in 1980 from The University of Tokyo, he worked for Tohoku University and the Asian Institute of Technology. His research area includes the management of greenhouse gas emissions from urban areas and urban material flow analysis.

Yasuaki Hijioka is a senior researcher in the Integrated Assessment Section of the Social and Environmental Systems Division at the National Institute for Environmental Studies.

xiv

Ai Hiramatsu is a project assistant professor in the Transdisciplinary Initiative for Global Sustainability, The University of Tokyo. She received her PhD in environmental engineering from the Department of Urban Engineering at The University of Tokyo. Her research interests are climate change, waste management and sustainability science. She has been engaged in projects on solid waste management in Bangkok and its vicinity.

Seiji Ikkatai is a professor in the Research Center for Advanced Policy Studies in the Institute of Economic Research at Kyoto University. Before that he worked for the Ministry of the Environment, the Ministry of Foreign Affairs and the Ministry of Finance, after graduating from The University of Tokyo in 1975.

Hideo Kawamoto is a professor of philosophy at Toyo University (Tokyo). His main research fields are system theory, philosophy and psychiatry.

Hiroyuki Kawashima is an associate professor in the PhD Graduate School of Agricultural and Life Sciences, The University of Tokyo.

So Kazama is a professor in the Department of Civil and Environmental Engineering, Tohoku University. His specialities are hydrology and water resources engineering.

Toshihiko Masui is chief of the Integrated Assessment Section, Social and Environmental Systems Division at the National Institute for Environmental Studies (NIES). He also works as an associate professor at the Department of Social Engineering, Tokyo Institute of Technology. He obtained his PhD in engineering from Osaka University in 1997, and his research interests include global warming, model analysis and environmental systems.

Shunji Matsuoka is a professor in the Graduate School of Asia-Pacific Studies, Waseda University. He earned his PhD in environmental management from the Graduate School of Biosphere Sciences, Hiroshima University. His specialities are environmental economics, environmental policy, international development and cooperation, international environmental cooperation and policy evaluation.

Nobuo Mimura is professor and director of the Institute for Global Change Adaptation Science, and assistant vice president at Ibaraki University. Through studies on the impacts of climate change and sea-level rise in Japan, China, Thailand, Vietnam and small island countries in the South Pacific, he contributed to policy development on climate change. He has served the IPCC as lead author and coordinating lead author.

Satoshi Murakami is associate professor of urban and civil engineering, Faculty of Engineering, Ibaraki University, Japan.

Hisamichi Nobuoka is associate professor of urban and civil engineering at Ibaraki University, Japan. He has surveyed the severe coastal disaster sites of the Indonesian tsunami in 2004, Hurricane Katrina in 2005, Cyclone Sidr in 2007 and so on.

Tatsuyoshi Saijo is a professor at the Institute of Social and Economic Research, Osaka University, and researcher at the California Social Science Experimental Laboratory, University of California, Los Angeles. He is also coordinator of Climate Design. Before that he taught at the University of Tsukuba, University of California at Santa Barbara and Ohio State University.

Shell International BV is a global group of energy and petrochemicals companies. With around 101,000 employees in more than 90 countries and territories, Shell helps to meet the world's growing demand for energy in economically, environmentally and socially responsible ways.

Akimasa Sumi is professor and executive director of the Transdisciplinary Initiative for Global Sustainability, Integrated Research System for Sustainability Science, at The University of Tokyo. Before that, he was the director of the Center for Climate System Research, The University of Tokyo, and has been conducting research on climate change and climate modeling.

Makoto Tamura is an associate professor at the Institute for Global Change Adaptation Science, Ibaraki University. He received his MA and PhD degrees from the Graduate School of Arts and Sciences, The University of Tokyo. His research interests are impact assessment and countermeasures for climate change, and the interrelationship between economic activity and the environment.

Yasuhiro Yamanaka is an associate professor at the Graduate School of Environmental Science, Hokkaido University. He developed an integrated physical-biogeochemical-ecosystem model to understand the dynamics of climate systems and ecosystems (including fish) from past to future, and is also coordinating public communications as a leader of Global COE Programs.

Tokuhisa Yoshida is a professor at the Graduate School of Environment and Energy Engineering, Waseda University, Japan.

Preface

This book forms part of a series on sustainability science. Sustainability science is a newly emerging academic field that seeks to understand the dynamic linkages between global, social and human systems, and to provide a holistic perspective on the concerns and issues between and within these systems. It is a problem-oriented discipline encompassing visions and methods for examining and repairing these systems and linkages.

The Integrated Research System for Sustainability Science (IR3S) was launched in 2005 at The University of Tokyo with the aim of serving as a global research and educational platform for sustainability scientists. In 2006 IR3S expanded, becoming a university network including Kyoto, Osaka, Hokkaido and Ibaraki Universities. In addition, Tohoku University, the National Institute for Environmental Studies, Toyo, Chiba, Waseda and Ritsumeikan Universities and the United Nations University joined as associate members. Since the establishment of the IR3S network, member universities have launched sustainability science programmes at their institutions and collaborated on related research projects. The results of these projects have been published in prestigious research journals and presented at various academic, governmental and social meetings.

The *Sustainability Science* book series is based on the results of IR3S members' joint research activities over the past five years. The series provides directions on sustainability for society. These books are expected to be of interest to graduate students, educators teaching sustainability-related courses and those keen to start up similar programmes, active

members of NGOs, government officials and people working in industry. We hope this series of books will provide readers with useful information on sustainability issues and present them with novel ways of thinking and solutions to the complex problems faced by people throughout the world.

Integrated Research System for Sustainability Science

Abbreviations

AGCM	Atmospheric General Circular Model
ALPI	Aleutian Low Pressure Index
AR4	IPCC Fourth Assessment Report
BaU	business as usual
BOD	biochemical oxygen demand
CAFE	Corporate Average Fuel Economy (USA)
CBDR	common but differentiated responsibilities
CCCC	Climate Change and Carrying Capacity Program
CCMF	climate change mitigation facility
CCS	carbon capture and storage
CCSP	Climate Change Science Program (USA)
CDM	clean development mechanism
CFC	chlorofluorocarbon
CGE	computable general equilibrium
CO_2	carbon dioxide
COP	Conference of Parties
CRESH	constant-ratio-of-elasticity-of-substitution-homothetic
CVM	contingent valuation method
DHM	degree heating month
DOE	Department of Energy (USA)
FAO	UN Food and Agriculture Organization
GASR	Grants-in-Aid for Scientific Research (Japan)
GCM	general circulation model
GDP	gross domestic product
GEF	Global Environment Facility
GETS	global emissions trading scheme

GHG	greenhouse gas
GIS	geographic information system
GLOBEC	Global Ocean Ecosystem Dynamics
GMO	genetically modified organism
GTAP	Global Trade Analysis Project
IEA	International Energy Agency
IPCC	Intergovernmental Panel on Climate Change
LCS	low-carbon society
L-Q	load-quality
MDG	Millennium Development Goal
MEF	major economic forum
METI	Ministry of Economy, Trade and Industry (Japan)
MIROC	Model for Interdisciplinary Research on Climate
MLIT	Ministry of Land, Infrastructure, Transport and Tourism (Japan)
MOE	Ministry of the Environment (Japan)
MOP	Meeting of Parties
MW	megawatt
NASA	National Aeronautics and Space Administration (USA)
NEMURO	North Pacific Ecosystem Model Used for Regional Oceanography
NGO	non-governmental organization
NHS	nature-harmonious society
NOAA	National Oceanic and Atmospheric Administration (USA)
NSF	National Science Foundation (USA)
OECD	Organisation for Economic Co-operation and Development
OPEC	Organization of the Petroleum Exporting Countries
PDO	Pacific Decadal Oscillation
PICES	North Pacific Marine Science Organization
ppm	parts per million
PPP	purchasing power parity
PRSP	poverty reduction strategy paper
RCS	resource-circulating society
RPM	Research Programs by Ministries (Japan)
SLR	sea-level rise
SPM	summary for policy-makers
SRES	IPCC Special Report on Emissions Scenarios
SS	suspended solids
SWE	snow-water equivalent
UNFCCC	UN Framework Convention on Climate Change
USGCRP	US Global Change Research Program
USGS	US Geological Survey
VSL	value of a statistical life
WG	working group
ZL	zooplankton

1

Introduction: From climate change to global sustainability

Akimasa Sumi and Nobuo Mimura

1-1 Global warming: What kind of problem is it?

In 2007 the Intergovernmental Panel on Climate Change (IPCC) Working Group I AR4 (Fourth Assessment Report) clearly declared that the contribution of human activities to recent global warming is certainly more than 90 per cent (IPCC, 2007). This view is widely accepted by global scientific and political communities, which means that we have entered into an important stage of the global warming issue: the age of action. However, various questions will arise on entering this decision-making stage, and there may be increased levels of scepticism. It is therefore necessary to reconsider what the global warming issue means for our future and evaluate the available courses of action.

1-1-1 Perturbation to the radiative energy balance

The Earth's climate system is determined by radiative energy and material balances. With regard to energy, Earth's climate can be considered an open system; however, it is a closed system as far as most materials are concerned. Energy is measured by temperature, while a typical example of material is water (precipitation), which is a reason why traditional climate classification is based on temperature and precipitation. Temperature in the Earth's climate system is determined by the budget between incoming and outgoing energy. If the former is larger, the temperature will increase, although its distribution in the system is determined by

Climate change and global sustainability: A holistic approach, Sumi, Mimura and Masui (eds), United Nations University Press, 2011, ISBN 978-92-808-1181-0

processes within the system. In reality, the Earth's climate consists of many interacting subsystems that influence the distribution of energy. Precipitation also results from interactions between many processes in the climate system. At the same time, it should be noted that the Earth's climate is dynamic rather than static. The Earth has experienced many dramatic climate changes, including several ice ages.

Following the Industrial Revolution, human beings have become a component in the Earth's climate system. Through modification of the environment, we possess the power to reduce environmental constraints around us. By changing land cover and land use, we have increased our food supply. Furthermore, car use has amplified our ability to move. Emission of global warming gases associated with these human activities has resulted in changes in the minor constituent concentration in the atmosphere. This disturbs the Earth's radiative energy balance, resulting in a warmer climate.

However, perturbation induced by humankind does not only affect the radiational energy balance, but happens in many other fields as well. Thus it is concluded that the environment around us consists of interaction between various subsystems. To summarize these interactions, Komiyama and Takeuchi (2006) introduce three subsystems – the global (natural), social and human – and the various problems around us (the Earth's environmental issues) that result from the imbalance between these subsystems (see Figure 1.1). Of course it is true that there are many other

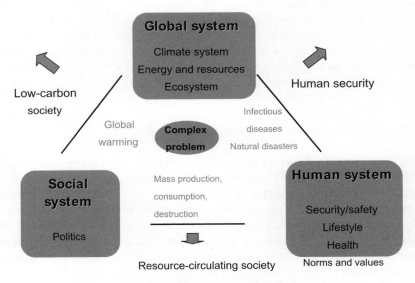

Figure 1.1 Relationship between three systems

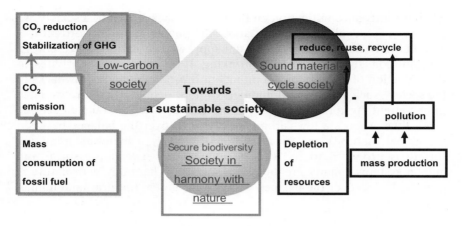

Figure 1.2 Integration of three societies

subsystems, but these three represent the three dimensions in a frame of thinking towards a sustainable society when each issue is considered.

The three societies, i.e. the low-carbon society, the resource-circulating society and the nature-friendly society, should be realized simultaneously, and an integration of each is proposed by Masui in Chapter 7. But even when action is taken to attain a low-carbon society, attention must be paid to these three interactions (Figure 1.2).

For example, the global warming issue is caused by the imbalance between the global (natural) and social systems. Greenhouse gases emitted by human activity have changed the concentration of the atmosphere, which perturbs the radiation balance in the Earth's climate system. Here it should be noted that the present climate is not the most ideal climate. The environment has evolved by adapting to climatic conditions. In other words, our society, natural resources and ecosystem services are under these climatic conditions – thus it is easy to understand that changes in the present climatic conditions will impact on our society. One result of the imbalance between the social and human systems is material circulation. Through production and consumption, we have produced many artefacts that have changed natural resources into waste. This waste production cannot continue indefinitely without consequences, and therefore a circulation of materials (recycling) is necessary.

Examples of the imbalance between the global (natural) and human systems are natural hazards such as earthquakes, tsunamis, typhoons and hurricanes. In addition to these hazards, we have to pay attention to issues in social and human systems, such as loneliness and the pursuit of a life worth living. Traditionally, issues relating to the human heart have been discussed separately from energy and material issues. However,

when we introduce mitigation and adaptation measures into a society, we have to make a value judgement about the people. In other words, if it is acceptable to make many people unhappy, we can easily reduce energy consumption. It is certain that shrinking of an economy contributes to the reduction of energy consumption; but it produces many drawbacks in the society, such as increased numbers of poor people. Therefore we have to pay attention to the well-being of individuals when we take an action.

We thus propose a low-carbon society to recover the balance between the global (natural) and social systems. Similarly, a material-circulating society is proposed to recover the imbalance between the social and human systems. Finally, creation of a society in harmony with nature is proposed to recover the balance between the global (natural) and human systems.

1-1-2 Equity between generations

Besides the natural phenomena outlined above, global warming exerts a strong influence on society, with one important issue being the resulting inequity between generations. The problems brought about by global warming are not currently urgent but will emerge in the future, suggesting that forecasting and backcasting are critical. Climate change is evaluated through climate model simulations. It should be noted that climate models depend on the scientific knowledge of the time, but uncertainties in future climate predictions are inevitable. Our climate system has a chaotic nature, and deterministic prediction for the future is, in principle, impossible. There are also interactions between human activities and the natural system which are difficult to quantify. For example, future energy use is strongly dependent on future socio-economic situations and technology development, which to some extent depend on taste and preference; people do not always base their decisions on economic factors. Human behaviour and social development involve many unpredictable aspects. However, we should not be caught in a trap of pessimism. The future is unpredictable, but there are areas in which consequences can be calculated. For example, it is certain that increased levels of carbon dioxide (CO_2) result in a warmer climate. Therefore, we have to take action based on reliable predictions and impact assessments.

1-1-3 Science and politics

It is often said that global warming is the first problem where science and policy sit at the same table. This does not mean that science has been out of politics; rather, in the past politics was the master and science the follower. This is best illustrated by the Manhattan Project in which the

world's first atomic bomb was developed during the Second World War. All scientific knowledge was mobilized to achieve a political goal. At present it is vital for politics to listen to the voice of science, but there remains a significant gap between the two fields. Politicians need all necessary knowledge, but policy usually requests more than science can provide. This provokes questions about the suitability of science for political decision-making, but it is clear that science is crucial. The present issues could not be addressed without scientific and technological knowledge. However, convincing politicians of scientific suggestions remains difficult because science relates the conclusions that follow logically from data and established theories. In contrast, politics has to pay attention to different aspects of human beings, such as desire, lust and economic values. The value system and mental situation of each individual must also be considered.

1-1-4 Understanding is critical, but action is also necessary

When issues emerge, scientists believe that we should attempt to gain a full understanding of each aspect and how it might interact with what is already known. While this is true, there are many problems that require action before complete understanding can be gained. Global warming is just such a problem.

When we take action before complete understanding, analysis of the criteria for action should be undertaken. It is easy to say that the present generation should take action on behalf of future generations, but full consideration of why and how we should act is imperative.

1-1-5 Freedom versus limitation

"Freedom, equality and fraternity" is a slogan from the French Revolution. However, these values cannot always be completely achieved simultaneously. Mankind is surrounded by many difficulties, and the conquest of nature has always been considered a victory. We now realize that human activity exerts a strong influence over our environment. Therefore, to adapt to the problems caused by global warming, we will have to introduce limits to our freedom. An example of this can be seen in the arms-reduction negotiations. To limit nuclear weapons, each country has to limit its freedom to increase its military power. To combat the problems caused by global warming, each society has to limit the freedom of maximizing its own economic interest.

People may insist upon their rights to pursue their own interests, but in some cases these may have to be forfeited. In brief, global warming creates a constraint to global politics and economics. The actions induced by

these issues need international diplomacy. The Nuclear Non-Proliferation Treaty has been created for reduction of nuclear weapons. For global warming, long-lasting international diplomacy is being procured through the activities of the UNFCCC Conference of Parties (COP)/Meeting of Parties (MOP), which has resulted in negotiation about future action following the Kyoto Protocol.

1-2 Now is the time for action

Social concern about global warming has now shifted from the scientific question of whether or not human activity contributes to climate change to real action such as adaptation and mitigation. However, on entering the stage of concrete action, we have to consider various aspects of society. In particular, there are distinct differences in position between developed and developing countries. We have to admit that developing countries have a right to develop, and the concept of "co-benefit" must be presented so that policies will be acceptable to nations at different levels of development. In the case of Japan, it is needless to say that the society is confronted with many issues, including resource scarcity, an aged society, poverty, public health and so on. It should be noted that all these issues require a solution. Each stakeholder has its own value criteria, and all are eager to have resources allocated to their own topic. Concrete action entails allocation of financial and human resources and numerous other assets, suggesting that time-consuming processes are required to reach a consensus on resource allocation among stakeholders. To reach this consensus, it is necessary for us to build a framework to tackle these problems.

1-3 Reliable tools are necessary for agreement

All action taken should be based on reliable estimates of future impacts and the probable effectiveness of any action. A reliable tool is needed for this purpose, because stakeholders naturally prioritize their own interests and profits. An objective framework is therefore necessary before a consensus can be reached, and one candidate for this is a reliable climate model combined with an integrated assessment model, as discussed by Sumi (2007). For example, recent advances in the technology of high-end super-computers are remarkable, and it is rumoured that the Exa (10^{13}) FLOPS super-computer will be available in the mid-2010s. This high-end computer will open a new era for climate modelling and increase the reliability of integrated assessment models. Many processes that are now

treated in a parameterization scheme in modelling will be given more advanced treatments. For example, clouds will be treated explicitly, which will reduce the uncertainty of climate sensitivity. Horizontal resolution will be increased, and there will be impacts at the local scale. In impact assessment modelling, various new factors including human behaviour and economics based on the tastes and actions of individual people will be added to the existing model. More reliable assessment may be possible.

Besides the advances in super-computing capability, significant advances in information network technology are expected. The success of the internet has increased the ease with which knowledge is accessed, which means that people all over the world can now easily access data describing the present status of our climate and environment. These IT contributions shape public opinion about the environment. Here, the role of the view from space via satellite remote sensing is particularly emphasized because this provides mankind with a platform to view the Earth from outside. It is also important that this view is transported to the public through the media. For example, deforestation in the Amazon, the hole in the ozone layer and the recent decrease of sea ice in the Arctic Ocean are all clearly demonstrated by satellite pictures and have thus become well known.

1-4 Structuring of knowledge

There are numerous issues resulting from global warming, and a huge volume of knowledge is produced every day. This knowledge must be structured properly to make maximum use of it. In the IPCC process, policy-relevant, rather than policy perspective, results are pursued, which is one example of an effort to structure knowledge. In this process, available peer-reviewed papers are collected and arranged by selected lead authors. Through the production process, manuscripts are reviewed by peers and governments. Finally, a summary for policy-makers is made line by line by government officials.

Another method of structuring knowledge is mapping the issues. For example, Hiramatsu, Mimura and Sumi (2008) have proposed a type of global warming mapping that provides a framework to arrange the existing knowledge.

These topics will be described in the following chapters.

1-5 Structure of this book

In this Introduction it is emphasized that global warming is a complicated issue where many factors interact with each other. In order to understand

the totality of the issue and find the weak points in our knowledge to overcome the issue, the structuring of knowledge is stressed. Our efforts to structure the knowledge of the global warming issue are described in Chapter 2, where a mapping of the global warming issue is proposed. It has a cycle with seven phases.

- Greenhouse gases are emitted due to anthropogenic socio-economic activities.
- Greenhouse gas concentration is determined through the natural carbon cycle.
- Climate change due to the change of the greenhouse gas concentration is estimated.
- Impacts due to climate change are estimated.
- Adaptation should be considered for the impacts.
- Mitigation should be considered for the impacts.
- These adaptation and mitigation options contribute to establishment of a new social structure.

This map describes a dynamic where the present structure of our society will be changed to a new structure of future society through mitigation and adaptation options relating to the global warming issue. Through this study, it is pointed out that research on adaptation and restructuring of society is weak and there are few definite images of the future society.

When we discuss the future, it should be given a time-horizon. Usually, this issue is handled in future simulation in models. There are many different types of models, from simple to complex, and it is very important to consider whether the model deserves future simulation. Regardless of the kind of model used, a degree of uncertainty is inevitable. When we consider an action for the future, we have to make a decision on criteria. Cost-benefit analysis is often used as a criterion. Then we have to estimate costs due to climate change resulting from global warming, where there are two different processes: estimate of the climate change and estimate of cost of impacts due to the climate change. Usually, climate change is estimated using a numerical simulation in a climate model. Here, accuracy of the estimate of climate change becomes important. As a final decision is made by society, it is very important to know the reliability of the estimate of climate change due to global warming. In other words, one must let society know the risk of global warming. With incomplete or imperfect information, exactly how to communicate this is very important. This aspect is discussed in Chapter 3.

As is described before, impacts of climate change due to global warming are a very difficult research theme, because there are many different topics and stakeholders. It often happens that a certain impact which is negative to one stakeholder is positive to another stakeholder. Then there is the question of the practical way to present estimates of impacts

to society. Various kind of impacts are discussed in different horizontal scales – Japanese, regional and global – in Chapter 4. Finally, optimization of adaptation and mitigation strategy is discussed.

In Chapter 5 we discuss several policy-related issues. When we take action, policy issues are inevitable. Various policy options within domestic legislation and an international framework are necessary. However, policy options alone are not sufficient. We need collaborations of many stakeholders, and among these the behaviour of private companies is important. As an example, the Shell energy scenario is presented to show how this private company is thinking about the future. Finally, the relationship between developed and developing countries becomes important. In other words, international development aid policy should be consistent with the climate change adaptation/mitigation policy.

Following policy options, we should take concrete action to transform our society. This issue is discussed in Chapter 6. It covers diverse topics, from the social system and life cycle to the role of journalism and eco-philosophy. This is inevitable when we think about reorganizing our society, because society consists of many levels with different characterizations.

Our future vision is presented in Chapter 7. It is often said that a low-carbon society should be established to overcome the global warming issue. However, we think this is not enough. As there are so many issues around us, it is not enough to pay attention to just one aspect. Given that the present situation resulted from an imbalance between the three societies – the global (natural), social and human systems – in order to realize a sustainable society we have to restore balances between these societies. You may ask why? One tentative approach is presented in Chapter 7, as the first step in this issue. This can be considered to be one of our conclusions regarding the future society, although its formulation is simple and more work will be necessary. In Chapter 8, a summary is given.

REFERENCES

Hiramatsu, A., N. Mimura and A. Sumi (2008) "A Mapping of Global Warming Research Based on IPCC AR4", *Sustainability Science* 3(2), pp. 201–213.

IPCC (2007) *Climate Change 2007: The Physical Science Basis*. Cambridge: Cambridge University Press, available at www.ipcc.ch.

Komiyama, H. and K. Takeuchi (2006) "Sustainable Science: Building a New Discipline", *Sustainability Science* 1(1), pp. 1–6.

Sumi, A. (2007) "On Several Issues Regarding Efforts toward a Sustainable Society", *Sustainability Science* 2(1), pp. 67–76.

2

Structuring knowledge of climate change

Ai Hiramatsu

2-1 Introduction

Sustainability science has emerged as a new academic field that seeks to link and integrate conventional disciplines to solve today's complicated problems in international societies and achieve a sustainable society. It is a problem-oriented discipline method and is expected to articulate visions for future society.

Climate change has become one of the most prioritized issues in both national and international arenas today. Climate change issues cover a broad range of disciplines and are a typical example of the advantages of sustainability science. So far, conventional disciplines and individual research have addressed these problems from specific viewpoints in a specific field. However, climate change cannot be solved by a single measure. It has been difficult to understand the whole picture of climate issues, and moreover it is very difficult to know what is happening in each region, what research and measures are implemented in each field and how they are related to each other.

To organize the enormous volume of knowledge, just listing keywords and showing causal connections or relationships among them is cumbersome and can result in confusion.

To get a comprehensive view of climate-related issues and design sustainable countermeasures for addressing climate change, a new method and approach are required, which are expected to be developed in sustainability science. The approach should unify the various aspects of

*Climate change and global sustainability: A holistic approach, Sumi, Mimura and Masui (eds),
United Nations University Press, 2011, ISBN 978-92-808-1181-0*

climate change, including natural and social sciences such as climate prediction, impact assessment, mitigation and adaptation technologies, economics, policies and social issues. The problem must be tackled from a wide range of viewpoints from different academic fields.

Since the early twentieth century, brainstorming has been a popular technique designed to let people generate creative ideas among large amounts of knowledge as a first step in the solution of a problem. However, brainstorming itself does not always lead to a solution, although it engages people to cooperate and improve teamwork. Around the end of the twentieth century new methods were developed which lead people to organize and reconstruct broad knowledge to understand the objects better. The KJ method, also known as the affinity diagram, was proposed by Kawakita (1991) to make brainstorming more effective. Its process consists of three steps: first, record data and ideas on labels in a brainstorming meeting; then group those labels and make teams with identified titles or concepts; thirdly, make a chart with these teams adding arrows to indicate their relationship, then discuss and conduct analysis. The KJ method has been widely used in Japanese business and administrative circles (Scupin, 1997). Mind maps, concept maps and other models have also been developed to activate people's brains and organize complex ideas. In mind maps, people draw their ideas and knowledge freely from a central idea. They are utilized in business, education and self-analysis (Buzan and Buzan, 1996). Concept maps focus more on the connection of concepts and try to capture knowledge more systematically and hierarchically (Novak and Cañas, 2008).

Here, as a tool of structuring knowledge, a mapping approach will be introduced. As mentioned above, mapping approaches are sometimes used to gain a systematic understanding of complex problems involving many diverse elements. There are some mapping approaches on sustainability. Kajikawa et al. (2007) drew a research overview map by analysing the citation network of papers published in academic journals which are related to sustainability science and detecting their research domains. Choucri et al. (2007) proposed a conceptual framework to guide the understanding of the elements of sustainability. They use a three-dimensional (3D) pillar map with an integrated frame system comprising slice (domain of core concept), ring (dimension of problem and solution) and cell (granular manifestation).

Climate issues can also be structured and visualized by mapping, so that people comprehensively recognize problems and implement well-designed policies and countermeasures. Framing examples on climate change are represented in the Intergovernmental Panel on Climate Change (IPCC) assessment reports, and in the reports of the Council for Science and Technology Promotion (Ichikawa, 2004; Koike, 2006). As well

as the integration of research disciplines, active communication and sharing of knowledge and experience among experts and organizations in different fields are important. In this chapter, a mapping framework of global warming issues is introduced: it is used to restructure our present knowledge by several universities and institutes in Japan participating in a project entitled Integrated Research Systems for Sustainability Science (IR3S). The map has seven phases in the global warming process, based on the interaction between human society and nature. The objective of this study is to reorganize current research results and clarify problems and solutions. It also aims to clarify certainties and uncertainties of scientific knowledge and identify higher and lower priority areas for future research (Hiramatsu, Mimura and Sumi, 2008).

2-2 Mapping framework for structuring global warming

2-2-1 Phase classification

To make it easier to understand the complex and wide-ranging elements related to global warming, an organizational mapping framework is used. The map is classified into seven phases; the sequence from phase 1 to phase 7 naturally follows the process of global warming and is easy to understand (Table 2.1). This cycle of phases is not at equilibrium but will continually change based on the dynamic interaction between nature and human society. Interactions between human society and natural systems will continue, and the issues raised in the process of global warming will be repeated. The change of social structure in phase 7 has the possibility of producing new problems, which means that we will have to tackle those problems again and again. The important thing is that we have to consider problems with the whole cycle continuously and the sequence of the phases is expected to repeat towards a low-carbon society, in which the CO_2 concentration is stabilized at a level that is not dangerous.

Based on this dynamic structure of seven phases, the mapping framework of global warming issues is created (Figure 2.1). This is conceptually clear and easy to understand, yet it is also comprehensive, encompasses a broad range of global warming elements and applies to various challenges and problems.

2-2-2 Identification of key questions

To catch the whole structure and core problem for seeking compatible countermeasures, it is useful to set key questions in each phase. Table 2.2

Table 2.1 Phase classification

Phase	Explanation
1 Socio-economic activity and GHG emissions	GHGs and aerosols are emitted and natural environments are changed by the economic activities of human society
2 Carbon cycle and carbon concentration	In the natural system, carbon circulates in the atmosphere, in the ocean and on land through photosynthesis, respiration, decomposition and other processes Emitted GHGs enter these circulation processes and finally determine the GHG concentration in the atmosphere
3 Climate change and global warming	GHGs in the atmosphere cause climate change, such as increases in air temperature and sea level
4 Impacts on ecosystems and human society	Climate change induces various effects on ecosystems and human society, such as submerging of low-lying areas, extinction of species and changing food production and water resources
5 Adaptation	To address the impacts of climate change, human society must promote policies and technologies to adapt to a warmer world
6 Mitigation	In addition to adapting to a warmer world, human society must reduce GHG emissions to decrease GHG concentrations in the atmosphere, and must therefore introduce various mitigating policies and technologies
7 Social systems	New social systems should be developed There must be changes in social values, lifestyles and education, and voluntary actions taken by society

shows representative key questions for each phase, which can be the highest on the list of concerns regarding climate change for that phase. There are many underlying issues and more detailed questions in each phase, and users can set the necessary level of questions depending on their needs.

In this chapter, these key questions and mapping classifications are used to measure the extent to which current scientific knowledge and research has provided answers to society.

2-2-3 Setting keywords

Users can divide each phase into several categories and put major keywords of climate issues into those categories. In Figure 2.1, two to four

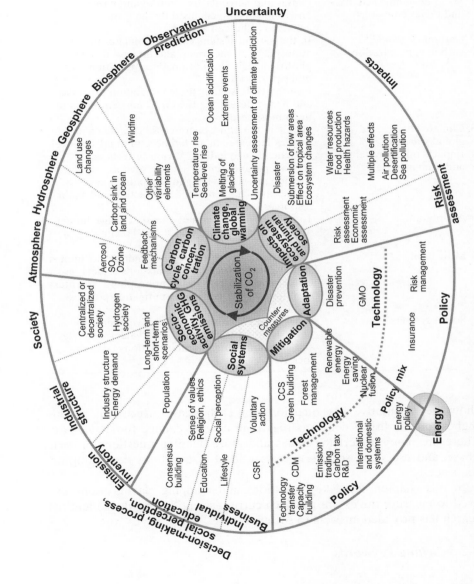

Figure 2.1 Map of the seven phases with keywords
Source: Hiramatsu, Mimura and Sumi (2008).

Table 2.2 Key questions for each phase

Phase	Key question
1 Socio-economic activity and GHG emissions	How will the amount of anthropogenic GHG emissions and their emission sources change?
2 Carbon cycle and carbon concentration	How do GHG concentrations change? What is the mechanism of the carbon cycle and what are the environmental variation factors relating to climate change?
3 Climate change and global warming	Does global warming occur? How will the climate change in the future?
4 Impacts on ecosystems and human society	What are the impacts of climate change? What level of climate change will put humans and ecosystems at risk?
5 Adaptation	What kinds of adaptation policies and technologies are required? By how much will adaptation measures reduce the risk?
6 Mitigation	What kinds of mitigation policies and technologies are required for reductions in GHG emissions? How much GHG emission reduction will be possible?
7 Social systems	How can human society change social systems to create a low-carbon society? Do the changes contribute to a sustainable society?

Source: Hiramatsu, Mimura and Sumi (2008).

categories are created in the phases and major keywords of current research programmes in the world are input in the map. The category names are shown in the circle around the map.

Phase 1 incorporates the industrial structure and basic social structure that determine GHG emissions and relate to the emission inventory, including population and society's energy demands. In phase 2 the carbon cycle was divided into the atmosphere, hydrosphere, geosphere and biosphere. The behaviours of GHGs and aerosols, mechanisms of the carbon cycle and other environmental elements affecting the carbon cycle are included. Phase 3 was divided into observation and prediction of climate change, as well as the related uncertainties. Observed global warming items and models predicting the future climate are included here. Phase 4 contains the categories of impacts and risk assessment. Impacts include the direct effects of global warming as well as the indirect or multiple effects associated with other causes. Categories for technology and policy for mitigation and adaptation are included in phases 5 and 6. In phase 5, adaptation technologies such as revetments against high storm surges or

flooding and improvement or introduction of genetically modified organisms (GMOs) to ensure crop yields in a warmer climate are posted. Adaptation policies include insurance schemes and other types of risk management. In phase 6, as mitigation technologies, energy saving, renewable energy and carbon capture and storage as well as forest management techniques are posted. Mitigation policies include creation of an international/national regime to reduce GHG emissions and economic measures, such as emissions trading and the clean development mechanism (CDM). There are some policies and technologies that relate to both phases 5 and 6. Although the energy sector has strong ties to climate change and plays an important role in mitigation, there are too many studies in this sector and the types of energy represented here are minimized. It mainly includes those that deal with climate change, energy saving, renewable energy and other related issues. Phase 7 includes philosophical aspects and the governance of society, such as the decision-making process, education system, social values and the behaviour of businesses and individuals.

As for keywords, items located closer to the centre represent more fundamental issues and items located further out are more applied, in general. The items closest to the centre of the map represent the most fundamental issues in phases 1, 2 and 7; the more serious phenomena and effects in phases 3 and 4; and the highest-priority options in phases 5 and 6. The items listed further from the centre are the more practical challenges on which society needs to work, especially in phases 1 and 7. These key questions and keywords are arbitrarily defined by experts and should be evaluated further or can be changed by users. But by using this mapping framework and considering the issues in each phase holistically, well-balanced countermeasures against global warming can be developed.

2-3 Application of IPCC findings

2-3-1 Classification of research findings

In this section, an application of this mapping framework for IPCC research findings is shown. The IPCC has provided detailed information to decision-makers and others interested in climate change at regular intervals, and the reports are a good source of comprehensive information to help understand current research findings. The latest report, the IPCC Fourth Assessment Report (AR4), was released in 2007, and this is used for organizing and restructuring the knowledge on global warming in this section (IPCC, 2007a, 2007b, 2007c).

The findings summarized by the bullets in the summaries for policy-makers (SPMs) of AR4, which are summaries of Working Groups (WG) I–III, are assumed to represent the essence of the current state of scientific knowledge. They are classified into the seven phases according the type of research findings to be applied to the mapping framework of Figure 2.1. The application of those results into each phase is shown in Figure 2.2. By this visual map, it becomes easy to grasp the distribution of research and which working group has strength in each phase. This first step can help to examine the current policies and develop the appropriate climate policies for the future.

To show the amount of findings in each phase in detail, the number of scientific findings obtained by each WG have been calculated and displayed in Figure 2.3. WGI research deals primarily with phases 2 and 3, WGII research with phases 4 and 5 and WGIII research deals with phases 1, 6 and 7.

The largest number of findings for WGI on a single phase (phase 3) was 48 (out of a total of 52 for the phase). These research findings are observations of global and regional climate change in the atmosphere, ocean and snow-covered areas, as well as future projections by climate models, primarily on the global level. The number of research findings obtained by WGI in phase 2 was 21. Most of these deal with radiative forcing of GHGs and aerosols and investigations of the causes of climate change, including mechanisms.

WGII mainly provided findings of impact research; its largest number of findings was 75 in phase 4. Most of the findings in phase 4 are related to the observed impacts of global warming and predictions of future impacts in regions and sectors, while a few cover risk assessment. The other topic of WGII is adaptation. In phase 5 there are only 10 research findings: the necessity of adaptation has been recognized and practical uses of adaptation have been introduced, but there are almost no practical findings on adaptation policy.

Phase 6 has the largest number of findings, 82, all of which are from WGIII which has mitigation as its main research focus. Findings in phase 6 mainly deal with various short- and medium-term mitigating technologies, policies, measures and methods and their economic costs, whereas fewer focus on long-term mitigation. Although it is also an important issue, there are only 15 findings dealing with emission sources and emission pathways for stabilization of GHG concentrations in phase 1. Even fewer research findings have been obtained in the social system – eight findings in phase 7.

The IPCC works are assumed to be policy relevant and the research was principally selected from the point of view of scientific and policy needs. The difference in the numbers of findings seems to represent these

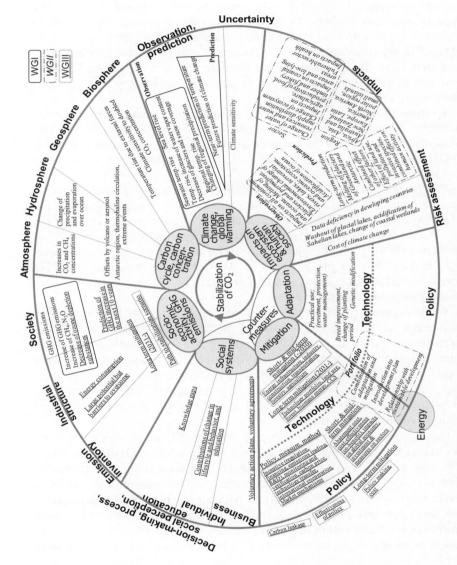

Figure 2.2 The mapping of scientific findings listed in IPCC AR4

Source: Hiramatsu, Mimura and Sumi (2008).

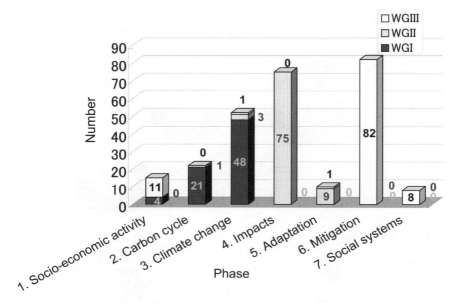

Figure 2.3 Number of scientific findings listed in IPCC AR4 for each phase
Source: Hiramatsu, Mimura and Sumi (2008).

characteristics. From the SPM analysis, it is found that a focus was placed on research such as acquiring scientific evidence of global warming and its causes, identifying the effects of climate change and backing up mitigation options argued by various nations. Therefore, the numbers of scientific findings for phases 2, 3, 4 and 6 are much higher than those of other phases.

2-3-2 Certainty of research findings to the key questions

Not only can the amount of research be compared, but the certainty of research findings can be evaluated. Among the research findings of IPCC AR4, those which can be scientific answers to the key questions in the seven phases in Table 2.2 were extracted and summarized (see the appendix in Hiramatsu, Mimura and Sumi, 2008, for detail). The answers were classified into the seven phases in the mapping framework and analysed for certainty (Figure 2.4). Considering the level of reliability placed by the IPCC on the findings, with the cooperation of two to three coordinating lead authors or lead authors from each WG, answers are ranked on the basis of expert judgement as follows.
- A: Answered with high certainty.
- B: Partly answered (incomplete).
- C: No answer or still uncertain.

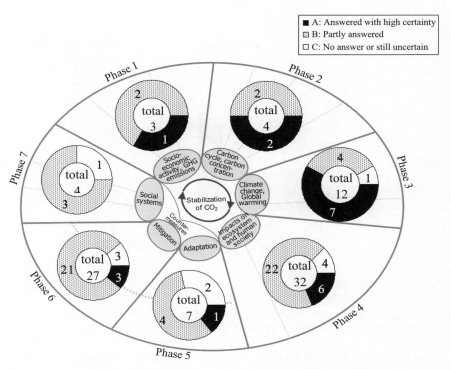

Figure 2.4 Certainty rankings for answers to the key questions in each phase
Note: The number of IPCC findings in each ranking category is shown for each phase.
Source: Hiramatsu, Mimura and Sumi (2008).

For the measurement of certainty, research findings described as "virtually certain", "very likely" and "high confidence" in the SPMs were almost always ranked A. If there was difficulty in deciding between A/B and B/C or the judgement of coordinating lead authors or lead authors was divided, the lower rank was chosen.

In phase 1 the answers clearly indicate that so far CO_2 emissions derived from fossil fuels have increased, from an average of 23.5 $GtCO_2$ per year in the 1990s to 26.4 $GtCO_2$ per year in 2000–2005. For the future, CO_2 emission scenarios for six alternative categories of stabilization levels (from 445–490 to 855–1,130 ppm CO_2 equivalent) have been proposed as emission pathways, and findings indicate that the lower the stabilization level, the sooner this peak and decline would need to occur. However, it is still uncertain which pathway to take because outcomes depend on action taken by the world and by individual nations. Therefore there is only one A in phase 1; to improve the certainty, more concrete

future scenarios for energy structure, industrial changes and other emission sources are required.

In phase 2 half the answers are fairly certain, although there are only a few answers in this phase. Answers to questions about the mechanism of climate change have become much clearer. New observational data, research on radiative forcing and model calculations have clarified the view that recent global warming can only be explained by combining natural changes with the increase in anthropogenic GHGs, leading to the conclusion that recent human activities have caused global warming. Answers to questions concerning changes in thermohaline circulation, other drivers and feedback systems have higher levels of uncertainty.

In phase 3 the proportion of answers with a high degree of certainty is more than 50 per cent. The question of whether global warming has occurred has been clearly answered. The climate has been getting warmer – the global average temperature has increased by 0.74°C in the past 100 years (1904–2005). Looking at the future climate, the estimated temperature increase ranges from 2.0 to 6.1°C, and an increased number of extreme events and other climatic changes have also been predicted. Predictions provide clear answers for the near-future climate, but are less clear for the long-term future climate.

In phase 4 the answers indicate the impacts of climate change on ecosystems and human society have already become apparent, most obviously changes in snow- and ice-covered areas and biological systems. Polar regions, high-latitude areas and coastal zones have been identified as being vulnerable to climate change in the future. Although the amount of research in this area has increased, impacts vary by sector and region, and there is still uncertainty in the answers. More studies are required for the detection of dangerous levels of impacts and the multiple effects of other drivers.

In phase 5 there are few research findings and few certain answers. Adaptation is recognized as a necessary measure and has begun with existing technology, such as coastal revetment and agricultural adaptation. Options for adaptation are being studied, but the practical effectiveness and costs are not yet clear. Although there is a need for more integrated study of adaptation to address the unavoidable impacts resulting from warming due to past emissions, a portfolio of adaptation and mitigation measures is also required to diminish the risks associated with climate change. The design of such a portfolio remains as a future challenge.

In phase 6 research findings show various mitigation measures have been studied and discussed. There is a good deal of potential for a reduction in emissions in each sector through the use of available technologies for mitigation in the near future, especially in the energy infrastructure and forest management sectors, with high reliability. Technology transfer

is also effective. However, there is still a good deal of uncertainty about cost-effectiveness, carbon pricing, emissions reduction by sector and policies for long-term mitigation. As a whole, in the absence of a clear global direction, the answers in this phase remain ambiguous despite the many suggestions.

In phase 7 the current answers on social systems provide low levels of certainty. To reduce GHG emissions drastically, a change in the structure of society itself is required and more cooperation and consensus-building among nations are needed to reach agreements; appropriate measures are necessary to penetrate down to the local level to guarantee effective policy implementation. However, even though there is solid potential and a demand for such research, findings are quite limited in this phase. To date, research has been conducted on contributions from businesses (e.g. voluntary actions resulting from voluntary agreements) and behavioural change.

2-3-3 Analysis of mapping IPCC findings

The research findings presented in IPCC AR4 represent a marked improvement and answer key questions to some extent, especially on the physical aspect of climate change. However, there still remains a need to improve the more practical studies and social science research if successful action is to be taken to address climate change. There is a need for the appropriate implementation of a portfolio of adaptation and mitigation strategies, and more concrete societal assumptions for stabilization. Research in the field of social systems has also been weak. There have been no systematic studies, and few certain scientific findings in relation to the social system have been reported throughout the WGs. Studies on improving the participatory process of citizens, the effects of culture, ethics and religion, and the cooperation of various actors are also required.

2-4 Application of governmental research programmes

2-4-1 Japan

In this section, the number and budgets of governmental research programmes on climate change are classified into the seven phases in the map and analysed.

Governmental research programmes can be divided into two types, bottom-up research and top-down research. In Japan, for bottom-up re-

Table 2.3 Keywords to extract research on climate change

Global warming	Greenhouse gas (GHG)	Kyoto initiative
Climate change	Carbon cycle	Kyoto mechanism
Climate change	Carbon capture and storage (CCS)	Clean development mechanism (CDM)
Climate prediction	Aerosol	Joint symposium (JI)
Climate model	UN Framework Convention on Climate Change (UNFCCC)	Emissions trading (ET)
Carbon circulation model	Intergovernmental Panel on Climate Change (IPCC)	Carbon tax
Climate scenario	Conference of Parties (COP)	Carbon sequestration
Greenhouse effect	Kyoto Protocol	(Carbon) sink

Table 2.4 Research on climate change in Grants-in-Aid for Scientific Research

Year	Number	Budget ($1,000)	% of total budget
FY 2004	147	5,176	3.78
FY 2005	151	6,953	4.58
FY 2006	137	7,108	4.60
FY 2007	140	7,604	5.15
FY 2008	166	10,783	7.64

Note: $1 = 94 yen (August 2009).

search, researchers apply with their individual topics to Grants-in-Aid for Scientific Research (GASR).

To know how many studies on climate change are registered with GASR, around 30 keywords related to climate change were used to analyse the titles of all research in the database. Keywords are listed in Table 2.3. Research which is assumed to contribute directly to addressing climate change was selected. As shown in Table 2.4, the number of studies on climate change seems stable until 2007. However, the budget has been increasing year by year: in 2008 it had doubled since 2004. Next the studies were classified into the seven phases of the mapping framework (Figure 2.5). There are many studies in the carbon cycle, impact assessment and mitigation. The budget for carbon cycle research is by far the largest; the budget in mitigation, especially in energy-related research, is the next largest. Recently impact assessment research is rapidly increasing. On the other hand, research in future social structure, adaptation and social systems is very limited. Sometimes adaption studies are included in other fundamental research as an extension of existing work, but such research is not extracted in this analysis.

Research Programs by Ministries (RPM) is funded by the Japanese government as top-down research: the government puts more priority on

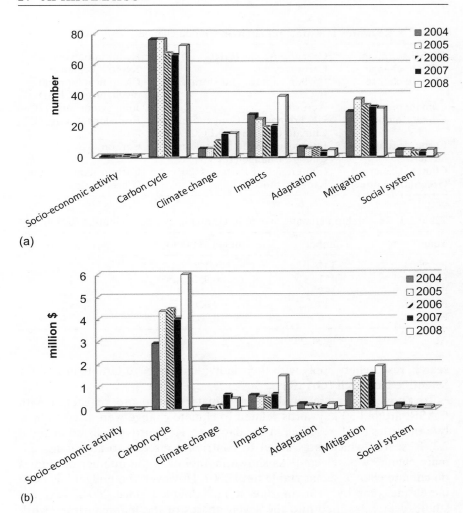

(a)

(b)

Figure 2.5 Number (a) and budget (b) of research on climate change in Grants-in-Aid for Scientific Research (bottom-up research)

the specific field and allocates a budget to it. RPM data are obtained from the Council for Science and Technology Policy, Cabinet Office and the websites of the ministries. Figure 2.6 shows the number of research projects and budget of each ministry in 2006 (energy research data of the New Energy and Industrial Technology Development Organization are excluded).

The RPM budget is almost 100 times as much as that of GASR. The fields the Japanese government currently focuses on are observation, cli-

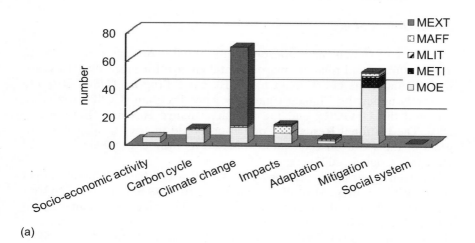

(a)

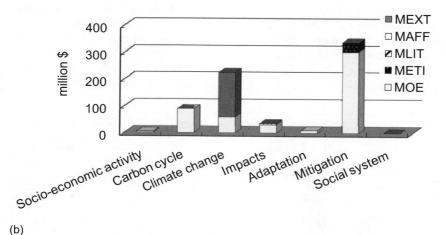

(b)

Figure 2.6 Number (a) and budget (b) of research on climate change in research programmes of Japanese government (top-down research), 2006
Note:
MEXT: Ministry of Education, Culture, Sports, Science and Technology
MAFF: Ministry of Agriculture, Forestry and Fisheries
MLIT: Ministry of Land, Infrastructure, Transport and Tourism
METI: Ministry of Economy, Trade and Industry
MOE: Ministry of the Environment

mate modelling and mitigating options, while there are few research resources distributed in adaptation and social systems.

2-4-2 United States

The US government has sponsored substantial coordinated research on global climate and related environmental change for more than 15 years, initially under the US Global Change Research Program (USGCRP) and currently under the Climate Change Science Program (CCSP), which integrated the USGCRP and the Climate Change Research Initiative in 2002. The National Research Council proposed metrics to measure progress of the CCSP in 2005, and evaluated its progress in 2007 (National Research Council, 2007).

Thirteen agencies participate in the CCSP, which has an annual budget of about $1.7 billion. Most of the budget is from NASA, the NSF, NOAA and the DOE. It is difficult to get details of the budget and management conditions in each agency, so evaluation was based on the knowledge and opinions of reviewers and interviews with agencies (ibid.). The CCSP is divided into three major components – overarching goals, research elements and cross-cutting issues – and is difficult to compare with the exact same elements in Japan. In Figure 2.7 the budget for research on climate change is classified into the research element of the CCSP.

A large part of the budget goes to research on the carbon cycle, atmospheric composition and climate variability and change, which almost

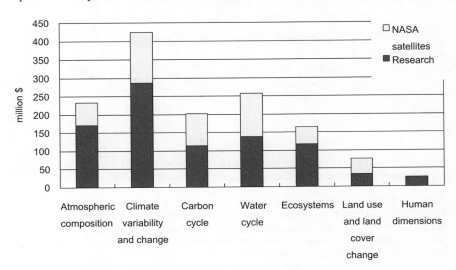

Figure 2.7 Budget of US governmental climate research, 2006
Source: National Research Council (2007).

correspond to observation and projection of climate change in Japan. Secondly, there is a large budget for research on water cycles and ecosystems related to climate impacts. The budget for human and social dimensions is small in both the United States and Japan. Mitigation (energy measures) is mainly covered by the US Climate Change Technology Program and cannot be analysed here.

2-4-3 Comparison of national research budgets on climate change

Japan mainly contributes to carbon cycle, observation and projection, mitigation and energy technology. In the United States understanding of climate systems has increased and climate projection has improved, too. On the other hand, there is little research in adaptation, social systems and future visions of society in Japan and little work on impacts on human and social systems, social science and support for policy decisions in the United States. It is pointed out that most of the US government's global change budget has focused on upstream uncertainties in the natural sciences, and little has been budgeted for social and behavioural sciences (Pielke, 1995; Nordhaus and Popp, 1997). The supply of and demand for science in decision-making have not been in alignment (Sarewitz and Pielke, 2007). Climate research in the European Union and other countries is not analysed here, but the same trend is seen in the IPCC AR4 results. There is deeper understanding of the carbon cycle, observation and projection of climate change, and impacts and mitigation options, but less research on social systems, socio-economic activity and future scenarios. It is important that scientific knowledge is communicated effectively within society, so that science can be utilized effectively and new technologies and policies that address climate change are accepted; this remains a challenge for us.

2-5 Conclusions

To get a complete picture of the current state of scientific knowledge regarding climate change, a mapping framework for climate change issues has been introduced. Mapping research findings in such a way has made it possible for us to understand better the overall state of current scientific knowledge regarding climate change. With the application of this type of mapping framework, we can identify which areas of research have progressed and which are lagging behind with regard to global warming. This is important when society decides future directions of research. The mapping approach also provides a framework that will be useful in organizing the various needs of society. Moreover, with this holistic mapping

framework, as well as taking effective measures against climate change, it is possible to assess whether these measures are compatible with other problems and contribute to the larger goal of achieving a sustainable society.

Acknowledgements

The author acknowledges the kind permission of Springer Science. The study was supported by Japan's Ministry of Education, Culture, Sports, Science and Technology (MEXT) through the Special Coordination Funds for Promoting Science and Technology.

REFERENCES

Buzan, Tony and Barry Buzan (1996) *The Mind Map Book: How to Use Radiant Thinking to Maximize Your Brain's Untapped Potential*. Harmondsworth: Penguin Books (reprint: Plume).

Choucri, N., D. Mistree, W. R. Baker, F. Haghseta, C. I. Ortiz and T. Mezher (2007) *Mapping Sustainability: Knowledge E-networking and the Value Chain*, Alliance for Global Sustainability Book Series Vol. 11. Berlin: Springer.

Hiramatsu, Ai, Nobuo Mimura and Akimasa Sumi (2008) "A Mapping of Global Warming Research Based on IPCC AR4", *Sustainability Science* 3(2), pp. 201–213.

Ichikawa, A. (ed.) (2004) *Global Warming – The Research Challenges, a Report of Japan's Global Warming Research Initiative*. Berlin: Springer.

IPCC (2007a) "Summary for Policymakers", in *Climate Change 2007: The Physical Science Basis*. Cambridge: Cambridge University Press.

IPCC (2007b) "Summary for Policymakers", in *Climate Change 2007: Impacts, Adaptation and Vulnerability*. Cambridge: Cambridge University Press.

IPCC (2007c) "Summary for Policymakers", in *Climate Change 2007: Mitigation*. Cambridge: Cambridge University Press.

Kajikawa, Y., J. Ohno, Y. Takeda, K. Matsushima and H. Komiyama (2007) "Creating an Academic Landscape of Sustainability Science: An Analysis of the Citation Network", *Sustainability Science* 2(2), pp. 221–231.

Kawakita, Jiro (1991) *The Original KJ Method*, revised edn. Tokyo: Kawakita Research Institute.

Koike, I. (ed.) (2006) *Chikyu ondanka wa doko made kaimei saretaka: Nihon no kagakusha no kouken to kondo no tenbou* (*To What Extent Has Global Warming Been Solved? Japanese Scientists' Contribution and Outlook*). Tokyo: Maruzen.

National Research Council (2007) *Evaluating Progress of the U.S. Climate Change Science Program: Methods and Preliminary Results*. Washington, DC: National Academies Press.

Nordhaus, W. D. and D. Popp (1997) "What Is the Value of Scientific Knowledge? An Application to Global Warming Using the PRICE Model", *Energy Journal* 18(1), pp. 1–46.

Novak, Joseph D. and Alberto J. Cañas (2008) "The Theory Underlying Concept Maps and How to Construct and Use Them", available at http://cmap.ihmc.us/ Publications/ResearchPapers/TheoryUnderlyingConceptMapsHQ.pdf.

Pielke, R. (1995) "Usable Information for Policy: An Appraisal of the U.S. Global Change Research Program", *Policy Science* 28, pp. 39–77.

Sarewitz, D. and R. Pielke (2007) "Neglected Heart of Science Policy: Reconciling Supply of and Demand for Science", *Environmental Science Policy* 10, pp. 5–16.

Scupin, Raymond (1997) "The KJ Method: A Technique Analyzing Data Derived from Japanese Ethnology", *Human Organization* 56(2), pp. 233–237.

3

Climate change risk communication

Seita Emori

From the standpoint of an expert on climate change projections, this chapter proposes a framework of "climate change risk communication" in which various stakeholders, including citizens, experts, industries and governments, communicate with each other on climate change risks. For communication to support adaptation policy-making, specific risk information for a particular region and sector is required. It is critical for stakeholders to have a proper understanding of the uncertainties in natural climate variability and scientific projections. For communication to support developing public opinion on mitigation policies and motivations for individual actions, comprehensive risk information is required for many sectors and aspects at the global scale. It is important for experts to provide unbiased information from a value-neutral standpoint, overcoming exaggerations seen in mass media as well as scepticism. Overall, it is important to distinguish supporting decision-making from decision-making itself, and to develop mutual trust among stakeholders through communication.

3-1 Introduction

It seems that awareness of climate change among the Japanese public has rapidly increased, thanks to the release of the 2007 film *An Inconvenient Truth*, the publication of the Intergovernmental Panel on Climate Change's (IPCC) Fourth Assessment Report and the 2008 Toyako G8

Climate change and global sustainability: A holistic approach, Sumi, Mimura and Masui (eds), United Nations University Press, 2011, ISBN 978-92-808-1181-0

Summit. During that time the author, as a climate scientist, was responsible for media presentations of the latest climate change projections from the Earth Simulator, which in 2004 was the world's fastest supercomputer; this brought about a deepening involvement in the arena of communicating facts about climate change and growing personal awareness of the communication gap over climate change between experts and non-experts, and of the difficulty and importance of closing that gap.

Under the Ministry of the Environment's Global Environmental Research Fund Strategic Research and Development Project S-5, "Integrated Research on Climate Change Scenarios to Increase Public Awareness and Contribute to the Policy Process" (also known as "Getting a 'Feel' for Future Climate Change", represented by Professor Akimasa Sumi, The University of Tokyo), which started in 2007, the author began practice and analysis of communication in earnest, with the cooperation of experts in the humanities and social sciences. From observing risk communication in other fields, these activities gradually led to advocating "climate change risk communication". This chapter will describe the climate change risk communication framework that can be proposed at this point in time, based on experience to date.

3-2 Climate change risk communication and its categorization

3-2-1 Defining climate change risk communication

Risk communication means providing for communication among stakeholders, including the public, experts, industry and government, regarding social risks such as environmental problems and disasters.

Regarding environmental problems, especially substantial initiatives have been made in the area of the risk to human health presented by chemical substances (e.g. Sekizawa, 2001). In a narrow sense, it seems that the "risk" presented by chemicals and disasters is understood as "the combination of the negative consequences of a certain phenomenon and the probability of its occurrence (more simply, the product of multiplying their values together)". However, if "a certain phenomenon" is considered as "climate change", then there is uncertainty in even answering what the associated consequences will be, and in some cases it is hard to conceive the possibility of occurrence in terms of quantitative probability. Therefore, one can define "climate change risk" as "the negative impacts caused by climate change, with uncertainty about the possibility of occurrence and the magnitude of the impacts".

Accordingly, the "climate change risk communication" in this chapter's title could perhaps be defined as "providing for communication among stakeholders, including the public, experts, industry and government, about the negative impacts of climate change while taking into consideration the uncertainty about the possibility of occurrence and the magnitude of the impacts". Additionally, climate change may conceivably have positive effects, as discussed below, and therefore we should probably understand "negative impacts" here to mean "net negative impacts" that also consider positive effects (while not necessarily calculated mathematically).

3-2-2 Climate change risk communication categories

The purposes of climate change risk communication can be divided roughly into three categories.

- On the occasion of government implementation of policies to reduce greenhouse gas (GHG) emissions in order to control climate change, risk communication can assist the formation of public opinion on whether or not to back such policies.
- On the occasion of judging whether industry and each member of the public will themselves take actions to reduce GHG emissions, risk communication can assist the motivation for those actions.
- As society adapts to the future climate so as to minimize negative impacts (and elicit positive effects to the maximum) when a certain extent of climate change is unavoidable, risk communication can assist the consideration of specific methods, mainly by government and industry.

The first two points are concerned with so-called mitigation policy (reducing GHG emissions), while the third concerns what is called adaptation policy. Because mitigation policies control climate change impacts in all world regions across the board, it is desirable that risk communication on such policy emphasizes determining climate change impacts as comprehensively and exhaustively as possible. On the other hand, adaptation policies mitigate certain kinds of impacts (or amplify positive effects) in certain regions, and it is therefore desirable that risk communication on adaptation policy emphasizes determining certain impacts in certain regions as concretely and quantitatively as possible.

Because the communication-related points of note for these two are totally different, they will be treated separately: first the chapter will discuss risk communication for adaptation policy, and then communication for mitigation policy.

In thinking through these categories, the author's perception is that "experts" are those who provide risk information, and they will not explicitly be presented as the entities who make social judgements.

However, because "communication" means a two-way exchange of information, one must not forget the importance of experts in becoming receivers of information, such as that on the risk perceptions of other stakeholders. And it goes without saying that when it comes to public opinion formation and motivation to enact measures, even experts have another role as members of the public.

3-3 Specific risk communication for adaptation policy-making

3-3-1 The nature of climate change risk with regard to near-future adaptation policy

Climate change adaptation policy to the greatest extent possible avoids certain climate change impacts (or amplifies positive effects) using means including providing physical and institutional infrastructure for society (e.g. Ministry of the Environment, 2008: 29–47). Examples are building levees to prepare for increased occurrences of flooding, setting up heatwave warning systems to prepare for rising incidence of heatstroke and, in agriculture, changing planting times and crop types in accordance with climate change.

According to the IPCC (2007: 12), over the next 20 years average global temperature is predicted to rise at an average rate of 0.2°C per decade, and it is thought that the magnitude of the rise during that period will not depend very much on measures to reduce GHG emissions. In other words, scientists predict that there will be a certain extent of warming in the near future regardless of emission reduction measures. For this reason people are beginning to perceive the need for adaptation policies in the near future.

Adaptation policy-making requires prediction information that is as specific and quantitative as possible, especially when it involves building physical infrastructure. That is to say, once the extent and location of the increased flooding are predicted, policy will determine what size of levees to build.

When considering near-future adaptation policy, it is deemed necessary to note the following characteristics of climate change risk.
• Because climate change risk gradually increases over several decades, over the short term (about 10 years), it is heavily influenced by the natural variability of climate.
• Long-term climate change risk projections themselves have scientific uncertainty.

While both are related to uncertainty of projections, the first is the uncertainty of natural climate change while the second is the uncertainty

of the science used in making the projections. These are explained in detail below.

3-3-2 The uncertainty of natural climate change, and how to communicate it

The climate change we actually experience year after year is a combination of anthropogenic climate change that proceeds slowly over the long term and year-by-year irregular natural variability (fluctuation) as typified by El Niño. As such, even if one implements policies for adaptation to climate change, the following year may by chance be a cold one. If stakeholders think that "because global warming is advancing, next year will definitely be hotter than this year", we first need communication that will eradicate that misunderstanding, and then have stakeholders properly understand the relationship between long-term climate change and short-term natural fluctuation.

In other words, it is definitely not the temperature itself that is higher next year as compared to this year, but the "probability of high temperature" (or, for example, the "probability of flooding"). For stakeholders to understand it in this way, perhaps they must to an extent understand the concept of probability. Or perhaps experts need to avoid explanations using probability concepts and use innovative explanations so that stakeholders understand things as intuitively as possible.

It is conceivable that some stakeholders understand the probability concept well enough and prefer to make decisions using more sophisticated scientific information. In such instances it is desirable for experts to estimate theoretically the quantitative range of the uncertainty arising due to natural fluctuation (for example, a 90 per cent confidence interval with a range of $\pm X°C$), and present that to stakeholders. Scientific attempts have been made to predict short-term climate variation (e.g. Smith et al., 2007); however, they are not treated in detail here.

3-3-3 Scientific uncertainty used in projections, and how to communicate it

Even if we consider climate change while excluding uncertainty due to natural climate variation, there is still a certain amount of uncertainty in climate change risk projections. Often, when performing quantitative climate change risk projections, the climate is first predicted using "climate models", which are mathematical simulations of the Earth's atmosphere and oceans based on physical principles. When necessary, this is followed by performing simulations of impact areas of interest, such as flooding or agriculture, using climate model results as input. Owing to the scientific uncertainty of these simulation models, uncertainty arises in climate

change risk projections. In other words, we can say that there is uncertainty in our scientific understanding of what is modelled (such as the atmosphere-ocean system, floods or agriculture), which is the basis for building models. A detailed treatment of the uncertainty in climate model projections is contained in Emori (2008: 173–210).

An easy-to-understand method of showing this uncertainty is to juxtapose the results of several different models. By doing so, a person does not have to be an expert to see immediately the differences among models, for example in the regional distribution of projected temperature rises. When it comes to projections of things like precipitation amount and agricultural crop yields, it is not unusual to see inter-model differences, even to the extent that the indications of change (increases or decreases) are different.

Therefore, for risk communication, it is crucial that stakeholders do not put too much faith in the details of projection results from a single model. When stakeholders consider adaptation policies using projection results from simulation models, it is desirable if possible to have experts on hand to offer advice on the reliability of the projection results. It is also important that experts make the effort to show objectively the range of scientific uncertainty by statistically using the results of multiple models (ibid.: 182–190).

If the detailed projection results from a single simulation model take on a life of their own without being accompanied by information on uncertainty, it is possible that information on the extent of danger posed to Japan or individual prefectures would be perceived too concretely by stakeholders, eliciting anxiety among the public in an inappropriate way, or affecting land prices and the like. At the same time, because in general stakeholders seek information that is as detailed as possible, a great challenge for risk communication is how to provide specific information while appropriately explaining the uncertainty.

Additionally, when assessing impacts and considering adaptation policies, it is necessary to note carefully the factors that increase the uncertainty of final consideration, such as the uncertainty of future regional distribution of population and assets, age composition and other socioeconomic factors relating to the vulnerability of society to climate change, and also factors such as the uncertainty in the cost and effectiveness of adaptation technologies.

3-3-4 Experts' expectations for stakeholders

In light of the climate change risk described above, there are two items which according to experts are important considerations for decision-making by stakeholders.

First, in response to the problem of the uncertainty of natural fluctuation, climate change adaptation policies are meaningful only when they consider plans on time scales longer than 10 years at the least. For that reason, decision-making by stakeholders must have a long-term perspective to ensure that adaptation policies are properly vetted. With industrial activities in particular, long-term planning often means up to five years at most, and because industry must address various short-term risks other than climate, assuring such a perspective is not necessarily easy. It is certainly not clear whether stakeholders are truly convinced of the importance of preparing at present for climate risk that will appear gradually over the long term, and it is likely that the effectiveness of that conviction depends on communication with experts. This is perhaps an important theme in climate change risk communication.

Second, to address the problem of uncertainty in the science used in projections, stakeholders must not place too much faith in the details of projections. The future is uncertain in the first place, but scientific projections can only show the direction with the highest probability. Accordingly, stakeholders need to be fully aware that this problem is essentially a matter of "decision-making based on uncertain information". In the case of industry, it is taken for granted that management judgements are made in the face of all kinds of uncertainties; therefore, there is no necessity to emphasize that point. If a projection proves wrong, it is undesirable for the implementation of adaptation policies to engender a bigger loss than when not implementing them. Therefore, when considering adaptation policies, rather than strategies that attempt optimization in response to projected future climate, strategies that eliminate vulnerabilities which appear to be especially problematic in the projected future climate should take precedence.

3-4 Comprehensive risk communication for public opinion formation and motivation to enact measures

3-4-1 Communication regarding climate change "scepticism"

Before treating risk communication regarding mitigation policies, we can touch on risk communication relating to so-called climate change "scepticism", because it is thought that this issue exercises no small effect on the formation of public opinion and the motivation of the public to enact measures.

"Scepticism" here is part, not all, of the argument against the mainstream perception of the IPCC and other entities on the science of global warming. In general, there is nothing wrong with arguing scientifically for

the possibility that a certain scientific persuasion is mistaken, and in fact this is essential for the advancement of science. However, when the argument is based on an obvious misunderstanding or distortion, and unjustly disparages the reliability of climate change science, that is here referred to as "scepticism" and is considered a problem.

As an expert of the "mainstream", the author is in a position to rebut "scepticism", but from the perspective of communication with the public, one must point out that mounting a rebuttal is not so simple.

First of all, from the standpoint of experts, there is a tendency to think that if one points out the misunderstandings and distortions in a sceptic's argument, the logical fallacies of scepticism are proven and that is sufficient. However, from the lay person's point of view, to outward appearances scepticism is pointing out the problems in the mainstream argument, and it appears to be proving its logical fallacies. Therefore it appears to lay people, who approach both arguments without the preconception that the mainstream is correct, that both views seem plausible (that is, the argument is going around in circles). It is often the case that discerning the differences requires verifying quotations and data sources and being literate in the field. Generally it is difficult to expect this of lay members of the public.

Next, on the level of preconceptions, one would think that many members of the public have the naive idea that the mainstream is supposed to be correct; however, when sceptics tell the public, for example, that "science should not be dogmatic" or "the science of global warming is political", it appears that more than a few members of the public are convinced that the mainstream is not necessarily right. And even if one tries to convince people that the mainstream is right on the grounds that "many scientists throughout the world support this", sceptics will rebut this with arguments such as "science is not a majority decision" or "Is there no freedom in scientific enquiry?" Therefore, this is not necessarily a decisive argument.

As this shows, experts face the essential communication difficulty of not being able to convince people even though they are providing credible information. While it is important that experts rebut sceptics, they must be aware that their communication strategies will be put to the test in presenting an effective refutation.

3-4-2 A comprehensive understanding of climate change risk

We can now discuss risk communication that helps formation of public opinion and motivation relating to mitigation policies. Communication for this purpose can be seen as helping stakeholders to understand in the best possible way "How serious a problem is climate change in the first

place?" or, expressed in another way, "How frightening is climate change?" Of course it is anticipated that the "more frightening" the public's perception of climate change, the easier it is for public opinion to support aggressive climate change policy, and the easier it is to motivate industry and each member of the public to enact measures on their own initiative.

Among the communication actors in society, those whose stance is to boost climate change measures as much as possible perhaps tend to spread the perception that "climate change is really frightening". As a backlash to this (which is also related to the scepticism discussed above), it seems that some people spread the perception that "climate change is not at all frightening". Under these circumstances it is important for experts to talk about how frightened we should actually be, while doing their best to exclude preconceptions.

Comprehensive information on climate change risk is a necessity for this purpose, in other words the "big picture" on climate change risk, and one can cite several perspectives to keep in mind when organizing that information.

(1) *The quantitative uncertainty of impact projections.* This was covered above. Numerical values of impacts projected by models actually have ranges.

(2) *The contribution of factors other than climate change.* Factors other than climate, such as population growth and urbanization, contribute to the impacts one is observing. For example, in addition to climate, population growth has a critical impact on increasing water shortages in the future.

(3) *Good and bad impacts.* Global warming might also have desirable (positive) impacts on society. For example, less cold stress is expected on agriculture, human health and the like in cold regions.

(4) *Direct and indirect impacts on Japan.* Not only will there be impacts due to changes in Japan's climate (direct impacts), but also impacts via those on other countries (indirect impacts). Some conceivable ones are impacts through trade, increases in the number of refugees and conflicts.

(5) *The effectiveness of adaptation, and the difficulty or ease of implementing it.* With regard to impacts that are easy to adapt to, it is inappropriate to emphasize their magnitude if no adaptive measures are taken. For example, if summers become hotter in cold regions where space cooling was formerly not required, people will start using air conditioners. Therefore it is anticipated that health damage due to heatwaves will be smaller than that extrapolated on the basis of previous experience.

(6) *Feedback and high-order impacts.* This means, for example, taking into consideration impact chains, like the increase in secondary dam-

age such as infectious diseases due to increased flooding, and continuing impacts on industrial activities.

(7) *The possibilities and impacts of surprises.* This is the problem of how much we should worry about heavy impacts that are not scientifically impossible, such as the sudden collapse of the Antarctic ice sheet or methane emissions from permafrost.

(8) *Thinking is partly dependent on values.* This refers to how people are emotionally affected by the extinction of wildlife species or disasters in other countries, and the degree of importance they attach to things such as impacts on future generations. These are dependent on value judgements of individuals.

Depending on how these perspectives are taken into account, the "scariness" of information on climate change risk can likely be adjusted to any extent. For example, if you emphasize the importance of factors other than climate change (2), positive impacts (3) and impacts to which it is easy to adapt (5), you can give the impression that climate change "isn't frightening". On the other hand, if you emphasize increases in refugees and conflict due to disasters in other countries (4) and the possibility of large-scale impacts such as the sudden collapse of the Antarctic ice sheet (7), you can give the impression that climate change is "extremely frightening".

Assuming here that experts try to be value-neutral, they should give the "big picture" that covers as much as possible in the range from "not frightening" to "frightening", and leave it to the public how they feel about it. Attempts such as this are the challenge awaiting climate change risk communication. Of course, since a perfectly neutral viewpoint is impossible, one must note that the "big picture" that is presented must necessarily be dependent on the sense of balance of the expert who prepared it.

3-4-3 Expert neutrality

The value neutrality or policy neutrality of experts can be discussed a little further. It is certainly not self-evident that experts are neutral in these senses, and realistically they have not achieved neutrality. It is natural for experts, as individuals, to have their own ideas on things such as the extent to which they desire to support climate change policy, and it is possible that these ideas are reflected consciously or unconsciously in their behaviour as experts when communicating with stakeholders.

Considering individual experts' communication strategies, the advantage of consciously conducting "non-neutral" communication is, of course, that experts can disseminate their own values and the policies they support to other stakeholders. However, if other stakeholders discern an expert's non-neutrality, it will likely engender the disadvantage that the

expert's message will be accepted only by those stakeholders whose values are roughly the same. Therefore, the strategic advantage of providing neutral communication is that the message will be readily accepted by stakeholders with various values.

For example, the IPCC describes its own stance as being "policy-relevant" but not "policy-prescriptive". There is a state called "policy-implicative" between these two. Even if experts' messages do not expressly prescribe or recommend certain policies, it is possible to suggest a certain policy orientation by selecting certain bits of objective information and adjusting the emphasis of their presentation. Realistically, it is difficult to provide information that is completely free of "implied policy"; however, it is important that experts whose intent is policy-neutral communication are aware of, and sensitive to, the possibility that their own information provision is policy-implicative.

In systems where communication is actually being carried out, it is likely that in addition to the difference between simply being neutral or not, there are various types of experts such as those who are intentionally non-neutral but pretend to be neutral, those who are intentionally neutral but cannot conceal their own thoughts and those who are not aware of their own neutrality. Additionally, many people who disseminate the results of research on climate change impacts are experts in certain fields (such as flooding, agriculture or health), and perhaps tend to emphasize the importance of their own fields of research. Because the public are probably often unconscious of the neutrality of experts when accepting their information, we should perhaps be aware that in reality it is very difficult for communication to be uniform.

3-4-4 Communication via the media

In actuality, opportunities for experts to communicate their information to the general public nearly always happen through the media. Therefore communication between experts and the media and communication between the media and the public are equally important.

There is frequent criticism that the media tend to emphasize the "scariness" of climate change (e.g. Takeda, 2008: 20–21). If this is a general trend, some conceivable reasons are as follows.

- Because the intention of media people responsible for addressing the climate change issue includes motivating the public to carry out certain measures, they tend to provide information from such a stance.
- Because of competition among media (such as TV station ratings) and within media (such as securing column space in a newspaper), the media are likely to express things in an exaggerated manner to get the public's attention.

- Because the media attempt to make things simpler for readers and viewers to understand, they tend to omit the detailed preconditions and exceptions in scientific knowledge.

The first reason means that the information provided by the media could be policy-implicative. Needless to say, this is presumably not limited to the climate change issue. If one allows media people to express themselves with some freedom, it is perhaps difficult – and there may be no need – to stop them from controlling the selection and emphasis of scientific knowledge in line with their own intentions and within bounds that are not scientifically mistaken. On the other hand, there is a view that, especially in the case of public media, always being policy-implicative in the same direction is problematic (ibid.). The debate on this point will be a challenge for climate change risk communication.

On the second and third reasons, the exaggeration and simplification that affect scientific accuracy must be corrected by proper communication between experts and media people, and this is to an extent possible. However, one imagines that as the range of expression supposedly acceptable to experts is generally narrower than the range of expression media people supposedly would like to have accepted, communication would require harmonizing them in particular.

With regard to communication between the media and the public, it is important for the time being that the public develop information literacy so as to, for example, be aware of the media tendencies described above, and exercise caution when incorporating information received from the media into the formation of their own views.

It appears as though this chapter cites only problems with the media, but when it comes to the possibility of involving people who previously had no interest in certain matters, the media play a major role in climate change risk communication. Obviously it is crucial to have the media do their job while overcoming these problems.

3-5 Concluding remarks

This chapter discusses the idea of "climate change risk communication" with emphasis on what should be communicated among stakeholders and points that should be carefully noted, especially from the stance of experts.

It has discussed communication methodology, because it appears that even risk communication in general has no established methodology at the present time, and the author's group cannot claim to have found a methodology that could be regarded as especially effective for the climate change issue. At this stage we are experimenting with dialogue on various scales with the public, industry people, media people and others.

Finally, there are two items that seem to be important to everything discussed here, and two items that are not discussed.

The two items that seem to be of general importance are probably common knowledge in the risk communication field, but will be noted here because front-line experts tend to forget about them. One is the need to make a clear distinction between "assisting decision-making based on scientific information" and "decision-making itself". In other words, it is not appropriate for experts to attempt decision-making themselves, nor for decision-makers to leave decision-making solely to the experts. It is important that, when providing information, experts carefully select the portions that depend on value judgements, and leave the judgements to decision-makers.

The second item is the importance of developing mutual trust among stakeholders. For example, imagine if experts had the preconception that "non-experts just don't get it even if something is accurately explained to them; they like exaggeration and are readily swayed by laughable scepticism". Or imagine if non-experts had the preconception that "experts don't properly explain things for us, and they always use hard-to-understand language". Effective communication would be impossible under such conditions. One cannot overemphasize the importance of eliminating such preconceptions and developing mutual trust, even if only little by little, through communication.

Two points were not discussed. In communication on climate change, and especially on mitigation policies, the risk perspective is just half the issue. The other half is what we might call "climate change policy communication". That is to say, on the matter of domestic emission reduction policy and Japan's approach in international negotiations such as on the UN Framework Convention on Climate Change, we need communication among stakeholders, including the public, experts, industry and government, regarding what impacts there will be on people's livelihoods, the domestic economy, international society and other sectors in the event that a certain policy is adopted. Because this is a perspective that is more directly connected to value judgements than in the case of risk, one can easily imagine that such communication is more difficult. In fact, in the policy communication process on Japan's mid-term target (reduction target up to 2020) in May–June 2009, it appeared that there were difficulties such as dialogue grinding to a halt due to clashes between industry and citizen groups. At any rate, it is only once we begin to conduct climate change risk communication in tandem with climate change policy communication that we can call Japan's climate change policy a decision-making process based on scientific information.

Finally, the second item not treated here is the importance of conceiving climate change as part of what might be called the problem of

sustainability within the connections between other broad groups of international and domestic problems. It goes without saying that climate change is closely related to problems such as those of energy, resources, wastes, pollution, environmental damage, food, water, security, nuclear proliferation, the global economy, poverty in developing countries, population ageing in developed countries, healthcare and population. Considering the climate change problem does not at all mean thinking that its solution will take precedence over solving these other problems. It would be difficult to say that we have a sufficiently good view of the connections among these problem groups at this time; however, in the future one hopes that humankind obtains a framework for "sustainable problems communication" that takes a bird's-eye view of these problem groups to assist decision-making, and that we will see the day when "climate change risk communication" fully plays a role as part of that.

Acknowledgements

The author's experiences and investigations, upon which this chapter is based, were obtained mainly through the Ministry of the Environment's Global Environmental Research Fund Strategic Research and Development Project S-5, "Integrated Research on Climate Change Scenarios to Increase Public Awareness and Contribute to the Policy Process". I wish to express gratitude to my co-researchers.

REFERENCES

Emori, S. (2008) *Are Climate Change Projections "Correct"? Science's Challenge to an Uncertain Future*. Kyoto: Kagaku Dojin.
IPCC (2007) *Climate Change 2007: The Physical Science Basis*. Cambridge: Cambridge University Press.
Ministry of the Environment (2008) "Smart Adaptation to Climate Change: Report of Research Committee on Climate Change Impacts and Adaptation", available at www.env.go.jp/earth/ondanka/rc_eff-adp/.
Sekizawa, J. (2001) "The Uncertainty of Chemical Risk Assessment", *Japanese Journal of Risk Analysis* 12(2), pp. 4–9.
Smith, D. M., S. Cusack, A. W. Colman, C. K. Folland, G. R. Harris and J. M. Murphy (2007) "Improved Surface Temperature Prediction for the Coming Decade from a Global Climate Model", *Science* 317(5839), pp. 796–799.
Takeda, K. (2008) *The Lie of an Environmental Problem 3?* Tokyo: Yosensha.

4

Climate change impacts and responses

4-1

Overview of climate change impacts

Nobuo Mimura

4-1-1 Emerging impacts

Climate change is a fundamental change in the Earth's physical systems; it has a range of effects on many systems and sectors that rely on climate, such as water resources, terrestrial and marine ecosystems, food production, natural disasters, coastal zones, industries and human health. These effects have apparently been occurring because climate change accelerated in the last decades of the twentieth century. Sea ice and permafrost areas have significantly shrunken in the Arctic, where the largest rise in atmospheric temperature is observed. Many species and ecosystems have started moving towards the poles and higher elevations in mountains. Several extreme events causing serious damage to human society have occurred in the twenty-first century, such as the heatwave in Europe in 2003, Hurricane Katrina in 2005, recent droughts in Australia and floods and droughts in Asia and Africa. Although the causal relationship between individual extreme events and global warming cannot be identified, the increase in the intensity of natural disasters resulting in further threats to human society has been a major concern.

It should be noted that the impacts of climate change can be both negative and positive; the fertilizing effect of higher CO_2 concentration on plants is a typical positive effect. However, the negative effects are considered overwhelming because global warming is progressing in the twenty-first century (IPCC, 2007c). Furthermore, these effects will be critical in developing countries, particularly in Africa, Asia and the Pacific. It

Climate change and global sustainability: A holistic approach, Sumi, Mimura and Masui (eds), United Nations University Press, 2011, ISBN 978-92-808-1181-0

is essential to understand where and when the effects will appear and how strong they will be. Many studies have been conducted to estimate future impacts of climate change on national, regional and global scales. The IPCC's Fourth Assessment Report (AR4) is a comprehensive summary of such efforts. This chapter deals with impacts induced by climate change and responses to them from various aspects. This section will present an overview of climate change impacts as an introduction to the chapter, based on the IPCC's AR4 (IPCC, 2007a, 2007b, 2007c). Although references are not explicitly shown, most information presented is from this report.

4-1-2 Impacts on major sectors: A global perspective

4-1-2-1 Freshwater resources and water environment

Water circulation is a part of the Earth's climate system. Therefore, climate change has a direct effect on the temporal and spatial distribution of water resources through changes in atmospheric temperature, precipitation, evaporation and sea level. A major conclusion of future estimates is that changes in runoff and water availability are highly variable with region. Runoff in the twenty-first century estimated by an ensemble mean of the outputs of climate models is shown in Figure 4.1.1.

In terms of water availability, runoff will increase at higher latitudes and in some wet tropics, including East and Southeast Asia, and decrease over much of the mid-latitudes and dry tropics. Areas that are currently semi-arid, such as the Mediterranean Basin, western USA and southern Africa, will suffer a further decrease in water resources due to climate change. Glacier- or snowmelt-fed regions inhabited by more than one-sixth of the world's population are also threatened. This issue is critical in South America, particularly in Bolivia, Peru, Colombia and Ecuador, where water availability has already been compromised. Furthermore, Andean inter-tropical glaciers are estimated to disappear over the next few decades. According to the IPCC SRES A2 scenario (IPCC, 2000), the number of people living in severely stressed river basins is projected to increase from 1.4–1.6 billion in 1995 to 4.3–6.9 billion in 2050.

With regard to the risks of natural disasters, both extreme precipitation and drought events are likely to increase in frequency and intensity. Drought-affected areas will probably increase; simultaneously, up to 20 per cent of the world's population living in river basins will be affected by increased flood hazards by the 2080s.

Water quality is another problem associated with climate change. Rising sea levels will expand areas of groundwater and estuary salinization,

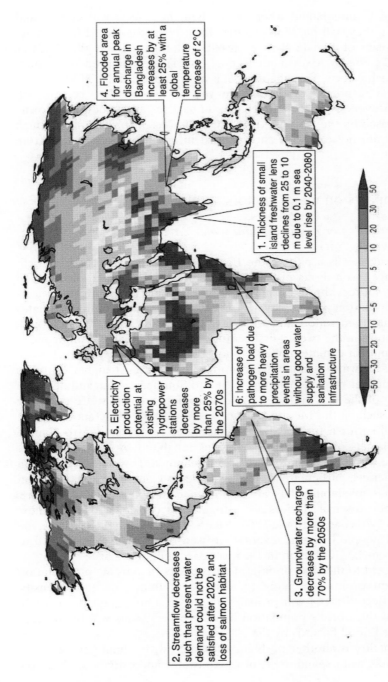

Figure 4.1.1 Illustrative map of combined mean change of annual runoff (%) between the present (1981–2000) and 2081–2100 for the SRES A1B emissions scenario

Source: IPCC (2007c).

Note: Please see page 309 for a colour version of this figure.

The text inside the figure's labelled boxes:

1. Thickness of small island freshwater lens declines from 25 to 10 m due to 0.1 m sea level rise by 2040–2080

2. Streamflow decreases such that present water demand could not be satisfied after 2020, and loss of salmon habitat

3. Groundwater recharge decreases by more than 70% by the 2050s

4. Flooded area for annual peak discharge in Bangladesh increases by at least 25% with a global temperature increase of 2°C

5. Electricity production potential at existing hydropower stations decreases by more than 25% by the 2070s

6. Increase of pathogen load due to more heavy precipitation events in areas without good water supply and sanitation infrastructure

Colour scale: -50 -30 -20 -10 -5 0 5 10 20 30 50

48

resulting in a decrease in freshwater availability for humans and ecosystems. Water pollution may be exacerbated by higher water temperatures, increased precipitation intensity and longer periods of low flow.

Changes in flooding and droughts and depletion and degradation of water resources are serious barriers for sustainable development, because they affect the well-being of regional and local societies by hindering safe access to sufficient quality water. As all the problems induced by climate change affect the function and operation of the existing water infrastructure and water management practices, many countries face challenges in improving water usage and risk management to respond to new conditions under climate change. Therefore, countermeasures against climate change for water will be a long-term challenge for many countries.

4-1-2-2 Ecosystems

Climate change will affect various ecosystems, such as forests, high mountains, freshwater, marine and coastal regions, wetlands and deserts. Some major impacts include extinction of species, loss of biodiversity, changes in ecosystem structure and degradation of goods and service supply. Simultaneously, we should pay attention to the fact that many ecosystems have already been stressed by human activities such as land-use change, pollution and over-exploitation of resources. Therefore, impacts on ecosystems are a complex combination of existing human activities, climate change and associated disturbances of flooding, drought, wildfire, insect intrusion and ocean acidification. In general, ecosystems already weakened by other drivers are particularly vulnerable to climate change. Since the space to explore the entire picture of the impacts presented in the IPCC AR4 is limited, this section describes only symbolic issues.

Forests are likely to undergo large-scale changes: Amazon forests, taiga forests of China and much of the Siberian and Canadian tundra forests would show major changes with more than 3°C increase in global mean temperature. While forest expansions are predicted in North America and Eurasia if temperature rise is less than 2°C, tropical forests will probably be severely impacted, including biodiversity losses. In oceans, coral bleaching will occur over the next 50 years, thereby causing major loss of corals, particularly from the Great Barrier Reef. Acidification of oceans due to increasing atmospheric CO_2 is expected, and surface ocean pH would further decrease by 0.5 by 2100. This will impair shell or exoskeleton formation of marine organisms such as corals, crabs, squids, marine snails, clams and oysters.

Analyses have identified the following ecosystems as most vulnerable: tundra, boreal forest, mountain and Mediterranean-type ecosystems on continents, mangroves and salt marshes along coasts and coral reefs and

sea-ice biomes in oceans. As a result of these combined effects, we will experience a large biodiversity loss because approximately 20–30 per cent of species assessed until now would be at high risk of extinction if global mean temperatures increase by more than 2–3°C.

Ecosystems are considered to be a basis to support the sustainability of human beings by providing biological products and services. These ecosystem services include regulation of climatic conditions, filtering and cleaning air and water, and presenting natural beauty and inspiration. If ecosystems are damaged drastically by the combined effects of climate change and other stresses, including development and land-use changes, the foundation for the well-being of human society would be seriously eroded. This is a primary concern about the impacts of climate change. However, we do not yet understand the comprehensive relationship between climate change and changes in ecosystem and biodiversity. How do ecosystems shift under changing climate? How much can we rely on ecosystem goods and services in the future? These are challenging research themes in sustainability science.

4-1-2-3 Food production

Food production is a major concern in terms of climate change impact. However, the emergence of effects of increasing temperature is not simple because the fertilizing effect of CO_2 promotes plant growth. Because of this, and preferred higher temperature conditions, the global food production potential of agriculture would increase with a rise in global average temperature up to approximately 3°C; however, when this level is exceeded, the production potential will begin to decrease. In mid- to high-latitude regions, moderate warming would benefit cereal crops and pasture yields, while even slight warming would decrease yields in seasonally dry and tropical regions.

In addition to the impacts of changes in mean climate, changes in the frequency and severity of extreme events, together with an increase in risks of fire, pests and disease outbreak, will have significant effects on food production. Imbalance between food supply and demand may be addressed through international trade. In response to climate change, many developing countries in Asia and Africa could try to increase food trade because population growth and changes in dietary habit are expected in these countries. This tendency increases the food import dependency of these countries.

A key question for food production is whether the number of people at risk of hunger will increase because of climate change. Since socio-economic development generally reduces the number of people at risk of hunger, the net result will be a balance of socio-economic development and climate change impacts. Today, 820 million people are undernour-

ished. In the IPCC SRES scenarios of socio-economic development assuming no climate change, it is predicted that 100–770 million will be undernourished by 2080. On the other hand, scenarios including climate change predict that 100–1,300 million will be undernourished by 2080. Although the effects are uncertain, the number of people at risk of hunger will tend to increase with increase in climate change. Climate change and socio-economic development will combine to alter the regional distribution of hunger, but sub-Saharan Africa will face the most negative impacts.

4-1-2-4 Coastal zones and low-lying areas

Coastal zones and low-lying areas are particularly vulnerable to climate change because it intensifies stresses acting on the coastal zones, such as tropical cyclones, rise in sea level, increase in water temperature and changes in wave conditions. On the exposed side, coasts include fragile ecosystems, such as mangroves, wetlands and coral reefs; and problems arise from increasing concentrations of population and socio-economic activities. Therefore, as global warming proceeds, coastal zones will be exposed to increasing risks because of climate change and sea-level rise, and the effect will be exacerbated by human-induced pressures on coastal areas.

As for the natural environment in coastal zones, corals will experience a major decline because they are vulnerable to thermal stress. A projected future increase in sea surface temperature of approximately 1–3°C will result in more frequent bleaching events and widespread mortality. Coastal wetlands, including salt marshes and mangroves, are sensitive to increasing sea level, and it is estimated that 33 per cent of the wetlands existing in the world would be lost with a 36 cm rise in sea level. The largest losses will probably be on the Atlantic and Gulf of Mexico coasts of America, the Mediterranean, the Baltic and small island regions.

Coastal flooding in low-lying areas will become a greater risk in future because of sea-level rise and more intense coastal storms. Without adaptation, more than 100 million people could experience coastal flooding each year by the 2080s. Particularly vulnerable areas are those with high exposure to coastal storms and low human adaptive capacity. These include deltas, particularly Asian mega-deltas (the Ganges-Brahmaputra in Bangladesh and West Bengal as well as the Mekong), low-lying coastal urban areas, particularly areas prone to natural or human-induced subsidence and tropical storm landfall (e.g. New Orleans and Shanghai), and small islands, especially low-lying atolls (e.g. the Maldives and Tuvalu).

Sea-level rise is caused by thermal expansion of seawater, melting land-based glaciers and snow and disintegration of ice sheets in Greenland and Antarctica. Because these phenomena have substantial inertia

compared to other climate change factors, sea-level rise will continue beyond 2100 for many centuries. Climate stabilization could reduce but not stop sea-level rise. Hence there is a need to consider long-term adaptation; this will be discussed more in a later section.

4-1-2-5 Industries, settlement and human health

In terms of socio-economic vulnerabilities, there are high-risk locations. Typical are coastal and riverine areas prone to extreme weather events and areas whose economies are linked with climate-sensitive resources such as agricultural and forest product industries; other factors are water demands, tourism and rapid urbanization. In general, because these areas are distributed in developing countries, vulnerability of the society is higher in these countries. Furthermore, within these countries, poor communities and households are particularly vulnerable to climate change because they are already under stress from climate variability and extreme events and tend to be concentrated in unsafe areas lacking sanitation. They also have only limited access to social services and resources for coping with these threats. For climate-related risk management, it is necessary to increase social ability for coping, i.e. adaptive capacity, including robust and reliable physical infrastructures.

Climate change will impact not only on society as a whole but also individuals, especially their health. Health impacts extend across wide areas: nutritional status, death and injuries caused by disasters, thermal stress and heat-related mortality, vector- and water-borne infectious diseases such as malaria and dengue and diseases related to urban air quality. These will affect the health status of millions of people; in particular, the effects will be severe for those with low adaptive capacity in developing countries and poor communities. For example, climate change may increase the frequency of malnutrition and consequent disorders, which will have implications for child growth and development. Climate change is expected to have some mixed effects on the range and transmission potential of malaria in Africa. Although it may bring some benefits, such as fewer deaths from exposure to cold, these benefits would overall be outweighed by the negative health effects of rising temperatures worldwide, especially in developing countries.

4-1-2-6 Changes in impact due to the magnitude of climate change, and the most vulnerable regions

Based on sector- and region-based assessment, the IPCC AR4 presented an entire picture of the magnitude of impact varying with the extent of climate change, as shown in Figure 4.1.2.

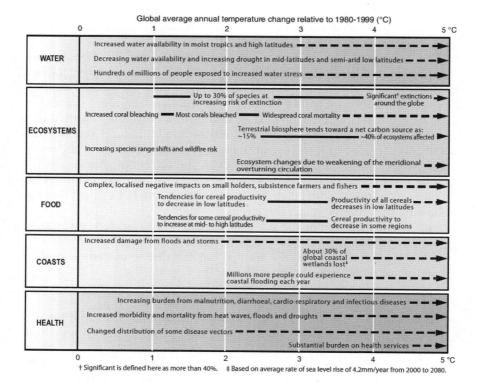

Global average annual temperature change relative to 1980-1999 (°C)

WATER
- Increased water availability in moist tropics and high latitudes
- Decreasing water availability and increasing drought in mid-latitudes and semi-arid low latitudes
- Hundreds of millions of people exposed to increased water stress

ECOSYSTEMS
- Up to 30% of species at increasing risk of extinction ── Significant† extinctions around the globe
- Increased coral bleaching ── Most corals bleached ── Widespread coral mortality
- Terrestrial biosphere tends toward a net carbon source as: ~15% ── ~40% of ecosystems affected
- Increasing species range shifts and wildfire risk
- Ecosystem changes due to weakening of the meridional overturning circulation

FOOD
- Complex, localised negative impacts on small holders, subsistence farmers and fishers
- Tendencies for cereal productivity to decrease in low latitudes ── Productivity of all cereals decreases in low latitudes
- Tendencies for some cereal productivity to increase at mid- to high latitudes ── Cereal productivity to decrease in some regions

COASTS
- Increased damage from floods and storms
- About 30% of global coastal wetlands lost‡
- Millions more people could experience coastal flooding each year

HEALTH
- Increasing burden from malnutrition, diarrhoeal, cardio-respiratory and infectious diseases
- Increased morbidity and mortality from heat waves, floods and droughts
- Changed distribution of some disease vectors
- Substantial burden on health services

† Significant is defined here as more than 40%.   ‡ Based on average rate of sea level rise of 4.2mm/year from 2000 to 2080.

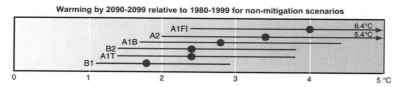

Warming by 2090-2099 relative to 1980-1999 for non-mitigation scenarios

A1FI ── 6.4°C
A2 ── 5.4°C
A1B
B2
A1T
B1

Figure 4.1.2 Examples of impacts associated with projected global average surface warming

Upper panel: Illustrative examples of global impacts projected for climate change associated with different increases in global average surface temperature in the twenty-first century. The black lines link impacts; broken-line arrows indicate impacts continuing with increasing temperature. Entries are placed so that the left-hand side of the text indicates the approximate level of warming that is associated with the onset of a given impact. Quantitative entries for water scarcity and flooding represent the additional impacts of climate change relative to the conditions projected across the range of SRES scenarios A1FI, A2, B1 and B2. Adaptation to climate change is not included in these estimations. Confidence levels for all statements are high.

Lower panel: Dots and bars indicate the best estimate and probable ranges of warming assessed for the six SRES marker scenarios for 2090–2099 relative to 1980–1999.

Source: IPCC (2007a).

The horizontal axis of Figure 4.1.2 indicates increasing global mean temperature, which is a measure of the amount of climate change. Natural systems would experience significant changes, such as glacier melting, species extinction and coral mortality, even with a temperature rise as low as 1°C. Industries such as agriculture and fisheries are also sensitive to a relatively low temperature rise because they rely on natural systems. The fertilizing effect of CO_2 will enhance plant productivity and thus be beneficial to agriculture and forestry. However, the effects of climate change will be negative when the temperature rise exceeds approximately 3°C.

In terms of the regional distribution of impacts, the IPCC identified the following particularly vulnerable areas.

- The Arctic, because of the effects of high rates of projected warming on natural systems.
- Africa, especially the sub-Saharan region, because of current low adaptive capacity as well as climate change.
- Small islands, because of high population and infrastructure exposure to risk of sea-level rise and increased storm surges.
- Asian mega-deltas, such as the Ganges-Brahmaputra and the Zhujiang, because of their large populations and high exposure to sea-level rise, storm surges and river flooding.

In other areas, even those with high incomes, some people can be particularly at risk, such as the poor, young children and the elderly.

A major issue for impact assessments is how to determine the dangerous level of global warming. In international forums such as the 2009 G8 Summit held in L'Aquila, Italy, and COP15 in Copenhagen, a 2°C increase was often referred to as a target of temperature stabilization. However, it is difficult to determine a specific value from the scientific viewpoint, because many sectors and countries have different critical temperatures as shown so far. Determination of the dangerous level is a matter of value judgement and highly subjective. For example, small island countries have insisted that a 2°C increase is too high because they face risks of inundation, while other countries may withstand a higher temperature increase. Therefore, this target should be determined based on social and political judgements in the international negotiations. In this regard, the role of science related to impact assessment is to provide a comprehensive and accurate picture of future risks caused by climate change.

4-1-2-7 Large-scale events causing abrupt change and large impacts

There is another concern regarding the key impacts of climate change: large-scale events which could possibly cause abrupt changes in the Earth's systems and have a major worldwide impact.

One of these is a very large rise in sea level that would result from widespread deglaciation of the Greenland and West Antarctic ice sheets. The IPCC AR4 indicated with medium confidence that at least partial deglaciation of the Greenland ice sheet, and probably the West Antarctic ice sheet, would occur over a period of time, ranging from centuries to millennia, with a global average temperature increase of 1–4°C (relative to 1990–2000) contributing to a sea-level rise of 4–6 m or more. Complete melting of the Greenland and West Antarctic ice sheets would lead to a sea-level rise of up to 7 m and 5 m, respectively. Since the major cities in the world, where population and economic activities are largely concentrated, are situated on the coasts, such a large sea-level rise would have tremendous effects on today's civilization and result in major changes in coastlines and ecosystems. Relocating populations, economic activity and infrastructure would be unaccountably expensive and challenging. Although the future estimates of such large phenomena involve high uncertainty, their impacts will be extremely significant if they occur. Therefore, a precautionary strategy should be applied to minimize the possibility of their occurrence. We should realize that our decisions today will determine the long-term future of society.

4-1-3 Countermeasures against climate change and its implications for sustainable development

4-1-3-1 Countermeasures against climate change

There are two basic countermeasures to address global warming: one is mitigation and the other adaptation. Mitigation involves measures to reduce emissions and strengthen the absorption of greenhouse gases (GHGs), while adaptation includes measures to increase preparedness for the adverse effects of climate change. To date, many efforts have been made to mitigate global warming, mainly in developed industrialized countries. Policies about mitigation will be discussed in Chapter 5. In the face of the emerging impacts of climate change mentioned above, people now realize the necessity and importance of adaptation. Adaptation is particularly important for the next 30 years because the effects of mitigation efforts will not be realized for several decades. However, this does not mean that mitigation is of no fundamental importance to stabilizing global warming in the long run. Therefore, measures against global warming should be a portfolio of mitigation and adaptation.

It is known that global warming cannot be suppressed completely, and impacts of climate change and extreme events will occur. The effects will be much more serious in developing countries because they lack social infrastructure to prepare for hazards and provide support for people's

well-being. These countries include small islands, such as Tuvalu, Kiribati and the Maldives, and countries situated on low-lying deltas, such as Bangladesh. In terms of the stock of social infrastructure, African countries are particularly problematic. Since their GHG emissions are low, the major countermeasure for these countries should be adaptation.

4-1-3-2 Adaptation and sustainable development

Adaptation requires society's ability to reduce adverse impacts of climate change and utilize its favourable effects. There have been intensive discussions on the concept and implementation of adaptation, mainly focusing on developing countries (Huq et al., 2003; Hay and Mimura, 2005, 2006; IPCC, 2007c). Countermeasures against current meteorological extreme events, such as droughts and floods, are also effective measures to adapt to future climate change. Since the projections of future climate change entail uncertainties, the entry point of adaptation options is no-regret measures, which are effective in improving preparedness for hazards today.

The success of adaptation depends on the adaptive capacity of each country and local community. Studies are necessary to identify the roles of factors that can strengthen adaptability. In communities, traditional mutual cooperation and consanguineous networks are important. Furthermore, it will be a major challenge to incorporate the traditional knowledge and technologies of the communities into modern science and technology. To date, the policies of central and local governments have rarely considered the local situation properly.

Mainstreaming adaptation is also emphasized, which means incorporating adaptation considerations into major policies, such as disaster prevention plans, water resource management, agricultural and food security policies and environmental management, rather than highlighting adaptation in isolation. Only this can ensure effective adaptation to climate change. Adaptation to climate change and sustainable development share the same direction of socio-economic development. Strengthening adaptive capacity includes many activities, such as reducing human pressure on resources, management of environmental risk and social resilience to hazards, which are important targets of sustainable development. Therefore, adaptation is considered an important component of sustainable development.

Human society faces problems other than climate change, such as environmental pollution, loss of biodiversity, changes in land use due to economic development, population growth and economic globalization. It is important to address these pressures together with global warming. The real world is under multiple stresses, and sustainable development

can be achieved by solving these problems in a holistic manner. This approach will pave the way to sustainable development. These aspects will be discussed in the following chapters, which deal with designing climate policy and integration of a low-carbon society with a resource-circulating and nature-harmonious society.

REFERENCES

Hay, J. E. and N. Mimura (2005) "Sea-level Rise: Implications for Water Resources Management", *Mitigation and Adaptation Strategies for Global Change* 10(4), pp. 717–737.

——— (2006) "Supporting Climate Change Vulnerability and Adaptation Assessments in the Asia-Pacific Region – An Example of Sustainability Science", *Sustainability Science* 1(1), pp. 23–35.

Huq, S., A. Rahman, M. Konate, Y. Sokona and H. Reid (2003) *Mainstreaming Adaptation to Climate Change in Least Developed Countries (LDCs)*. London: International Institute for Sustainable Development.

IPCC (2000) "Emissions Scenarios 2000", in N. Nakicenovic and R. Swart (eds) *Special Report of the Intergovernmental Panel on Climate Change*. Cambridge: Cambridge University Press.

——— (2007a) *Climate Change 2007: Synthesis Report*. Geneva: IPCC.

——— (2007b) *Climate Change 2007: The Physical Science Basis*. Cambridge: Cambridge University Press.

——— (2007c) *Climate Change 2007: Impacts, Adaptation and Vulnerability*. Cambridge: Cambridge University Press.

4-2

Climate change impacts in Japan

Yasuaki Hijioka

4-2-1 Impact assessment of climate change in Japan

There are a number of research projects in progress focusing on climate change impacts in Japan. One of these is titled Project for Comprehensive Projection of Climate Change Impacts. This study developed risk maps to represent quantitatively nationwide and regional climate change impacts in Japan by field (Project Team for Comprehensive Projection of Climate Change Impacts, 2008).

The results, focusing on the projected physical impacts in five fields – water resources, forests, agriculture, coastal zone/disaster prevention and human health – are summarized below.

4-2-1-1 Water resources

The frequency and intensity of torrential downpours will increase, flood damage will expand and landslide disasters and dam sedimentation will worsen. The costs of water supply purification will rise due to increased turbid runoff during periods without rainfall. On the other hand, decreases in snow-water resources will cause shortages of agricultural water at the time of ploughing and irrigation of fields on the Pacific side of the Tohoku region, and the risk of water shortages will increase in various areas, including southern Kyushu and Okinawa, due to changes in precipitation.

Climate change and global sustainability: A holistic approach, Sumi, Mimura and Masui (eds),
United Nations University Press, 2011, ISBN 978-92-808-1181-0

4-2-1-2 Forests

Forests in Japan will suffer severe consequences as a result of increased temperature and changes in rainfall from global warming. The distribution of suitable habitats for Siebold's beech (*Fagus crenata*) forests, dwarf bamboo (*Sasa kurilensis*), Japanese stone pine (*Pinus pumila*) and Abies shikokiana will sharply decrease, and from around the middle of the twenty-first century the Shirakami mountain range will no longer be a suitable habitat for beech forest. There will also be increased risk of pine-wilt damage with a temperature rise of 1–2°C, resulting in the area of risk expanding to the northern tip of Honshu where such damage has not yet occurred.

4-2-1-3 Rice yield

Rice yields will increase in northern Japan, while yields in the southwest of the country from the Kinki region westward will be roughly the same as or slightly lower than at present. Agriculture will be significantly affected by deterioration in rice quality, a northward shift in areas suitable for the cultivation of other cereals, fruit trees and other crops, and decreases in their yields.

4-2-1-4 Coastal zones

Rising sea levels and increasing storm surges will result in increased flood damage to vulnerable areas and populations even when current shore protection measures are considered. The risk of flooding will be particularly high in semi-enclosed sea areas, such as the Seto Inland Sea, and land areas bordering the inner parts of Japan's three major bays (Tokyo Bay, Ise Bay, Osaka Bay), which were reclaimed long ago, as well as their environs. Moreover, rising sea levels will weaken river embankments through the expansion of brackish waters and increase the risk of liquefaction in coastal zones.

4-2-1-5 Human health

Global warming will result in increased threats to human health. With rising temperatures, especially the daily maximum temperature, the mortality risk from heat stress and the incidence of heatstroke will drastically increase. In particular, the risk to people of advanced age will become greater. The occurrence of atmospheric pollution (photochemical oxidants) due to changes in weather will increase. The potential range of

distribution of vector mosquitoes for infectious diseases (dengue, malaria and Japanese encephalitis) will also expand.

The results of this research indicate that Japan will experience significant impacts even with a relatively small temperature increase.

4-2-2 Integrated assessment model and stabilization scenarios

Under the Project for Comprehensive Projection of Climate Change Impacts, the integrated assessment model AIM/Impact[Policy] has been developed for the assessment of global warming control targets. These targets include the stabilization of GHG concentrations and global mean temperature increase as well as economically efficient paths to emission abatement for realizing these targets and their consequent impacts and risks (Hijioka et al., 2006, 2008; Hijioka and Takahashi, 2006). Figure 4.2.1 illustrates the structure of AIM/Impact[Policy].

Using AIM/Impact[Policy], impacts in a time series can be calculated for established policy targets, such as climate stabilization levels or emis-

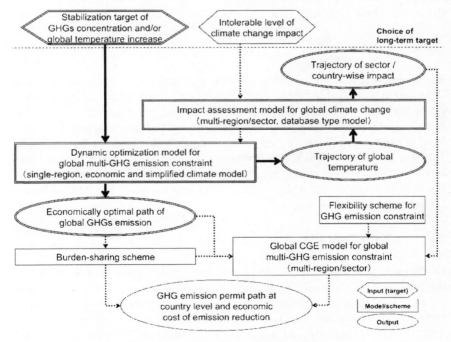

Figure 4.2.1 Structure of AIM/Impact[Policy]

sion reduction targets. This model makes it possible to determine whether unacceptable levels of serious climate change impacts can be avoided by achieving a certain climate stabilization target. As such, the model is an effective tool for evaluating global warming mitigation policies while also considering global warming impacts.

4-2-2-1 Integrated assessment model

AIM/Impact[Policy] comprises many models that are linked via input and output data. The model can quantitatively show national and prefectural global warming impacts by sector, with the input condition being the global mean temperature change that is estimated under the assumed temperature rise and GHG concentration stabilization target. To integrate several types of detailed impact assessment models for climate change, the model adopts impact response functions for sectors of individual countries and Japan. Impact response functions are aggregates (databases) that result when the aforementioned detailed model is used to perform many repeated simulations, while primary factors such as temperature and precipitation are varied, as in sensitivity analysis, and the output averaged according to region.

4-2-2-2 Stabilization scenarios

AIM/Impact[Policy] was used to perform a comprehensive assessment of sectoral global warming impacts with Japan as the region (Project Team for Comprehensive Projection of Climate Change Impacts, 2009). To prepare the climate scenarios for this purpose, we used normalized climate change databases created by MIROC3.2hires, which is a high-resolution atmosphere-ocean coupled general circulation model with a horizontal resolution of 1.125° (about 100 km). This model was developed by a joint research team from The University of Tokyo Center for Climate System Research, the National Institute for Environmental Studies and the Japan Agency for Marine-Earth Science and Technology's Frontier Research Center for Global Change. To assess global warming impacts, we conducted an analysis of GHG emission control policies to examine the stabilization of GHG concentrations and GHG reduction timings under "business as usual" (BaU) conditions and two additional constraints, as follows.

- BaU: Temperature increase of approximately 3.8°C in 2100.
- 450s: 450 ppmv cap on total GHG concentrations (CO_2 equivalent concentration). Equilibrium temperature increase of approximately 2.1°C compared with pre-industrial levels.

- 550s: 550 ppmv cap on total GHG concentrations (CO_2 equivalent concentration). Equilibrium temperature increase of approximately 2.9°C compared with pre-industrial levels.

We performed constraint optimization calculations in which equilibrium global temperature increase did not exceed the constraint between 1990 and 2200. We used the SRES B2 scenario prepared by the IPCC for future population and future economic growth. An equilibrium climate sensitivity of 3.0°C was applied. The carbon feedback effect was not considered.

4-2-3 Impact assessments by stabilization level of atmospheric GHG concentration

Table 4.2.1 outlines the sectoral impact assessment using the integrated assessment model.

We calculated the sectoral impacts in Japan under the BaU scenario and the two GHG concentration constraint scenarios (Figure 4.2.2). In this assessment, the adaptation effect is not considered. The impacts of global warming are the increments relative to 1981–2000 (or 1990) as the base period or year.

4-2-3-1 Impacts of floods: Flooded area

The lower the level at which GHG concentration is stabilized, the smaller will be the flooded area. Even under the 450s scenario, however, damage is expected to increase substantially. Large differences in the nationwide flooded area under the 450s, 550s and BaU scenarios are not evident until around mid-century (up to the 2050s). Thereafter, differences appear according to the scenario, with the maximum flooded area expected to reach approximately 1,000 km^2, 1,100 km^2 and 1,200 km^2 under scenarios 450s, 550s and BaU, respectively.

4-2-3-2 Impacts of floods: Flood damage cost potential

The lower the level at which GHG concentration is stabilized, the smaller will be the flood damage cost potential. Even under the 450s scenario, however, damage is expected to increase, accompanying the progress of global warming.

Significant differences among scenarios are not seen until around mid-century (up to the 2050s), and by around 2050 the flood damage cost potential is slightly less than 5 trillion yen/year. Approaching the end of the century (up to the 2090s), significant differences appear according to the

Table 4.2.1 Sectoral impact assessment using an integrated assessment model

Outline of impact assessment by field

Flood area

– Climatic variables: annual daily maximum precipitation.
– Japan's average level of protection corresponds to that for downpour rainfall occurring once every 50 years under the present circumstances.
– Three major metropolitan areas have a higher level of protection, corresponding to that for downpour rainfall occurring once every 150 years under the present circumstances.
– The level of protection remains unchanged in the future.

Flood damage cost potential

– Flood damage cost potential is estimated as follows.
  (1) Establish method for calculating the cost of damage according to each land-use type, with reference to "assets subjected to direct damage" in the *Manual for Economic Evaluation of Flood Control Investment* of the Ministry of Land, Infrastructure, Transport and Tourism.
  (2) Extract distribution of flood depth and flood period from the flood calculations.
  (3) Calculate flood damage costs, applying the method described in (1) above, considering the land-use classification of each grid cell.
– The level of protection remains unchanged in the future.
– Depreciation of asset values due to damage is not considered.

Probability of slope failure

– Climatic variables: annual daily maximum precipitation.
– Probability of slope failure when rainfall exceeds 50 mm/day (one assumption in terms of model analysis).

Slope failure damage cost potential

– Economic loss calculation: Amount of economic loss = Economic value (basic economic unit) × Scale (area) of land use × Probability of slope failure.
– Depreciation of asset values in areas that have suffered from such a disaster in the past and future changes in asset values are not considered.

Suitable habitats for F. crenata *forest*

– Climatic variables: cumulative temperature (warmth index), daily minimum temperature of the coldest month, winter precipitation (December–March) and summer precipitation (May–September).
– The migrations of *F. crenata* forests and land use are not considered.

Cost of damage from decrease in suitable habitats for F. crenata *forest*

– The environmental economic value of *F. crenata* forests is estimated by the contingent valuation method (CVM), focusing on their biodiversity maintenance function.
– The value is the non-market value (the value of items not traded on the market).

Table 4.2.1 (cont.)

Outline of impact assessment by field

Areas at risk of pine wilt

– Climatic variables: annual mean temperature increase.
– Considering present land-use types, the changes in areas at risk of pine wilt accompanying global warming are estimated by an impact function that estimates risk based on the cumulative mean temperature of each month, with a threshold of 15°C (MB index).

Rice yield

– Climatic variables: changes in accumulative insolation in the warm season (May–October), mean temperature change in summer (July, August), mean temperature change and CO_2 concentration in the warm season excluding summer (May, June, September, October).
– The biomass of rice plants is determined by the balance between the decrease accompanying the reduction in growing season due to temperature rise and the increase accompanying the CO_2 fertilization effect. The final rice yield is determined by the positive effect due to the reduction in cold-weather damage in currently cool regions, and the negative effect due to high temperature-induced sterility in currently warm regions.

Economic value of sandy beach loss

– Given future sea-level rises, the area of beaches encroached on is estimated by prefecture.
– Sea-level rises by the 2090s: 0.15 m (450s), 0.19 m (550s) or 0.24 m (BaU).
– Differences in sea-level rises among regions are not considered; it is assumed that sea-level changes occur uniformly throughout Japan.
– The use value of sandy beaches is 2,179 yen/visit.

Affected population, area and cost of damage due to storm-surge flooding in western Japan

– The affected population, area and cost of damage due to storm-surge flooding in western Japan are estimated using a storm-surge flood model that incorporates storm-surge protection facilities and combines the impact functions of affected population, area and cost of damage due to storm-surge flooding obtained from numerous storm-surge flood calculations for various typhoon intensities and sea-level rises, as well as sea-level rise scenarios by stabilization level as estimated by the integrated assessment model.
– The damage occurring every year is estimated.
– Sea-level rises by the 2090s: 0.15 m (450s), 0.19 m (550s) or 0.24 m (BaU).
– The typhoon intensity is varied linearly to reach 1.3 in 2100, with 1990 = 1.

Affected population, area and cost of damage due to storm-surge flooding in Japan's three major bays

– The affected population, area and cost of damage due to storm-surge flooding in Japan's three major bays are estimated using a storm-surge flood model that incorporates storm-surge protection facilities and combines the impact

Table 4.2.1 (cont.)

Outline of impact assessment by field

functions of affected population, area and cost of damage due to storm-surge flooding obtained from numerous storm-surge flood calculations for various typhoon intensities and sea-level rises, as well as sea-level rise scenarios by stabilization level as estimated by the integrated assessment model. The degree of damage caused by the strongest category of typhoon (per occurrence) towards the end of the century is estimated.
– Sea-level rises by the 2090s: 0.15 m (450s), 0.19 m (550s) or 0.24 m (BaU).
– The typhoon intensity is varied linearly to reach 1.3 in 2100, with 1990 = 1.

Heat stress mortality risk

– Climatic variables: change in annual mean temperature.
– The probability of a person dying of heat stress during a year is estimated using a model for estimating excess mortality due to heat stress and its input data (that is, changes in the number of days with temperature higher than optimal temperature).
– Population data: the value for 1990 is used, with future values remaining unchanged.
– Population composition is not considered.
– Only changes in excess mortality at high temperatures due to temperature rise are examined, and changes in excess mortality at low temperatures are not targeted.

Cost of damage due to heat stress (heatstroke) mortality

– Focusing on the mortality risk due to heatstroke, which is one of the typical causes of death on hot days, the cost of damage is measured by the CVM.
– Changes in heatstroke mortality are estimated by multiplying the current average mortality due to heatstroke by the future changes in risk estimated using a model for estimating excess mortality due to heat stress, and this result is multiplied by the value of a statistical life (VSL) to estimate the cost of damage from mortality due to future heat stress (heatstroke).

scenario, with the maximum flood damage cost potential expected to reach approximately 6.4 trillion yen/year (450s), 7.6 trillion yen/year (550s) or 8.7 trillion yen/year (BaU).

4-2-3-3 Impacts of floods: Probability of slope failure

The lower the level at which GHG concentration is stabilized, the lower is the probability of slope failure. Under the 450s scenario, the increase in probability of slope failure shows a tendency to reach a ceiling.

Significant differences in the probability of slope failure nationwide under the 450s, 550s and BaU scenarios are not seen until around mid-century (2050s). However, by around the end of the century (2090s) differences in the probability of slope failure appear according to the

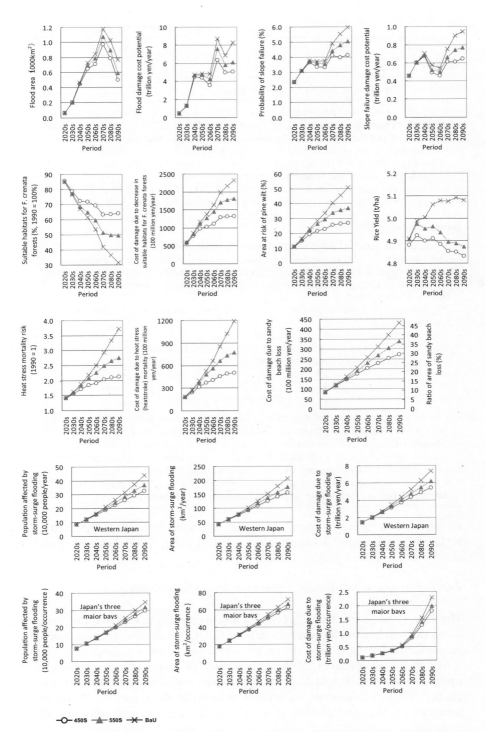

Figure 4.2.2 Impacts of climate change through the twenty-first century in Japan by sector

66

scenario, with expected maximum increases of approximately 4 per cent (450s), 5 per cent (550s) or 6 per cent (BaU).

4-2-3-4 Impacts of floods: Slope failure damage cost potential

The lower the level at which GHG concentration is stabilized, the lower will be the slope failure damage cost potential. Under the 450s scenario, the damage cost is expected to reach a ceiling.

Significant differences in slope failure damage cost potential nation-wide are not seen among the three scenarios until around mid-century (up to the 2050s). By the end of the century (up to the 2090s) significant differences appear depending on the scenario, with the value under the 450s scenario not varying noticeably from the value around mid-century (about 0.50 trillion yen/year), in contrast to maximum expected values reaching approximately 0.77 trillion yen/year under the 550s scenario and approximately 0.94 trillion yen/year in the case of BaU.

4-2-3-5 Impact on forests: Suitable habitats for F. crenata forest

Slight differences in the decrease in suitable habitat area for *F. crenata* forests under the 450s, 550s and BaU scenarios are expected around mid-century (2050s), with decreases of 28, 35 and 39 per cent, respectively. Large differences among the scenarios appear around the end of the century (2090s), with decreases of 36 per cent (450s), 50 per cent (550s) and 68 per cent (BaU). Under the strictest stabilization scenario (450s), the rate of decrease in suitable habitat area slows towards the end of the century. However, an unavoidable decrease of about 36 per cent is expected, so monitoring for conservation will become important.

4-2-3-6 Impact on forests: Cost of damage due to decrease in suitable habitat for F. crenata forest

Under the 450s and 550s GHG concentration stabilization scenarios, the rate of increase in the cost of damage is expected to decline towards the end of the twenty-first century. Slight differences are seen in the cost of damage under the three scenarios around mid-century (2050s), with costs of 103.4 billion (450s), 127.3 billion (550s) and 138.1 billion yen/year (BaU). Significant differences appear among the scenarios by the end of the century (2090s), with costs of 132.5 billion, 181.1 billion and 232.4 billion yen/year, respectively.

4-2-3-7 Impacts on forests: Areas at risk of pine wilt

Irrespective of the stabilization level, areas at risk of pine wilt are expected to continue to expand in the future. However, under the 450s

scenario with the lowest stabilized GHG concentration, it is possible that the trend of expansion will be halted around the end of the century. Slight differences in the proportion of area at risk of pine wilt nationwide under the 450s, 550s and BaU scenarios are seen around mid-century (2050s), at approximately 22, 26 and 28 per cent, respectively. Substantial differences appear among the scenarios around the end of the century (2090s), when the percentages of area at risk are expected to reach 27, 37 and 51 per cent, respectively.

4-2-3-8 Impacts on agriculture: Rice yield

Until around mid-century (up to the 2050s), increases in rice yield are expected because the negative effects of the reduction in growth period are less than the CO_2 fertilization effect and also because of the reduction in cold-weather damage. Thereafter, under scenarios 450s and 550s the trend reverses to one of decreasing yields towards the end of the century (2090s) because the negative effects from the reduction in growth period are greater than the CO_2 fertilization effect and yields are reduced due to higher temperatures. In contrast, under the BaU scenario, although the trend will not reverse to become a reduction in yield, the rate of increase is expected to become gradually lower.

Increases in yield can be expected due to global warming. However, this trend is forecast to reach a ceiling at a certain level of temperature rise, and a trend of increasing inter-annual variations in yield is projected due to the relationship between temperature and sterility rate. There are also concerns regarding the impacts of climate change on quality and taste.

4-2-3-9 Economic value of sandy beach loss

Even under the 450s scenario, the area of sandy beach loss due to sea-level rise continues to increase until the end of the century (up to the 2090s), with expected losses of approximately 29 per cent of the sandy beach area. Under scenarios 550s and BaU, losses are expected to reach approximately 37 and 47 per cent, respectively, over the same period. The cost of damage due to sandy beach loss by the end of the century is expected to reach approximately 27.3 billion yen/year (450s), 33.8 billion yen/year (550s) or 43.0 billion yen/year (BaU). When compared with BaU, a substantial damage reduction effect can be expected under the 450s scenario. However, damage due to the rise in sea level is expected to continue for a long period, even under the 450s scenario; therefore, long-term adaptation measures are important.

4-2-3-10 Affected population and area and cost of damage from storm-surge flooding in western Japan

With rising sea level and more powerful typhoons accompanying the progress of global warming, damage is expected to increase in western Japan. Damage in this region by the end of the century (2090s) in terms of the population and area affected and the cost could reach the following levels:

- 450s: approximately 320,000 people/year, 155 km²/year, 5.4 trillion yen/year
- 550s: approximately 370,000 people/year, 176 km²/year, 6.2 trillion yen/year
- BaU: approximately 440,000 people/year, 207 km²/year, 7.4 trillion yen/year.

4-2-3-11 Affected population and area and cost of damage from storm-surge flooding in Japan's three major bays

Storm-surge damage is also expected to increase in Japan's three major bays, as follows:

- 450s: approximately 300,000 people/event, 63 km²/event, 1.8 trillion yen/event
- 550s: approximately 320,000 people/event, 67 km²/event, 2.0 trillion yen/event
- BaU: approximately 350,000 people/event, 72 km²/event, 2.3 trillion yen/event.

4-2-3-12 Heat stress mortality risk

The lower the level at which GHG concentration is stabilized, the smaller the heat stress mortality risk. Under the 450s scenario, the rate of increase in mortality risk is expected to become gradually lower towards the end of the century.

Differences in heat stress mortality risk under scenarios 450s, 550s and BaU remain comparatively small around mid-century (2050s), at approximately 1.8, 2.1 and 2.2 times baseline (current) levels, respectively. At the end of the century (2090s), however, larger differences are expected depending on the scenario, at approximately 2.1, 2.8 and 3.7 times current levels, respectively.

4-2-3-13 Cost of damage from heat stress (heatstroke) mortality

The lower the level at which GHG concentration is stabilized, the lower the cost of damage due to heat stress (heatstroke) mortality. Particularly

in the case of the strictest stabilization level (450s), the cost of such damage is expected to reach a ceiling near the end of the twenty-first century, at approximately 50 billion yen/year.

Differences in the cost of such damage remain comparatively small around mid-century (2050s), at approximately 37.3 billion yen/year (450s), 48.0 billion yen/year (550s) and 52.9 billion yen/year (BaU). By the end of the century (2090s) large differences are expected according to the stabilization level, reaching approximately 50.1 billion yen/year (450s), 77.5 billion yen/year (550s) or 119.2 billion yen/year (BaU).

4-2-4 Conclusion

In Japan, as in the rest of the world, greater impacts of global warming are expected in the future in a broad range of fields related to people's lives. If a significant reduction in global GHG emissions is achieved, a considerable reduction in the damage to Japan can be expected. However, even when the GHG concentration is stabilized at 450 ppm CO_2-equivalent concentration, a certain amount of damage is unavoidable.

Global warming is expected to progress over the next 20 years irrespective of whether additional mitigation measures are implemented. However, differences in impacts reflecting differences in the global climate stabilization level are expected to become larger from around mid-century onward. Therefore, in addition to the active implementation of mitigation measures for stabilizing the climate, it is necessary to study and implement without delay long-term adaptation measures in preparation for certain levels of adverse impacts.

In this chapter, general and overall climate change impacts in Japan have been discussed, considering future GHG stabilization targets. Chapters 4-3–4-6 introduce detailed sectoral impacts of climate change.

REFERENCES

Hijioka, Y. and K. Takahashi (2006) "Integrated Assessment of Greenhouse Gas Stabilization Concentrations, Emission Pathways, and Impact Threshold Values for Control of Global Warming", *Global Environmental Research* 10(2), pp. 261–270.

Hijioka, Y., T. Masui, K. Takahashi, Y. Matsuoka and H. Harasawa (2006) "Development of a Support Tool for Greenhouse Gas Emissions Control Policy to Help Mitigate the Impact of Global Warming", *Environmental Economics and Policy Studies* 7(3), pp. 331–345.

Hijioka, Y., Y. Matsuoka, H. Nishimoto, T. Masui and M. Kainuma (2008) "Global GHG Emission Scenarios under GHG Concentration Stabilization Targets", *Journal of Global Environment Engineering* 13, pp. 97–108.

Project Team for Comprehensive Projection of Climate Change Impacts (2008) "Global Warming Impacts on Japan – Latest Scientific Findings", available at www.nies.go.jp/s4_impact/seika.html#seika1.

―――― (2009) "Global Warming Impacts on Japan – Long-Term Climate Stabilization Levels and Impact Risk Assessment", available at www.nies.go.jp/s4_impact/seika.html#seika3.

4-3

Water resource problems due to climate change

So Kazama

Water resource problems have had a discernible influence on many fields, directly in terms of food and ecosystems and indirectly in terms of water-borne infectious diseases, coastal erosion and so forth. Here we present four examples of climate-driven changes related to water resources: flood impact, sedimentation disaster, snow-water resource depletion and water quality problems in Japan. Water-related disasters are sometimes independent of water resources; however, Japan has struggled for a long time with regard to both flood control and sustainable water use because it frequently experiences floods and droughts due to its steep, mountainous terrain and high levels of rainfall. The following sections depict the vulnerability of social, environmental and economical sectors of Japan to climate change. Some of the adaptation measures that should be implemented are discussed in these sections.

4-3-1 Flood and adaptation

According to the Fourth Assessment Report of the Intergovernmental Panel on Climate Change (IPCC AR4), the magnitude of global climate change in the latter part of the twenty-first century is expected to be higher than that in the twentieth century (IPCC, 2007: 11). It is predicted that rainfall intensity will increase and cause more frequent and serious flood damage. Furthermore, Atmospheric General Circular Model (AGCM) results show that rainfall will increase in Japan and cause more

Climate change and global sustainability: A holistic approach, Sumi, Mimura and Masui (eds), United Nations University Press, 2011, ISBN 978-92-808-1181-0

frequent and serious flood damage (JMA, 2005). The severity or impact of flood hazards depends on the preparedness and implementation of adaptation measures beforehand.

In general, climatic parameters, geology and topography as well as socio-economic activities differ greatly from one local setting to another. To encourage spatial adaptation mechanisms at the local scale, we estimated the national costs of flood damage by numerical simulations based on digital map data and the flood control economy investigation manual prepared by the Ministry of Land, Infrastructure, Transport and Tourism (MLIT, 2004) in Japan. Simulation was performed using a flood model incorporating representative precipitation data for the whole of Japan. The flood model comprises general hydraulic concepts, 2D non-uniform flow and elevation and land-use data for determination of hydraulic surface roughness (Kazama, Sato and Kawagoe, 2009). AGCM results were incorporated into the analysis, predicting a probable change in future precipitation patterns in the respective areas. Local-scale precipitation was estimated from AGCM projections using a statistical downscaling technique. This technique statistically links AGCM output and several local morphological factors, such as elevation and surface aspects, using factor analysis and applies the relationship to smaller grid cells on a digital map. Flood damage caused by extreme rainfall for the return periods of five, 10, 30, 50 and 100 years was estimated with respect to the linear relationship between monthly AGCM rainfall obtained using the statistical downscaling technique and extreme rainfall calculated at observed points.

To decide the investment cost for disaster adaptation by infrastructure construction, it is important to estimate the benefits of hazard risk reduction in terms of reduced property damage. We performed cost-benefit analyses for several future precipitation scenarios and estimated the economic benefit of flood protection measures (ibid.), which is expected to guide decision-making towards more resilient decisions. Table 4.3.1 shows the potential damage cost for each return period.

In the same approximation of flood defence completion for 50-year flooding (current flood control can prevent damage of US$910 billion), the benefit of protecting from flooding for 100 years is the difference in the damage cost between return periods of 50 and 100 years, which is approximately US$210 billion (1,120–910 in Table 4.3.1). Furthermore, the numerical simulation results depict that the nationwide distribution of potential damage cost increases by shifting extreme rainfall from a 50-year to a 100-year return period, as shown in Figure 4.3.1.

Increase in potential damage cost is the same as the benefit of protecting from 100-year flooding. Urban areas receive the most benefits because of the high cost of flood damage in densely populated areas.

Table 4.3.1 Annual expected damage costs and return periods

Return period (years)	Annual extreme probability	Damage cost (US$ billion)	Interval average damage	Interval probability	Average annual expected damage cost (US$ billion)
5	0.200	380			
10	0.100	550	470	0.100	47
30	0.033	770	660	0.067	44
50	0.020	910	840	0.013	11
100	0.010	1,120	1,020	0.010	10
150	0.007	1,130	1,130	0.003	3

Note: Interval average damage is estimated from damage costs associated with two return periods. For example, interval average damage, interval probability and average annual expected damage cost of the 30-year return period are $(770 + 550)/2.0$, $0.100–0.033$ and 660×0.067, respectively.

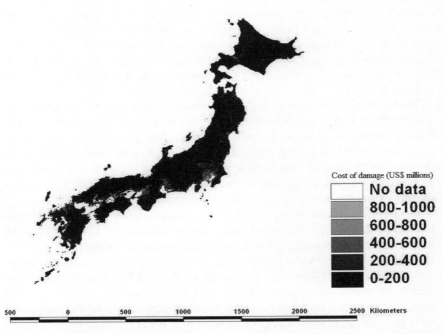

Cost of damage (US$ millions)
No data
800-1000
600-800
400-600
200-400
0-200

500   0   500   1000   1500   2000   2500 Kilometers

Figure 4.3.1 Distribution of increase in potential damage cost from rainfall with 50- to 100-year return periods
Note: Please see page 310 for a colour version of this figure.

Table 4.3.1 also shows the relationship between average annual expected damage costs and return periods. In this calculation, interval average damage is the average value of damage costs in both return periods, interval probability is the difference between both annual average extreme probabilities and the product of these values is the average annual expected damage cost. The extreme rainfall shift from 50- to 100-year return periods results in damage of approximately US$10 billion per year, which is equal to the benefit of constructing infrastructure for flood protection. Annual expenditure for flood control in the regular MLIT budget is nearly US$10 billion, which is similar to the expected damage costs. Analysis of cost-benefit ratios (B/C) is necessary to estimate the construction costs for flood control, which are calculated by dividing benefit (expected damage cost) by B/C. Construction cost is the countermeasure cost and will increase as part of the MLIT budget in response to climate change.

There are various options with different costs for flood countermeasures. These countermeasures should be evaluated according to regional differences, social structure and culture. Although the absolute cost of damage or infrastructure investment estimated in this simulation is insufficient for decision-making, the model does indicate the relative distribution of damage costs, which is helpful for discussing countermeasures to floods caused by climate change. Because of the economic implications of flooding, the areas susceptible to major damage require complete flood defences, including super-dykes or underground channels. On the other hand, areas less vulnerable to flood damage require mitigation measures, warning systems or evacuation plans. Urban areas have a high potential for damage because of the concentration of assets and variety of damages, due to the complicated urban system. Although megacities have huge flood control structures such as dykes and underground diversion channels, urban areas are vulnerable because of the very high expected damage costs and wide-range effects.

Recently, the MLIT has started discussing measures to protect against flooding caused by climate change, and has presented many options for countermeasures (MLIT, 2008). However, no discussions have dealt with measures tailored to specific regions of the country. Distribution maps of damage, such as that shown in Figure 4.3.1, should prove helpful in developing such regional countermeasures to protect against flooding due to climate change.

4-3-2 Sedimentation disasters

Landslide occurrence as a result of steep terrain and high frequency of heavy rainstorms is a common phenomenon in Japan; these landslides are

among the costliest hazards. To evaluate the frequency and distribution of landslides over Japan, a probabilistic model based on multiple logistic regression analysis, with particular reference to physical parameters such as hydraulic, geographical and geological parameters, was used. The hydraulic parameter, i.e. hydraulic gradient, is the main dynamic factor that includes the effect of heavy rainfall and its return period. A multiple logistic regression model was applied, and landslide susceptibility maps showing the spatial-temporal distribution of landslide hazard probabilities over Japan were produced using 1 × 1 km resolution grid cells. To represent probability over different temporal scales, extreme precipitation for five-, 30- and 100-year return periods was used for evaluation. The landslide hazard probability map developed was verified using past landslide events of 12 July 2004 in Tochio city, Niigata prefecture, located in a landslide-prone region.

Results of the probability model and spatial distribution of landslide hazard probability based on the hydraulic condition, geographical conditions and geological conditions of the area are portrayed on landslide hazard probability maps using geographic information system (GIS) technology. To evaluate temporal changes, the probability is estimated by changing the hydraulic factor using different return periods of extreme precipitation: five years, 30 years and 100 years. The hydraulic factor is the gradient of groundwater in the calculation of unsaturated-saturated subsurface flow by Richard's equation. Change in the return period could explain the temporal change in the probability of the landslide hazard. Landslide hazard probability maps for extreme precipitation over five-, 30- and 100-year return periods are shown in Figure 4.3.2. For all precipitation conditions, the mountain range on the Japan Sea side shows the highest landslide hazard probability, i.e. more than 95 per cent in the Iide, Asahi, Hida and Kiso ranges. Furthermore, when considering extreme precipitation over a 100-year return period (Figure 4.3.2c), some urban areas such as Iwaki, Hiroshima and Fukuoka approach 95 per cent or more landslide hazard probability. Since Japan has one of the highest life expectancy rates in the world (average 90 years), when a 100-year return period is considered, residents of the high landslide hazard probability regions (more than 95 per cent probability) are likely to experience a landslide once in a lifetime.

Most sedimentation disasters occur in rural areas with low population densities, as shown in Figure 4.3.2. These disasters isolate rural communities by blocking routes for traffic. Mountainous villages are very vulnerable to sedimentation disasters. We should plan emergency aid in preparation for these disasters.

The landslide hazard probability maps will assist authorities as well as policy- and decision-makers responsible for infrastructural planning and development, because they can identify landslide-susceptible areas and

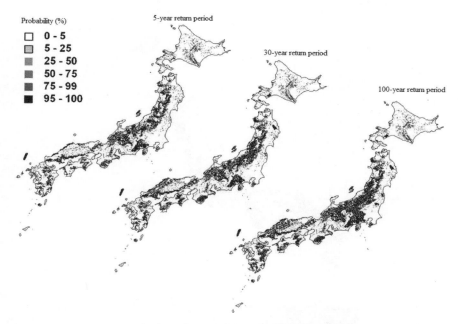

Figure 4.3.2 Landslide hazard probability maps for extreme precipitation in various return periods

thus reduce landslide damage by proper preparation. The overall distribution of landslide hazard probabilities as well as comparison of the changes in extreme precipitation for different return periods is very important because the return period dictates the time frames and design guidelines for countermeasures and indicates the order of priority of mitigation processes and financial fund allocations.

4-3-3 Snow-water resources

4-3-3-1 Impact on snow-water resources

Owing to its mountainous topography, snowmelt runoff plays an important role in stable river discharge and groundwater levels, and it is a key source of water for agricultural use in Japan. Global warming is very likely to affect snow-dominant water resources with changes in the timing and availability of water, which will intensify the stress among its numerous dependants.

Spatial and temporal distribution of snow-water equivalent (SWE) as well as snow density and depth were estimated by a combined method of

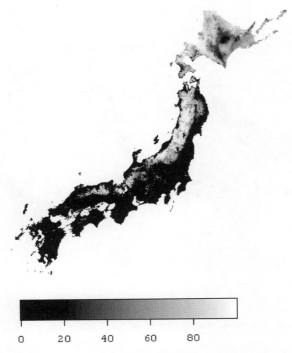

Figure 4.3.3 Percentage difference in SWE between light and heavy snow years to maximum SWE on 15 March

remote-sensing technology and degree-day techniques in Japan. Simulation worked very well for SWE estimations and helped to separate clearly less snowy areas from areas with heavy snow (Kazama et al., 2008). Vulnerable areas were detected from differences in the quantity of snow between heavy and light snow years. These areas are vulnerable because of a lack of irrigation water for rice production caused by climate change. The model developed in this study could contribute to water management activities and be used to provide recommendations for adaptation to future climate change. Areas with large variations in yearly snow are a vulnerable snow-water resource; these areas are unstable in terms of water supply.

Based on the simulation results, we can discuss the vulnerability of snow-water resources. The difference in snow distribution during light and heavy snow years (1993 and 2000, respectively) was calculated. To provide a better illustration, we considered the ratio of the difference between heavy and light snow amounts to the maximum snow amount. This shows the relative difference with respect to the total snow amount of the year or the normalized value. Figure 4.3.3 shows the distribution of the difference ratio between heavy and light snow amounts to maximum

Table 4.3.2 Comparison of snow-water resources, snow-water resource amount per paddy-field area and its ratio to water demand during the irrigation period in three typical basins

	Type of snowfall year	SWE (m³)	Rice acreage (km²)	SWE per acreage (m³/m²)	Ratio of SWE to water demand during irrigation period
Mogami River	Less	8.83×10^8	717 (Yamagata prefecture)	1.23	0.82
	Heavy	32.0×10^8		4.46	2.97
Kitakami River	Less	0.96×10^8	795 (Miyagi prefecture)	0.12	0.08
	Heavy	4.05×10^8		0.51	0.33
Shinano River	Less	32.1×10^8	1,210 (Niigata prefecture)	2.65	1.76
	Heavy	78.5×10^8		6.49	4.32

snow. This reveals that many areas are susceptible to change in expected snow-water resources in terms of climate and are vulnerable in these resources, including the north island, Hokkaido, and northeastern Japan, Tohoku, which show large ratios. Some of the central regions also have a high percentage of vulnerable snow-water resources. In fact, these districts rely on many dams and reservoirs for water management, and hence they will face difficult situations when there is less snowfall because of global warming.

4-3-3-2 Vulnerable areas for snow-water resources in Japan

Snowmelt water spreads over huge paddy fields in the spring season. This is similar to inundation. To understand the impact of decrease in snow caused by global warming, snow-water resources for paddy-field areas in typical rice basins were estimated for light and heavy snow years. The study basins were those of the Mogami, Kitakami and Shinano Rivers. The results are shown in Table 4.3.2.

Snow-water resources in the heavy snow year are more than double those of the light snow year in each basin. For example, the Mogami River has a 3.6-fold (4.46/1.23) difference in snow-water resources between heavy and light snow years. The Kitakami River basin has less snow amount and the lowest ratio compared with other basins, and has 0.33 as the ratio of SWE to water demand for irrigation even in the heavy snow year. The Shinano River basin has rich snow-water resources for irrigating rice fields in both years, although the decrease in the amount of snow-water resources, 3.85 m³/m² (6.49 to 2.65), is large. The Mogami

River is sensitive to change in the amount of snow and is critical in light snow years, with a ratio of 0.82. This type of basin is vulnerable to global warming and thus requires urgent measures such as construction of agricultural reservoirs or ponds.

4-3-4 Water quality problems

Climate change poses a threat to river water quality by altering the intensity, duration and time of rainfall, which may have serious impacts on water use and aquatic life. This problem can be overcome by precautionary assessments, predictions and appropriate choices of control measures, such as new water-treatment plants. Increased frequency and intensity of rainfall as well as early spring discharge due to temperature increase will result in severe erosion and introduce more pollutant and sediment loads to the rivers.

We tried to project the water quality change due to climate change, such as heavy rainfall and extension of the no-rain period, and analysed the variation ratio of turbidity loadings such as biochemical oxygen demand (BOD) and suspended solids (SS) in typical Japanese rivers according to the return period of extreme precipitation. Load-quality (L-Q) rating functions and organic pollutant sedimentation models were applied to evaluate water quality during heavy rainfall and drought periods, respectively (Kawagoe et al., 2008). Only the drought impact on water quality in rivers in Japan is discussed here.

SS concentration and BOD were estimated using a simple model, which involves storage of atmospheric fall-out and its discharge by rainfall under the conditions of no rainfall for more than three days and less than seven days and rainfall of more than 10 mm/day after the no-rainfall period. Furthermore, the no-rainfall duration was calculated from past records, and the duration and return periods were estimated for each region in Japan. Figures 4.3.4 and 4.3.5 show the changes in SS and BOD loads over 10- to 50-year return periods for important large river basins in Japan.

The increase is different in regions influenced by change in the pattern of rainfall. The tendency of increase in both qualities can be seen in downstream areas. Figure 4.3.4 shows that the Teshio, Agano, Kitakami and Ara Rivers have higher SS increase rates, i.e. more than 5 per cent. Figure 4.3.5 shows that the downstream regions of the Ara, Tone, Teryu, Gouno and Shinano Rivers have high BOD increases, i.e. more than 5 per cent.

Based on the results of this simulation, we can indicate high-risk rivers where water quality may worsen as a result of climate change in Japan.

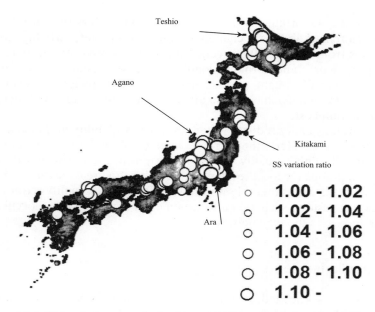

Figure 4.3.4 SS load change ratio for 10- and 50-year return periods of drought

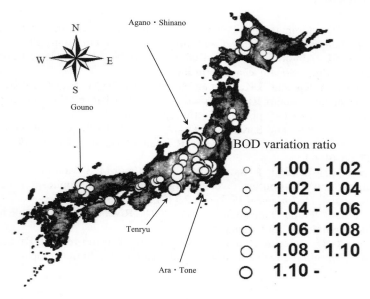

Figure 4.3.5 BOD change ratio for 10- and 50-year return periods of drought

Some of the important findings are that in some rivers turbidity loading increases remarkably with changing rainfall conditions; turbidity loading increases from 200 to 300 per cent with heavy rainfall caused by climate change in Japan; and turbidity loading increases about 110 per cent in cases of longer drought periods due to climate change. According to these results, climate change also affects river water quality and increases its adaptation costs.

Poor water quality reduces water resource availability and increases its adaptation costs. Here, the increase rates of SS and BOD are not very large, but declining quality increases the purification cost and depletes living conditions for local residents. The high-ratio areas shown in Figures 4.3.4 and 4.3.5 are vulnerable water areas. Poor water quality requires adaptation measures such as water-treatment plants or more flocculation, which increases the expenditure.

Acknowledgements

The author acknowledges the kind permission of Springer Science + Business Media and John Wiley & Sons.

REFERENCES

IPPC (2007) "Summary for Policy-makers", in *Climate Change 2007: Impacts, Adaptation and Vulnerability*. Cambridge: Cambridge University Press.

JMA (2005) "Abnormal Climate Report", available at www.data.kishou.go.jp/climate/cpdinfo/climate_change/ (in Japanese).

Kawagoe, S., Y. Kikuchi, S. Kazama and S. Takizawa (2008) "Effect of Water Quality on Japanese Major Rivers Caused by Climate Change", *Environmental Engineering Research* 45, pp. 467–474 (in Japanese).

Kazama, S., A. Sato and S. Kawagoe (2009) "Evaluating the Cost of Flood Damage Based on Changes in Extreme Rainfall in Japan", *Sustainability Science* 4(1), pp. 61–69.

Kazama, S., H. Izumi, P. R. Satukkalige, T. Nasu and M. Sawamoto (2008) "Estimating Snow Distribution Over a Large Area and Its Application for Water Resources", *Hydrological Processes* 22(13), pp. 2315–2324.

MLIT (2004) "Flood Damage Statistics of 2004", River Bureau, available at www.mlit.go.jp/index_e.html (in Japanese).

——— (2008) "Interim Report of Adaptation of Water-related Disasters for Global Warming", available at www.mlit.go.jp/index_e.html (in Japanese).

4-4

Climate change and world food production in the twenty-first century

Hiroyuki Kawashima

4-4-1 Introduction

The executive summary of the IPCC (2007) report relating to climate change and world food production reads as follows:

(1) In mid- to high-latitude regions, moderate warming benefits crop and pasture yield, and even slight warming decreases yield in seasonally dry and low-latitude regions (medium confidence).
(2) Projected changes in the frequency and severity of extreme climatic events have significant consequences for food and forest production as well as food insecurity, in addition to impacts of projected mean climate (high confidence).

The IPCC report only examined the influence of climate change on world food production. However, when the trend over the past 50 years is considered, there is a strong economic influence on food production. The influence of extreme climatic events on food production is small in advanced countries but large in developing countries. In general, the influence of climate on food production is smaller than that of the economy. Therefore, we first consider the trends of the world economy in the twenty-first century, and then add the influence of climate change to this.

As the world economy does not develop uniformly, we must think about the economy of each region. From food supply and demand in the twentieth century, we divided the world into the following five regions.

Climate change and global sustainability: A holistic approach, Sumi, Mimura and Masui (eds), United Nations University Press, 2011, ISBN 978-92-808-1181-0

- *The West* comprises Europe, North America, the former Soviet Union and Oceania. There are no food supply problems in this group. These are the food export regions.
- *Latin America* comprises Central America, South America and the Caribbean islands. Poverty exists in this region; however, food production potential is huge, especially in South America.
- *Asia* comprises Japan, China, Southeast Asia, India, etc. The food supply improved in the latter half of the twentieth century.
- *West Asia* comprises Iran, Turkey and the Arab and Maghreb countries. Many types of foods are now imported.
- *Sub-Saharan Africa* comprises Ethiopia, Nigeria, the Democratic Republic of Congo, etc. Poverty exists in this region, and the food supply is insufficient.

4-4-2 Trends in the past 50 years

4-4-2-1 Population

The world population reached 6.45 billion in 2005. The population in the West is 1.16 billion, Latin America is 0.56 billion, Asia is 3.53 billion, West Asia is 0.45 billion and sub-Saharan Africa is 0.75 billion. More than half of the world population lives in Asia, which thus has a big influence on population growth. The trends in population increase are shown in Figure 4.4.1 according to the five regions. This is the middle variant of the UN forecast. The population in 1950 is assumed to be 1.0 in the figure.

The population hardly increases for the period 1950–2050 in the West. It increases from 1950 to about 2010 in Asia; however, growth slows down after that. The population increase rate also decreases in Latin America, but rises in West Asia and sub-Saharan Africa. The population of West Asia in 2050 is predicted to increase to 1.8 times the population in 2005. This is 2.3 times in sub-Saharan Africa.

The population is currently increasing rapidly in sub-Saharan Africa and West Asia. However, these two regions account for only 20 per cent of the world population. The total population of Asia and the West constitutes 73 per cent of the world population. However, the rate of increase in both Asia and the West is declining. Therefore, the world population is not expected to increase considerably in the twenty-first century.

4-4-2-2 Cereal production

World cereal production is shown in Figure 4.4.2. High production is seen in Asia and the West. The production in 2005 was 912 million tonnes in

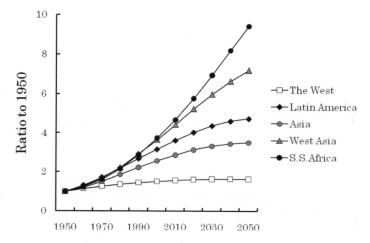

Figure 4.4.1 Population growth, ratio to 1950
Source: FAO FAOSTA, available at http://faostat.fao.org/default.aspx.

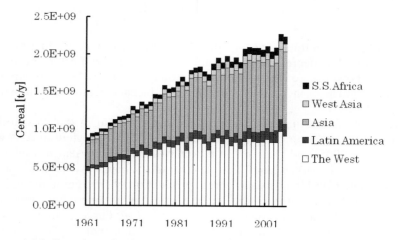

Figure 4.4.2 Cereal production
Source: FAO FAOSTA, available at http://faostat.fao.org/default.aspx.

the West, 158 million tonnes in Latin America, 965 million tonnes in Asia, 106 million tonnes in West Asia and 97 million tonnes in sub-Saharan Africa. Cereal production increased almost linearly from 1961 to around 1990. World production, however, has increased only gradually since 1990.

Comparison of cereal production in 2005 with that in 1990 shows that, in contrast to the West where production is almost the same, production has increased 1.6-, 1.2-, 1.3- and 1.4-fold in Latin America, Asia, West

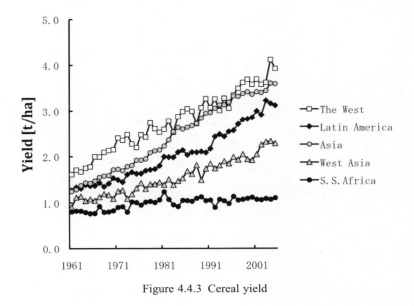

Figure 4.4.3 Cereal yield

Asia and sub-Saharan Africa, respectively. The increasing production rate in the West has decreased remarkably since the 1980s. Furthermore, the cereal harvest area of the world has not increased since 1961, so why has cereal production increased? Cereal yields in each region are shown in Figure 4.4.3.

The cereal yield in Asia is almost the same as that in the West today, although it was lower than that in the West in 1961. The yield in Asia was 3.6 t/ha in 2005, and that in Latin America and West Asia has also increased. On the other hand, the yield in sub-Saharan Africa has not increased since 1961, so why has cereal production of the region increased? The cereal harvest area of the entire world has not increased; however, that of sub-Saharan Africa has increased. The harvest area of sub-Saharan Africa in 2005 was 1.87 times larger than that in 1961. Production in sub-Saharan Africa has increased because of this increase in harvest area. This shows that the agriculture of sub-Saharan Africa accompanies deforestation because farmland is created by deforestation.

There is a good relationship between nitrogen fertilizer application and cereal yield (Figure 4.4.4). The yield is highest in areas where large amounts of nitrogen fertilizer are applied; it is relatively high in Latin America but low in West Asia. This shows that there is abundant land suitable for agriculture in Latin America but only a little in West Asia. Because nitrogen fertilizer application in sub-Saharan Africa is currently low, cereal yield is low. Cereal yield increases in sub-Saharan Africa if

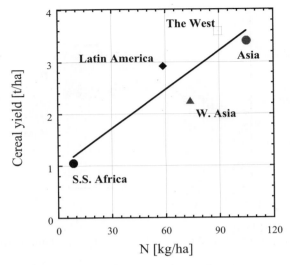

Figure 4.4.4 Relationship between nitrogen fertilizer input and cereal yield
Source: FAOFAOSTA, available at http://faostat.fao.org/default.aspx.

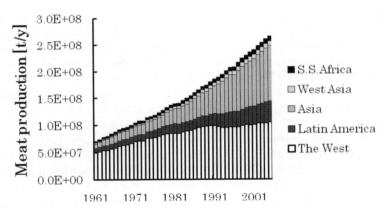

Figure 4.4.5 Meat production
Source: FAO FAOSTA, available at http://faostat.fao.org/default.aspx.

more nitrogen fertilizer is used, and thus the region could produce more cereal using the present arable land.

4-4-2-3 *Meat production*

Meat production has increased over the past 50 years (Figure 4.4.5). It has quadrupled, even though the world population has only doubled in

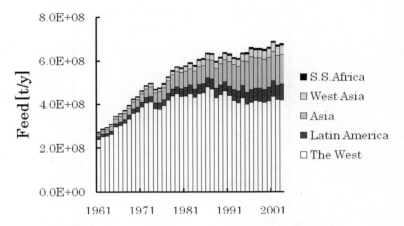

Figure 4.4.6 Cereal feed
Source: FAO FAOSTA, available at http://faostat.fao.org/default.aspx.

the same period, thus meat production per person has doubled. Meat production in Asia has increased particularly well, and the increase in China is remarkable.

Fodder is necessary to produce meat. Maize has been used as fodder worldwide; wheat is used in Europe. Worldwide fodder consumption since 1961 is shown in Figure 4.4.6. The West accounts for more than half of the entire consumption. However, consumption in the West has not increased since the 1970s; on the other hand, consumption has increased in Asia. Cereal fodder consumption in Latin America and West Asia has also increased, although cereal fodder is hardly used in sub-Saharan Africa today.

Cereal fodder consumption seems to be almost constant after the 1980s. However, according to Figure 4.4.5, the production of meat has increased since the 1980s. Meat production was 139 million tonnes and cereal fodder consumption was 579 million tonnes in 1981. The ratio of meat to cereal fodder was 4:2. This ratio has decreased; it was 2:7 in 2003. What is the reason for this decrease? First, beef production, which requires a lot of fodder, has hardly increased, while chicken production requiring small amounts of fodder has increased. Second, the productive efficiency of pork and chicken has improved, and soybean meal has been introduced as fodder.

Soybeans are produced to make vegetable oil. The solids left after extraction of the oil is called soybean meal, which is high in protein and used as fodder. Cereal fodder consumption has not increased since the introduction of soybean meal. Worldwide soybean production has increased rapidly (Figure 4.4.7); the main producers are the United States,

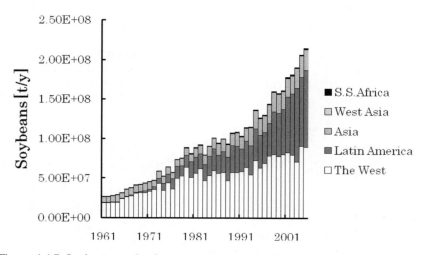

Figure 4.4.7 Soybean production
Source: FAO FAOSTA, available at http://faostat.fao.org/default.aspx.

Brazil and Argentina. Production has increased remarkably in South America, while that in the United States has hardly increased.

4-4-2-4 Trade

Cereal is consumed domestically and traded. World trade is about 300 million tonnes per year, corresponding to 13 per cent of world production. Cereal is mainly imported from the West to Asia, Latin America and West Asia. Sub-Saharan Africa also imports small amounts. Imported cereal was used as fodder in Asia, Latin America and West Asia, but has now been replaced by soybean meal, thus the amount of cereal trade remains constant after the 1980s.

Soybeans are mainly exported to Asia from the United States, Brazil and Argentina. Soybean trade was 58 million tonnes in 2004, corresponding to 27 per cent of world production. The export ratio of soybean is higher than that of cereals. China, in particular, imports large quantities of soybeans – 22 million tonnes in 2004.

The amount of meat trade increases rapidly, although the increase in cereal trade is not as much. Meat is mainly exported from the West, although export from Latin America has also increased. The West imports a large amount of meat, indicating that it trades in meat. However, the amount imported to Asia has increased in recent years. Meat production using imported fodder is decreasing gradually; however, the import of meat has increased in Asia. Development of freezing techniques has contributed to meat trade.

4-4-2-5 Amount of food supply per person

Domestic production plus import minus export represents supply. Supply per person is supply divided by the population. The cereal and meat supply per person are shown in Figures 4.4.8 and 4.4.9, respectively.

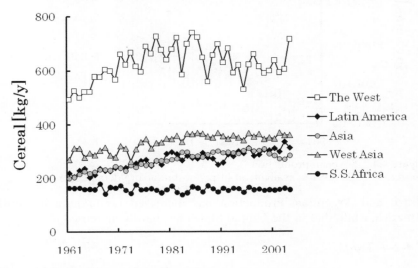

Figure 4.4.8 Annual cereal supply per person
Source: FAO FAOSTA, available at http://faostat.fao.org/default.aspx.

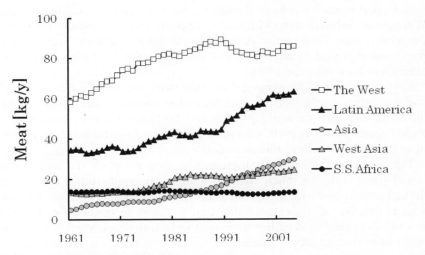

Figure 4.4.9 Annual meat supply per person
Source: FAO FAOSTA, available at http://faostat.fao.org/default.aspx.

The supply per person differs considerably according to the region. There is a large cereal and meat supply in the West. Much cereal in the West is used for meat production. In contrast, Asia has low levels of meat consumption, and meat supply in Asia is less than that in the West. Meat supply in Latin America is larger than that in Asia, although the cereal supply is almost equal – meat is produced by pasturing in Latin America. However, the supply in Asia has been increasing gradually since the 1980s. The increase in meat supply in China is remarkable. Meat consumption in Asia has increased, and continues to do so in the twenty-first century. However, because of the different cultures, meat consumption in Asia is not predicted to reach the same levels as in the West. Both cereal and meat production per person in sub-Saharan Africa have hardly increased because the rate of population increase is the same as the rate of increase in food supplies. Problems associated with food supply in sub-Saharan Africa have not improved in the past 50 years.

4-4-3 World food production in the future

First, the food supply and demand in the twenty-first century were forecast from the population increase and economic trends of the past 50 years. Then the influence of climate it was added, using the IPCC (2007) report to determine the influence of climate change.

4-4-3-1 Forecast without climate change

Patterns for the twenty-first century were considered in each region based on their past trends.

The West

There is little problem with food supply in the West because the population increase will not be much in the twenty-first century. Gene modification technology, environmentally friendly pesticides, herbicides and fungicides, effective fertilizer supply systems and many other agriculture-related technologies will be developed in this region. Ethanol production from maize will hardly influence the demand and supply of food because the price of maize is higher than that of crude oil. Only the United States makes ethanol from maize. To prevent falling maize prices, ethanol will continue to be prepared in the United States. The West will keep exporting food in the twenty-first century.

Latin America

The population increased in the twentieth century; however, the rate of increase is now decreasing and Latin America no longer has a rapidly

increasing population. South America can produce more food. Since Brazil has large areas of suitable land for agriculture, food production will increase in the twenty-first century. Soybean production will also increase in Brazil. In the near future, soybean export by Brazil will increase to more than that by the United States.

Argentina is also a big agricultural country. However, agricultural production here will not expand much in the twenty-first century because most of the land was developed in the twentieth century, and there is little unutilized land suitable for agriculture.

Asia

Asia currently imports a large amount of cereals from the West. This will continue in the twenty-first century. However, it seems that the amount of import will not increase in future because the transition to a healthier diet in China is almost complete and meat consumption in India will not change.

Today, there are many poor peasants in China and India. Addressing the problems of poverty is an important task in both countries. Capital investment in agriculture by the government will increase in China and India, and as a result they will probably become food-exporting countries, especially India. Although Asia has a large population, there seems little possibility that it will face food shortages in the twenty-first century.

West Asia

Saudi Arabia, Kuwait and Iraq export oil and it is therefore easy to import food. West Asia is a food import region. The population increases rapidly in this region; it was 110 million in 1950, is 450 million today and will be 800 million in 2050. If the population reaches 800 million, it would be about 10 per cent of the world total. West Asia has a large arid zone and less farmland. Water is necessary to produce food, and hence conflict related to water may occur.

Sub-Saharan Africa

Cereal production has increased because of the increase in planting area, but cereal yield has not increased for the past 50 years in this region. The rate of increase in food production is almost equal to the rate of increase in population. Therefore, the amount of food supply in the region has not increased.

The population is predicted to increase rapidly: it was 750 million in 2005 and will reach 1.7 billion in 2050. Food supply will become more difficult in future. There are 200 million ha of farmland in sub-Saharan Africa. If this is utilized effectively, enough food can be produced in the region. Nitrogen fertilizer usage is currently limited; production could be in-

creased by increasing its use. Nitrogen fertilizer usage facilitated the increase in production in Asia; it is necessary for African agriculture.

4-4-3-2 Forecast with climate change

The West

The influence of global warming on food production in the West has both positive and negative aspects.

There is a possibility that the US Mid-West will become drier with global warming. As this area produces the most grain in the United States, this will have a big influence on world food supplies. The United States currently exports about 100 million tonnes of cereals. Most cereal fodder used in Japan is produced there. Droughts may occur frequently in Australia as a result of global warming. Because Australia exports a large amount of wheat, this will also influence the world food supply.

Because of global warming, the arable land area in Canada and Russia may increase. The two countries comprise about 20 per cent of the world land area. Land that is frozen now is unsuitable for agriculture. However, there is abundant land in Russia and Canada, even if the frozen soil is excluded. Though capital investment is necessary, farmland area may increase. This will increase worldwide food production.

Latin America

This region is located from low to mid latitudes, and the influence of climate change on food production will be small. The population density in Latin America is comparatively low. More food can be produced, particularly in Brazil. Food production in countries such as Brazil will not decrease even if climate change occurs.

Asia

Drought may occur frequently in India because of global warming. Climate change will have a negative influence on Indian agriculture. However, the Indian economy is developing well, and it seems that India will be able to adjust to climate change. There are great opportunities for increasing cereal yield in future because the present yield is low. As a whole, the probability of India facing a food crisis in the twenty-first century is low.

Floods may occur frequently in Bangladesh because of rising sea levels. The population of Bangladesh is predicted to reach 240 million in 2050, from the current level of 140 million. The population density is high even today, and there is little possibility of an increase in the area of arable land. Global warming will have a great influence on food supply in the country.

Food production in northeast China will increase with global warming. However, drought is feared in inland China. Global warming has both positive and negative aspects for agriculture here, but as the population increase ceases and the economy develops well, the possibility of China facing a food crisis in the twenty-first century seems low.

West Asia

Food production will decrease as global warming progresses because West Asia is a dry region even today. Food import will increase as the population increases. Climate change will promote this tendency further.

Sub-Saharan Africa

Food production can barely match present population growth. There are worries about the aridity of the inland area. Political systems will continue to be unstable in most sub-Saharan African countries even in the twenty-first century. It will therefore be difficult for them to develop technology that will help in adapting their agriculture to climate change. If food production becomes unstable because of climatic change, sub-Saharan Africa will suffer the most damage in the world.

4-4-4 Conclusions

Global warming will have a positive influence on countries located in northern Eurasia. Most countries of the West are located in this region. The West can adapt agriculture to climate change because of the rapid development of gene modification technology. This means that a large amount of food will be produced in the West in the twenty-first century. Most countries in Asia will not face a food crisis in the twenty-first century because the population growth rate will decrease rapidly. However, the food supply in Bangladesh seems uncertain.

Latin America will not have a problem with food supply. West Asia will also not have problems with food supply if it can continue importing food.

Unlike the abovementioned regions, food production in Africa does not match its population increase, even without any climate change. Climate change will further exacerbate this problem. From a macro aspect, climate change will have the biggest influence on sub-Saharan Africa.

REFERENCE

IPCC (2007) *Climate Change 2007: Impacts, Adaptation and Vulnerability*. Cambridge: Cambridge University Press.

4-5

Effects of climate change and global warming on marine ecosystems and fishery resources

Yasuhiro Yamanaka and Masahiko Fujii

4-5-1 Introduction

This chapter overviews the results of previous studies on the impacts of climate change, such as climate regime shifts and global warming, on marine ecosystems and fishery resources. Furthermore, our ongoing modelling studies to predict future changes in natural marine environments due to global warming and their influence on human activities are introduced. Such simulation studies, together with observations, can be a powerful tool to link climate change systematically with marine ecosystems and fishery resources and provide a guideline for adaptation of human activities to future global warming, especially for fisheries and tourism.

Marine ecosystems and fishery resources are affected by various natural factors and human impacts (Figure 4.5.1), which include global warming and ocean acidification through anthropogenic CO_2 emission, eutrophication and fishing.

These impacts affect marine biogeochemical cycles, marine ecosystems and fishery resources as well as the climate system in many ways. For example, global warming modifies the climate system, producing changes in ocean currents, storm events and rainfall. It also strengthens the stratification of sea surface waters, leading to decrease in surface nutrients. On the other hand, rise in seawater temperature tends to enhance growth rates of lower and higher trophic level ecosystems. Modification of oceanic phytoplankton activity by global warming may help to regulate such warming by altering anthropogenic CO_2 concentrations through modified

Climate change and global sustainability: A holistic approach, Sumi, Mimura and Masui (eds), *United Nations University Press, 2011, ISBN 978-92-808-1181-0*

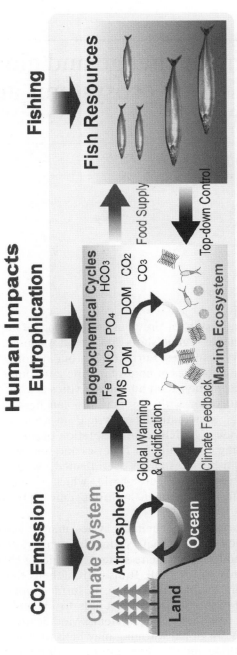

Figure 4.5.1 Components of natural marine environments
Note: The climate system is modified by global warming because of anthropogenic CO_2 emission. Climate change, particularly global warming and ocean acidification, and man-made eutrophication affect marine biogeochemical cycling and ecosystems. They also give feedback to the climate system by modifying the anthropogenic CO_2 absorption ability of phytoplankton. Changes in marine ecosystems and fishing pressure control the amount of fishery resources, which is a key factor determining lower trophic level ecosystems, such as zooplankton and phytoplankton.

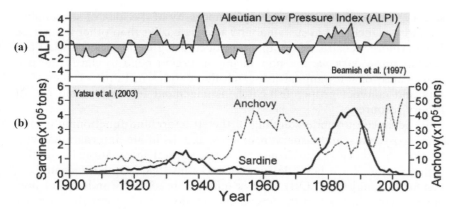

Figure 4.5.2 Time series of (a) Aleutian Low Pressure Index (ALPI); and (b) sardine and anchovy catches in seas close to Japan
Source: Beamish, Nebille and Cass (1997); Yatsu, Nagawasa and Wada (2003).

photosynthetic ability. Man-made eutrophication alters nutrient concentration and affects biodiversity in coastal regions. Fishing directly alters commercial fish stocks and determines lower trophic level biomass, such as zooplankton and phytoplankton, as prey.

Previous observational studies have examined the links between the components of natural marine environments (Figure 4.5.1), particularly the climate system and fishery resources. For example, small pelagic fish catches, such as anchovy and sardine, are reported to fluctuate by a factor of 10s, in accordance with the climate regime shift (Figure 4.5.2).

Figure 4.5.2 shows a good relationship between the Aleutian Low Pressure Index (ALPI; Beamish, Nebille and Cass, 1997) and sardine and anchovy catches in seas close to Japan (Yatsu, Nagawasa and Wada, 2003), i.e. more anchovy catches with lower ALPI (during warmer periods) and more sardine catches with higher ALPI (during colder periods), and an abrupt shift of dominant fish species from anchovy to sardine after the 1976/1977 climate regime shift in the western North Pacific. The shift of dominant fish species from anchovy to sardine was also evident during colder periods in the 1920s–1930s. The reason for this shift is still controversial; however, the optimal growth temperature hypothesis of Takasuka, Oozeki and Aoki (2007) provides the reasonable explanation that sardines with lower optimal growth temperatures are more suited to cold waters and vice versa.

Compared to agriculture and the livestock industry, the produce of the fishery industry is less predictable in both amount and species, because all fishery production, except aquaculture, inevitably depends on natural marine environments and is relatively unstable. As a result, fisheries

science has long been exposed to the necessity of the idea of sustainability and was included in sustainability science earlier than other industries. Furthermore, because of an apparent decreasing trend in worldwide fish catches these days, we are now facing an urgent need to clarify the primary cause of inter-annual fish-catch fluctuations in terms of many factors and conduct proper fish-catch management for sustainable use of fishery resources.

To advance our understanding of the structure and functioning of marine ecosystems and fishery resources and facilitate international collaborative fishery resource management, several international scientific collaborations have been developed since the 1990s. Global Ocean Ecosystem Dynamics (GLOBEC) was initiated in 1991 to understand how global change will affect the abundance, diversity and productivity of marine populations comprising a major component of oceanic ecosystems (www.globec.org/). North Pacific Marine Science Organization (PICES) is an inter-governmental scientific organization including Canada, Japan, the People's Republic of China, the Republic of Korea, the Russian Federation and the United States. It was established to promote and coordinate marine research in the northern North Pacific and adjacent seas (www.pices.int/). In 1994 the PICES Climate Change and Carrying Capacity (CCCC) Program, a regional programme of GLOBEC, was developed to provide a framework for examining climate-ecosystem linkages in the North Pacific.

4-5-2 Simulation of marine ecosystems and fishery resources

Under the framework of PICES/GLOBEC CCCC, a marine ecosystem model NEMURO (North Pacific Ecosystem Model Used for Regional Oceanography; Kishi et al., 2007) and a fish bioenergetics-based population dynamics model coupled with NEMURO (NEMURO For Including Saury and Herring (NEMURO.FISH); Figure 4.5.3) were developed to describe seasonal and inter-annual variability in lower trophic level (phytoplankton and zooplankton) and higher trophic level (small pelagic fish) ecosystems, respectively (Ito et al., 2004, 2007; Megrey et al., 2007; Rose et al., 2007).

Recently, several coupled lower-higher trophic level models have been developed and applied to various oceanic regions (Fulton, Smith and Punt, 2004). NEMURO.FISH is one of the most advanced models that can represent physical processes, nutrient cycling and lower and higher trophic level ecosystems as a whole. NEMURO was named after Nemuro City (Hokkaido, Japan), where the first model task team workshop was held in 2000. Recently, many studies have included NEMURO or

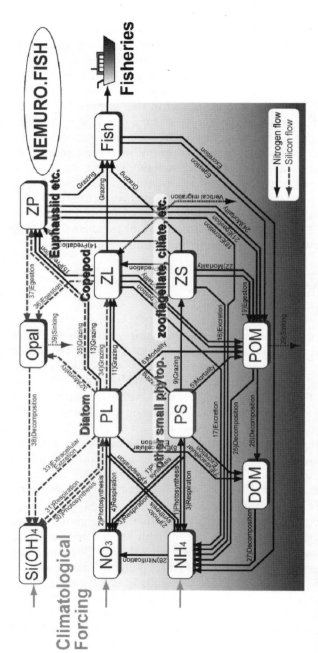

Figure 4.5.3 Schematic view of NEMURO.FISH

Note: PS (mmol N m^{-3}) is non-diatom smaller phytoplankton biomass; PL (mmol N m^{-3}) is diatom biomass; ZS (mmol N m^{-3}) is non-diatom-grazing microzooplankton biomass; ZL (mmol N m^{-3}) is diatom-grazing microzooplankton or mesozooplankton biomass; ZP (mmol N m^{-3}) is predatory macrozooplankton biomass; Fish is small pelagic fish (mmol N m^{-3}); NO$_3$ (mmol N m^{-3}) is dissolved nitrate; NH$_4$ (mmol N m^{-3}) is dissolved ammonia; Si(OH)$_4$ (mmol Si m^{-3}) is dissolved silicate; POM (mmol N m^{-3}) is particulate organic matter; DOM (mmol N m^{-3}) is dissolved organic matter; and Opal (mmol Si m^{-3}) is opal or biogenic silica frustules of diatoms. Solid and dashed arrows indicate nitrogen and silicon flows, respectively. Dotted arrows represent exchange or sinking of materials between the model domain and below.

Source: Ito et al. (2007); Megrey et al. (2007).

NEMURO.FISH in physical models, from a simple three-box model (Ito et al., 2004, 2007) to a complicated ocean general circulation model (Aita, Yamanaka and Kishi, 2007; Hashioka and Yamanaka, 2007; Hashioka, Sakamoto and Yamanaka, 2009; Okunishi et al., forthcoming).

Okunishi, Yamanaka and Ito (2009) developed a 2D individual-based model coupled with fish bioenergetics to simulate migration and growth of Japanese sardines (*Sardinops melanostictus*) in the western North Pacific. In the model, fish movement is assumed to be controlled by feeding and spawning migrations with passive transport by simulated ocean current. Their noteworthy originality is that spawning migration was modelled by an artificial neural network with an input layer composed of five neurons that receive environmental information, i.e. surface water temperature, water temperature change experienced, current speed, day length and distance from land. They revealed that of the five factors, water temperature and day length are more important for the orientation cues of Japanese sardines during spawning migration.

4-5-2-1 Simulated responses of marine ecosystems and fishery resources to climate change

Using National Centers for Environmental Prediction, NOAA National Weather Service/National Center for Atmospheric Research reanalysis six-hourly datasets of sea surface temperature, freshwater flux, surface wind stress and solar radiation obtained from 1948 to 2002, Aita, Yamanaka and Kishi (2007) simulated inter-annual variation with Pacific Decadal Oscillation (PDO), particularly focusing on the 1976/1977 climate regime shift (Figure 4.5.4).

The model results reproduce the observed decrease in primary production and diatom-grazing microzooplankton or mesozooplankton (ZL) biomass. Wet weight of individual saury in the western North Pacific is simulated to have decreased after the 1976/1977 climate regime shift, primarily due to cooling (Ito et al., 2007).

On the other hand, the model results show that the climate regime shift caused different responses of herring growth in the mid and late 1970s in the northeastern Pacific, i.e. herring growth rate decreased off the West Coast Vancouver Island and in Prince William Sound and increased in the Bering Sea (Rose et al., 2007). This is because the responses of water temperature and ZL (as a prey) abundance differ locally. The herring growth rate is positively correlated with two factors, and the more dominant factor change determines the herring growth rate in each oceanic region.

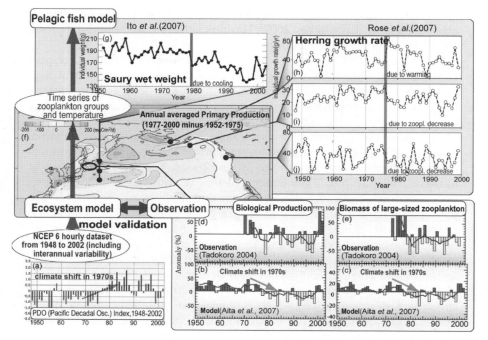

Figure 4.5.4 Inter-annual variation of primary production and biomass, 1948–2002
Note: (a) Anomaly of annually averaged Pacific Decadal Oscillation (PDO) index. Anomaly of annually averaged (b) modelled and (d) observed primary production and (c) modelled and (e) observed diatom-grazing microzooplankton or
mesozooplankton (ZL) biomass. Observational data from the PH line (41.3°N,
144–147°E), which crosses the Oyashio current, and model results from 41.3°N,
144–147°E. The solid line shows the five-year running mean. (f) Annually averaged primary production (1977–2000 minus 1952–1975). (g) Modelled wet weight
of individual saury in the western North Pacific. Modelled herring growth rate
(three to four years old) and annual average in (h) the Bering Sea, (i) Prince William Sound and (j) the West Coast Vancouver Island.
Source: Aita, Yamanaka and Kishi (2007); Tadokoro (2004); Ito et al. (2007); Rose et
al. (2007).

4-5-2-2 Lower trophic levels

Using predicted physical fields of velocity, water temperature and salinity,
vertical diffusivity and solar radiation (Sakamoto et al., 2005) obtained
by a climate model (a high-resolution set-up of the Model for Interdisciplinary Research on Climate (MIROC) version 3.2; K-1 Model Developers, 2004) under global warming scenarios, several modelling studies
with NEMURO have recently projected the effects of global warming

on marine biogeochemical cycling and ecosystems as well as pelagic fish (Hashioka and Yamanaka, 2007; Hashioka, Sakamoto and Yamanaka, 2009; Okunishi et al., forthcoming).

Applying 3D NEMURO to the western North Pacific near Japan, Hashioka and Yamanaka (2007) predicted increases in vertical stratification due to rising temperatures and subsequent decreases in surface nutrient and chlorophyll concentrations and a shift in the dominant phytoplankton group. The spring bloom is predicted to occur 1.5 months earlier than the present bloom because of strengthened stratification; however, the maximum biomass in the spring bloom is predicted to decrease drastically compared to the present bloom because of decreases in nutrient concentration. They concluded that the impacts of global warming on marine ecosystems do not appear uniformly in all seasons, but are particularly important at the end of spring and in the autumn bloom.

Their latest study including NEMURO in an eddy-permitting 3D model (Hashioka, Sakamoto and Yamanaka, 2009) shows that the model predictions correspond well to the observed time of an onset of the spring bloom (Figure 4.5.5). They also demonstrated that the maximum biomass during the spring bloom occurs 10–20 days earlier because of strengthened stratification, which is consistent with Hashioka and Yamanaka (2007), and that the maximum chlorophyll concentration in the spring bloom increases and decreases in the northern parts of the Kuroshio Extension region and the subarctic and subtropical regions, respectively, due to global warming.

They suggest that these responses to global warming are statistically significant compared to natural variations (Figure 4.5.5), and that these projected changes in the lower trophic level ecosystem may affect migration routes or abundance of adult pelagic fishes.

4-5-2-3 Higher trophic levels

Similar efforts to predict the impacts of global warming on fishery resources have been conducted in several studies.

Okunishi et al. (forthcoming) developed a multi-trophic level ecosystem model including Japanese sardines by coupling physical, biogeochemical plankton and fish models, including NEMURO. They demonstrated the possible impacts of global warming on the growth and migration pattern of Japanese sardines. The frequency of four-months-old low-weight sardines (<1 g) in the main spawning ground was projected to be significantly higher in the global warming simulation than that in the present simulation (Figure 4.5.6).

This is because sardine juveniles are mostly exposed to temperatures higher than the optimal temperature for feeding consumption and have a

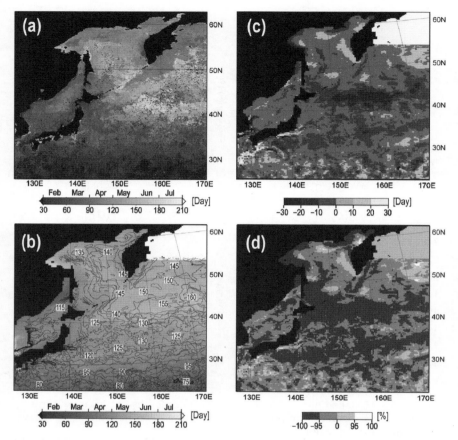

Figure 4.5.5 Time of maximum chlorophyll concentration in the spring bloom in Julian days
Note: (a) satellite (derived from NASA's Sea-viewing Field-of-view Sensor); (b) simulated; (c) projected changes (global warming condition minus present condition) in time of day; (d) significant levels (*p*-values) from Student's *t*-test for time.
Source: Hashioka, Sakamoto and Yamanaka (2009).

lower recruitment rate in the current main spawning region under global warming conditions. As a result, sardines were predicted to shift their spawning ground northwards and avoid a collapse in their recruitment. During the northward migration in summer, geographical distribution of the fish was projected to shift north by 1–2° under the global warming condition, since the optimal temperature region for feeding shifted northward (ibid.).

Global warming and the subsequent rise in water temperature are considered crucial factors for corals, inducing coral habitat migration towards

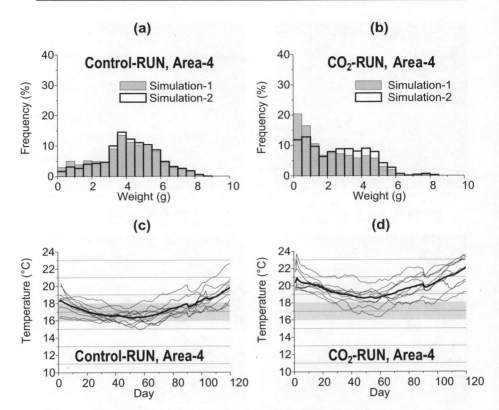

Figure 4.5.6 Modelled histogram of weight of four-months-old Japanese sardines and averaged temperature in present and global warming simulations in the current main spawning region

Note: Modelled histogram of weight of four-months-old Japanese sardines (a, b) and averaged temperature (c, d) in present (a, c) and global warming (b, d) simulations in the current main spawning region (Area-4) near Tosa Bay, south of Shikoku Island, Japan. Thin and thick lines in (c) and (d) denote average values for each simulation year and nine-year average values, respectively. Grey-hatched domains in (c) and (d) show the range of optimum temperature of feeding consumption of sardine (16–18°C). Furthermore, (a) and (b) show results of both simulation-1 and simulation-2, and (c) and (d) show results of simulation-1. Simulation-1 does not consider the effect of the mortality rate, while simulation-2 considers this effect.

Source: Okunishi et al. (2009).

higher latitudes and intensifying the chances of coral bleaching and death. Using projected monthly mean sea surface temperature in the twenty-first century obtained by MIROC version 3.2 (K-1 Model Developers, 2004) and simplified indices for coral bleaching and the northern limit of coral and coral reef distribution, Yara et al. (2009) quantitatively

evaluated the anticipated effects of global warming on corals in seas close to Japan (Figure 4.5.7).

They showed that the northern limit of the coral habitat, which is currently located in Niigata and Chiba prefectures in eastern Japan, is expected to move northward, up to Aomori and Iwate prefectures in northern Japan, and that the northern limit of subtropical coral reefs, currently located in southern Kyushu, is estimated to move to northern Kyushu by the end of the twenty-first century. On the other hand, the frequency and area of coral bleaching or death are expected to intensify around the Ryukyu Islands. In particular, high water temperatures, which result in coral death, will appear in the latter half of the twenty-first century.

4-5-3 For more realistic future projection of fishery resources

Most previous modelling studies have focused on pelagic marine ecosystems and fishery resources. However, if we consider the link with human activities, we also need to focus more on marine ecosystems and fishery resources in coastal regions because these regions are more strongly related to our everyday lives. Furthermore, many coastal species live among rooted marine species such as corals, sea grasses and mangroves. Most rooted species cannot migrate and are therefore considered to be sensitive to local environmental changes such as rise in seawater temperature due to global warming. To accomplish more realistic simulation of the coastal biogeochemical cycle and ecosystems, finer spatial models, such as those incorporating the runoff of materials from rivers, are required. Such models will also allow us to simulate two-way nutrient transport between land and ocean by anadromous fish species, such as salmon, through rivers.

The impacts of climate change and global warming on marine ecosystems and fishery resources are anticipated to emerge differently according to space, season and species. Hashioka, Sakamoto and Yamanaka (2009) suggest that even if global warming weakly affects annually averaged quantities, it could strongly affect certain marine species and biogeochemical processes that depend on seasonal events such as phytoplankton blooms. Okunishi et al. (forthcoming) stressed the importance of remembering that current models do not consider any future changes in marine ecosystem structure. No existing marine ecosystem models have considered the impacts of higher trophic level interactions, which may be modified by global warming. For example, the predation risk from fish predators, such as skipjack tuna (*Katsuwonus pelami*), that prefer warm water may increase with global warming and reduce the biomass

Figure 4.5.7 Anticipated effects of global warming on corals in seas close to Japan

Notes:

(a) Projected northern limit of coral and coral reef distribution in seas close to Japan in 2000–2099. Three simplified indices expressing the northern limit of coral and coral reef distribution are introduced: the isothermal lines of 18°C (lower lines), 13°C (middle lines) and 10°C (upper lines) in the coldest month represent the northern limit of sub-tropical coral reefs, high-latitude coral reefs and high-latitude coral habitat, respectively. Thin and thick lines denote the model results in each year and the 10-year average, respectively.

106

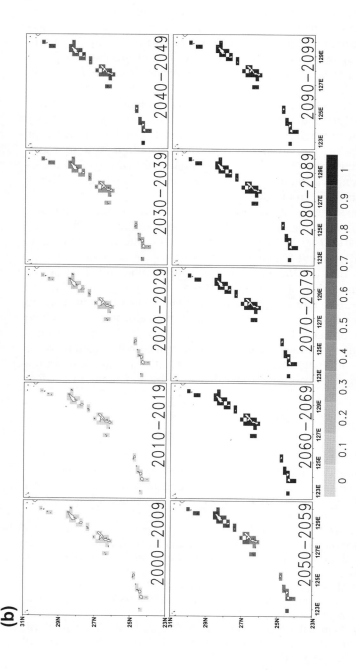

Figure 4.5.7 (cont.)
(b) Projected probability (frequency) of high seawater temperature occurrence that potentially induces severe bleaching or death of corals in the Ryukyu Islands, Japan, from 2000 to 2099. Degree heating month (DHM) is introduced as a simplified evaluation metric for coral stress on the water temperature. In this index, severe bleaching or death of corals is assumed to appear when water temperature >1°C (or >2°C) higher than the warmest-month climatology lasts for >2 months (or >1 month; DHM >2). A scale for probability (frequency) is shown at the bottom of the figure. Probability of 1 or 0.5 represents that such high seawater temperatures appear every year or every two years, respectively. Probability is only shown in oceanic regions in which corals exist currently.
Source: Yara et al. (2009).

107

of Japanese sardines or accelerate the northward migration of sardine (ibid.). Furthermore, Japanese sardines seem to compete in prey plankton with other pelagic fish such as Pacific saury (Ito et al., 2007). Therefore, changes in Japanese sardine biomass may reflect marine ecosystem structure, which may lead to feedbacks to Japanese sardine (Okunishi et al., forthcoming).

Biological adaptation to changes in marine environments, such as rise in seawater temperature due to global warming, is crucial but has hardly been clarified. For example, it is still controversial how long it takes or how many generations are necessary for corals to adapt to a seawater temperature higher than their current optimal one. Biological studies based on gene identification are ongoing, and the results will be reflected in future marine ecosystem and fish models.

Changes in marine ecosystems and fishery resources due to climate change and global warming, in turn, affect various human activities. For example, most coastal regions in Japan are located in the temperate zone, and the biological gradient between the subtropical or subpolar region is steep. This means that the local marine ecosystem could shift to a different one in response to climate change and global warming. Such changes in marine species may affect local human activities such as fisheries and tourism, including fishing and scuba diving, and relocation of marine parks and marine protected areas (Yara et al., 2009). It is essential to improve the predictive accuracy of models to find sustainable fisheries and minimize future unfavourable impacts of climate change and global warming on marine ecosystems and fisheries, which will in turn affect human activities.

REFERENCES

Aita, M. N., Y. Yamanaka and M. J. Kishi (2007) "Interdecadal Variation of the Lower Trophic Ecosystem in the Northern Pacific between 1948 and 2002, in a 3-D Implementation of the NEMURO Model", *Ecological Modelling* 202(1/2), pp. 81–94.

Beamish, R. J., C. E. Nebille and A. J. Cass (1997) "Production of Fraser River Sockeye Salmon (*Oncorhynchus nerka*) in Relation to Decadal-scale Changes in the Climate and the Ocean", *Canadian Journal of Fisheries and Aquatic Sciences* 54, pp. 543–554.

Fulton, E. A., A. D. M. Smith and A. E. Punt (2004) "Ecological Indicators of the Ecosystem Effects of Fishing: Final Report", Report No. R99/1546, Australian Fisheries Management Authority, Canberra.

Hashioka, T. and Y. Yamanaka (2007) "Ecosystem Change in the Western North Pacific Associated with Global Warming Using 3D-NEMURO", *Ecological Modelling* 202(1/2), pp. 95–104.

Hashioka, T., T. T. Sakamoto and Y. Yamanaka (2009) "Potential Impact of Global Warming on North Pacific Spring Blooms Projected by an Eddy-permitting 3-D Ocean Ecosystem Model", *Geophysical Research Letters* 36(20), L20604, doi: 10.1029/2009GL038912.

Ito, S.-I., M. J. Kishi, Y. Kurita, Y. Oozeki, Y. Yamanaka, B. A. Megrey and F. E. Werner (2004) "Initial Design for a Fish Bioenergetics Model of Pacific Saury Coupled to a Lower Trophic Ecosystem Model", *Fisheries Oceanography* 13, pp. 111–124.

Ito, S.-I., B. A. Megrey, M. J. Kishi, D. Mukai, Y. Kurita, Y. Ueno and Y. Yamanaka (2007) "On the Interannual Variability of the Growth of Pacific Saury (*Cololabis saira*): A Simple 3-box Model Using NEMURO.FISH", *Ecological Modelling* 202(1/2), pp. 174–183.

K-1 Model Developers (2004) "K-1 Coupled Model (MIROC) Description", in H. Hasumi and S. Emori (eds) T-1 Technical Report 1, Center for Climate System Research, University of Tokyo, Tokyo, p. 34.

Kishi, M. J., M. Kashiwai, D. M. Ware, B. A. Megrey, D. L. Eslinger, F. E. Werner, M. N. Aita, T. Azumaya, M. Fujii, S. Hashimoto, D. Huang, H. Iizumi, Y. Ishida, S. Kang, F. A. Kantakov, H.-C. Kim, K. Komatsu, V. V. Navrotsky, S. L. Smith, K. Tadokoro, A. Tsuda, O. Yamamura, Y. Yamanaka, K. Yokouchi, N. Yoshie, J. Zhang, Y. I. Zuenko and V. I. Zvalinsky (2007) "NEMURO – A Lower Trophic Level Model for the North Pacific Marine Ecosystem", *Ecological Modelling* 202(1/2), pp. 12–25.

Megrey, B. A., K. A. Rose, R. A. Klumb, D. E. Hay, F. E. Werner, D. L. Eslinger and S. L. Smith (2007) "A Bioenergetics-based Population Dynamics Model of Pacific Herring (*Clupea harengus pallasi*) Coupled to a Lower Trophic Level Nutrient-phytoplankton-zooplankton Model: Description, Calibration, and Sensitivity Analysis", *Ecological Modelling* 202(1/2), pp. 144–164.

Okunishi, T., Y. Yamanaka and S.-I. Ito (2009) "A Simulation Model for Japanese Sardine (*Sardinops melanostictus*) Migrations in the Western North Pacific", *Ecological Modelling* 220(4), pp. 462–479.

Okunishi, T., S.-I. Ito, T. Hashioka, T. T. Sakamoto, N. Yoshie, H. Sumata, Y. Yara, N. Okada and Y. Yamanaka (forthcoming) "Impacts of Climate Change on Growth and Migration of Japanese Sardine (*Sardinops melanostictus*) in the Western North Pacific", submitted to *Climatic Change.*

Rose, K. A., F. E. Wener, B. A. Megrey, M. N. Aita, Y. Yamanaka, D. E. Hay, J. F. Schweigert and M. B. Foster (2007) "Simulated Herring Growth Responses in the Northeastern Pacific to Historic Temperature and Zooplankton Conditions Generated by the 3-Dimensional NEMURO Nutrient-phytoplankton-zooplankton Model", *Ecological Modelling* 202(1/2), pp. 184–195.

Sakamoto, T. T., H. Hasumi, M. Ishii, S. Emori, T. Suzuki, T. Nishimura and A. Sumi (2005) "Responses of Kuroshio and Kuroshio Extension to Global Warming in a High-resolution Climate Model", *Geophysical Reseach Letters* 32, L14617.

Tadokoro, K. (2004) "Marine Ecosystem Changes Related to the Climatic Regime Shifts in the Oyashio Waters", in T. Sugimoto (ed.) *Ocean Currents and Biological Resources.* Tokyo: Seizando, pp. 208–216 (in Japanese).

Takasuka, A., Y. Oozeki and I. Aoki (2007) "Optimal Growth Temperature Hypothesis: Why Do Anchovy Flourish and Sardine Collapse or Vice Versa Under the Same Ocean Regime?", *Canadian Journal of Fisheries and Aquatic Sciences* 64, pp. 768–776.

Yara, Y., M. Fujii, Y. Yamanaka, N. Okada, H. Yamano and K. Oshima (2009) "Projected Effects of Global Warming on Coral Reefs in Seas Close to Japan", *Journal of the Japanese Coral Reef Society* 11, pp. 131–140 (in Japanese with English abstract).

Yatsu, A., K. Nagawasa and T. Wada (2003) "Decadal Changes in Abundance of Dominant Pelagic Fishes and Squids in the Northwestern Pacific Ocean Since the 1970s and Implications to Fisheries Management", *Transactions of the American Fisheries Society Symposium* 38, pp. 675–684.

4-6

Vulnerability of coastal zones in the twenty-first century

Hisamichi Nobuoka and Satoshi Murakami

Coastal zones are vulnerable to natural fluctuations, making these areas sensitive to climate change. There are two major reasons for their vulnerability: the land elevations are low, so natural disasters are easily caused by any rise in sea level, storm waves, storm surge and tsunamis; and many coastal zones have high population density or high levels of economic activity, so the disasters which break through protection systems cause huge damage. Based on these factors, the Working Group II report of the IPCC AR4 (IPCC, 2007b) addressed six concerns regarding coastal zones and climate change.

1. Coasts are experiencing the adverse consequences of hazards related to climate and sea level (very high confidence).
2. Coasts will be exposed to increasing risks, including coastal erosion, over coming decades due to climate change and sea-level rise (very high confidence).
3. The impact of climate change on coasts is exacerbated by increasing human-induced pressures (very high confidence).
4. Adaptation for the coasts of developing countries will be more challenging than for coasts of developed countries, due to constraints on adaptive capacity (high confidence).
5. Adaptation costs for vulnerable coasts are much less than the costs of inaction (high confidence).
6. The unavoidability of sea-level rise, even in the longer-term, frequently conflicts with present-day human development patterns and trends (high confidence).

Climate change and global sustainability: A holistic approach, Sumi, Mimura and Masui (eds), United Nations University Press, 2011, ISBN 978-92-808-1181-0

In this chapter, global coastal submerged/flooded area and affected population due to rising sea level are projected for detailed and quantitative impact assessment. Next, a more detailed impact study for the Chao Phraya delta is presented.

4-6-1 Impact on world coastal areas

It is believed that the rise in sea level due to the thermal expansion of seawater and fusion of ice sheets caused by global warming will amplify the effect of severe disasters in coastal zones. Historically, flood disasters due to impact from seawater have been generated by storm surges and tsunamis. Typical examples are the storm surge from an extratropical cyclone along the Dutch and British coasts around the North Sea in 1953, Typhoon Isewan, near Nagoya in Japan, in 1958 and Hurricane Katrina around the Mississippi delta in the United States in 2006. The biggest disaster of the latter type is the Indian Ocean tsunami in 2004. In the case of rising sea level, the population affected by these disasters must increase in low-lying delta areas and small archipelagic countries. Moreover, the world population is expected to increase to about 10 billion people by 2050. This population growth will increase the number of people affected by disasters in coastal zones.

Although many vulnerability assessments have been conducted in coastal areas, there are few global or regional assessments. The first global vulnerability assessment on coastal zones is reported by Hoozemans, Marchand and Pennekamp (1993). This study assessed coastal disasters and also issues such as ecosystem changes and rice production. However, the spatial resolution of the study was poor – it was conducted at a country level. Coastal disasters due to seawater were also projected only by an empirical method based on the relationships between winds and wind waves at some points. Nicholls, Hoozemans and Marchand (1999) improved some of the calculation techniques of the earlier study, such as by adapting the sea-level rise projected in a general circulation model (GCM) for climates, and conducted global vulnerability assessments along the coastal zones. Mimura (2000) and Nobuoka, Mimura and Fukuhara (2007) implemented vulnerability assessments in Asia and Oceania, with resolution as high as 60 arc-seconds. However, none of these studies had sufficient accuracy concerning astronomical tides and storm surges along coasts because the heights were calculated by a simple empirical method.

Furthermore, considering the uncertainty of climate, population and economic scenarios, these assessments did not have enough spatio-temporal accuracy. Chapter 6 of Working Group II of the IPCC AR4 (IPCC, 2007b), titled "Coastal systems and low-lying areas", described

only some fragmentary results, such as that the population in coastal zones will increase from 1.2 billion in 1990 to 1.8–5.2 billion in 2080. It is possible that the rising sea level and increasing intensity of tropical cyclones will add negative impacts for many coasts. Specific areas that might be seriously affected are the mega-deltas of Asia, which have a huge population, and developing countries, which do not have coastal defence systems even in the present scenario. These factors were projected for affected populations for annual storm surges in the 2020s, 2050s and 2080s. This projection assumed that new coastal defences will continue to be constructed at the present rate. This means that there is no construction for any adaptation to climate change. In Asia and Africa the affected population will increase. Under scenario A2 of the IPCC (2000) *Special Report on Emissions Scenarios* (SRES), the affected population will reach 25 million in the 2080s; the impact of a rise in sea level contributes only 7 million of this number. The method used for this projection was almost the same as that used by Nicholls, Hoozemans and Marchand (1999).

The purpose of this chapter is to project detailed and precise increases in the area and population affected by submergence/flood for the entire world coastal zone in the twenty-first century, considering the sea-level rise and the general population growth. This assessment used a detailed spatial grid – 60 arc-seconds – over the entire world. The storm surge and astronomical tides were calculated by numerical simulation. The projected sea-level rise, population and economic growth for three SRES scenarios (IPCC, 2000) were employed. No coastal defences were taken into account, so the projected results in this assessment are called the potential area and the potential population affected by the impacts.

4-6-1-1 Methodology of the vulnerability assessment

Global assessment was performed at intervals of 25 years from 2000 to 2100. The spatial resolution of the calculated assessment was 60 arc-seconds. Variations in the twenty-first century considered in this assessment are sea-level rise, population growth and economic growth accompanying global warming based on an SRES scenario. The time series of sea-level rise due to global warming was projected by multiplying thermal expansions of seawater volume, which were obtained from MRI-CGCM2 (Yukimoto and Noda, 2002) and MIROC3.2 (Hasumi and Emori, 2004), by an average rate between the thermal expansions and the total rising height in 2100, as expressed in the IPCC AR4 (IPCC, 2007a). The height by thermal expansion calculated by MRI-CGCM2 and MIROC3.2 is almost the maximum and the minimum, respectively, for all results of the general circulation model in IPCC AR4 (ibid.). Therefore, the average height of both models is a representative value. The population

in each 60 arc-seconds grid was calculated from the GPWv3 model and population growth according to SRES scenarios was provided by CIESIN (2002a). The value of GDP in each country was obtained from the results from CIESIN (2002b). In this study the major SRES scenarios, comprising A1B (low population growth and very high economic growth), B1 (low population growth and high economic growth) and A2 (high population growth and medium economic growth), over the entire world are used for all projections.

The impact from the sea was of two types. The first is the astronomical tide added to the increase in sea-level rise to project submergence areas. The other is the height of storm-surge deviation on the astronomical tide added to the sea-level rise for projections of flooded areas. The NA-OTIDE model (Matsumoto, Takanezawa, and Ooe, 2000), which is an ocean tide model developed by assimilating TOPEX/POSEIDON, was employed for calculations of the astronomical high tides along the world coasts, with observed tides at tidal stations. The heights of storm-surge deviations were calculated by a numerical simulation model based on the linear long-wave theory. Winds and atmospheric pressure on sea surfaces were hindcasted from the best tracks of tropical cyclones since 1951, distributed by JMA and IBTrACS of the NOAA. The spatial grid size and integral time of the calculation were two arc-minutes and five minutes, respectively. The height used in the assessment was storm surges downscaled to 60 arc-seconds.

The submergence area due to astronomical tide and sea-level rise and the flood area due to these factors as well as the storm surge were calculated using a simple method of level comparison between ground elevations and coastal water levels, taking into account a route from each coast. GTOPO30 of the USGS served as the base for ground elevations. The elevations of SRTM30 of NASA were substituted at a point that fulfils one of the following conditions:

- when the altitude by SRTM30 is 20 m higher than that by GTOPO30
- when the altitude by SRTM30 is lower than that by GTOPO30.

As artificial coastal defences were not considered in this analysis, the area where water reached should be called the *potential submergence area* and *potential flooded area*. Finally, the population in the submerged area and the flooded area was calculated.

4-6-1-2 Assessment results of coastal vulnerability

The distribution of storm-surge deviation is shown in Figure 4.6.1a. The storm-surge ranges of 0.5–1 m, 1–2 m, 2–3 m, 3–4 m and over 4 m are represented by crosses, grey diamonds, black squares, grey circles and black circles, respectively, on the map. The land with elevation lower than 20 m is grey. The distribution of storm surge deviation is in agreement with the known

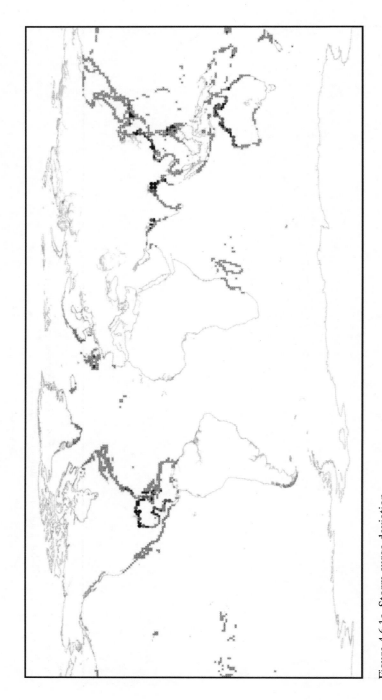

Figure 4.6.1a Storm-surge deviation
Notes: 1. A deviation of 0.5~1 m is shown as a cross, 1~2 m as a grey diamond, 2~3 m as a black square, 3~4 m as a large grey circle, 4 m and above as a large black circle; elevation under 20 m in grey.
2. Please see page 311 for a colour version of this figure.

Figure 4.6.1b Potential flooded area
Notes: 1. LR is 0.51 m. Flooded area is shown in black; elevation under 20 m in grey.
2. Please see page 311 for a colour version of this figure.

hotspots of storm surge. The only points where the storm surge deviation is larger than 4 m were the areas around the Mississippi and Ganges-Brahmaputra deltas and Hangzhou Bay. Other areas with large deviation are the coasts of the Philippines, the northern coasts of Viet Nam, the southern coasts of China and coasts of Japan in the northwestern Pacific Ocean, the northwestern coasts of Australia and several islands in the South Pacific, the coast around the Gulf of Mexico in the North Atlantic Ocean, the deltas of Bangladesh, Myanmar and Pakistan in the north Indian Ocean and the coast of Madagascar in the south Indian Ocean.

For the A2 scenario in 2100, which has a worst-case sea-level rise of 51 cm in this study, the areas flooded by storm surge at high tide are shown in black in Figure 4.6.1b. Though it was the worst-case scenario, the flooded areas are quite narrow compared with the size of the continents, so only some areas can be clearly identified on the map. The main areas are the deltas of the Mississippi, Ganges-Brahmaputra, Irrawaddy, Indus, Changchiang and Mekong. Some areas where tropical cyclones do not pass are submerged by rising sea levels with a high astronomical tide, such as in northeastern Sumatra, Borneo and the Amazon and Rhine-Meuse-Scheldt deltas.

Figure 4.6.2 shows the extended area of potential submergence area from 2000 to 2100 for every region and the world – the base is the area in 2000. Sea-level rise (SLR) is also shown on the right-side axis in the same figure. The potential submergence area of the world in the present climate becomes 1,300,000 km^2.

The extended areas according to the A1B, A2 and B1 scenarios become about 230,000, 220,000 and 160,000 km^2, respectively. Although the extended area for each scenario is slightly larger in Asia and North America, the difference by area is not so great in all regions. The trend of increase in the extended area of the world and of rise in sea levels is almost the same. When adding the impact of storm surge, the projected extension of the flooded area is shown in Figure 4.6.3.

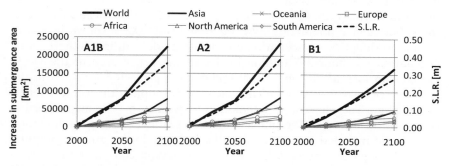

Figure 4.6.2 Increase in submergence area, 2000–2100
Note: SLR is average of the values of the two GCMs.

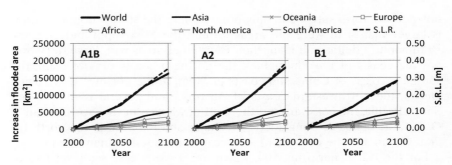

Figure 4.6.3 Increase in flooded area, 2000–2100
Note: SLR is average of the values of the two GCMs.

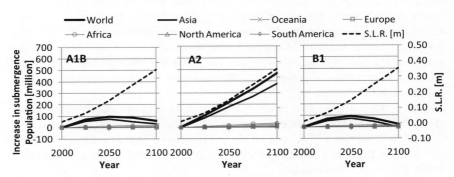

Figure 4.6.4 Increase in submergence population, 2000–2100
Note: SLR is average of the values of the two GCMs.

The base area is 1,770,000 km² in 2000. The extended areas for 2000 to 2100 in the A1B and A2 scenarios become about 160,000 and 180,000 km², respectively. The extended areas in Asia and North America are slightly larger than in other regions – the same trend as for the submerged areas in each scenario. The trend of the extension for 2000–2100 over the world is the same as that for the sea-level rise. The increase in the submergence population by 2100, based on 2000, is shown in Figure 4.6.4 according to each scenario and climate model. Although there was a population of about 257 million in the submergence area of the world in 2000, an increase to about 470 million was projected for 2100 in the A2 scenario, which is most of the increase in population in the twenty-first century. The increase in population of Asia forms the major portion of the world increase. The impacts of both sea-level rise and population growth are included in determining the increase in the affected population. Although the increase in affected population continues till 2100 in the A2 scenario, which also continues positive population growth, the increase is restrained in the A1B and B2 scenarios, in which population

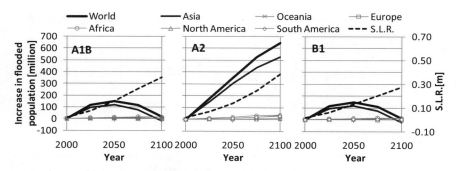

Figure 4.6.5 Increase in flooded population, 2000–2100
Note: SLR is average of the values of the two GCMs.

growth becomes negative after 2050. The population growth scenario in China, Bangladesh, Viet Nam and India greatly affected the results in Asia. This effect appears to reduce the affected population after 2050 in the A1B and A2 scenarios, unlike the trend of sea-level rise. The contribution of sea-level rise and population growth to the size of the affected population is described later.

The increase in the flooded population from storm surge with a sea-level rise is shown in Figure 4.6.5. The changing trend of the affected population for each SRES scenario is the same as that of the submerged population. However, the increase in the rate of flooded population precedes the increase in the rate of sea-level rise. At present, 436 million people in the world are affected by the potential impact of floods; the A2 scenario projects an increase in this number to about 600 million people by 2100.

Figure 4.6.6 shows the relative change in the population increase of submerged areas over the twenty-first century as a proportion of the total population of that region; in other words, the relative increase in population in submerged areas. The relative increase in population in flooded areas is shown in Figure 4.6.7.

Both figures show the results of the A1B and A2 scenarios of SRES with differing population growth. The effects of population growth and sea-level rise on these results are also separated by considering the increase in flooded population as if the population were fixed at that of the year 2000 as the effect of sea-level rise, and other increases were attributed to the impact of population growth.

The results of relative increase in total submerged population (Figure 4.6.6) indicate that for the A2 scenario, Oceania and Asia are affected in approximately the same proportions. In all scenarios and regions the impact of sea-level rise becomes significant in the latter half of the twenty-first century. Up to this point, the increase in population living in

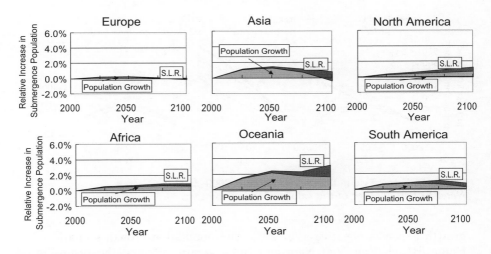

a) A1B scenario

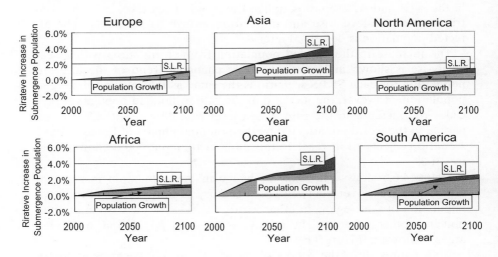

b) A2 scenario

Figure 4.6.6 Relative increase in submergence population in each region

potentially submerged areas is due to population growth. In Asia, in the
A1B scenario, it is clear that the proportion of the submerged population
is reduced because of negative population growth. The increase in flooded
population (Figure 4.6.7) has the same trend as in the submerged population results. These results show the increasing proportion of the total impact in North America occurring in areas affected by hurricanes, and the
larger effect due to population growth in Asia.

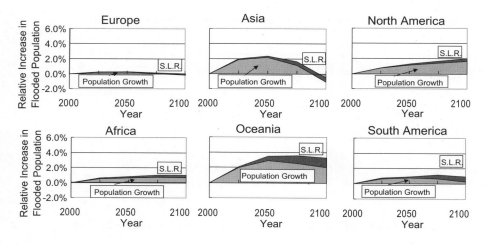

a) A1B scenario

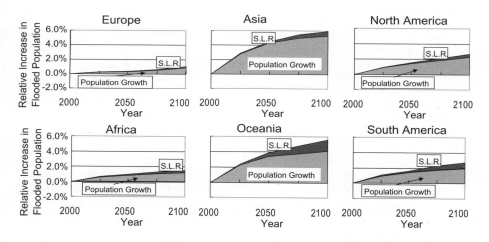

b) A2 scenario

Figure 4.6.7 Relative increase in flooded population in each region

The countries strongly affected in the results of scenario A2 for 2100 are shown in two perspectives to investigate their relative vulnerability. The values for each country were obtained from a global vulnerability assessment and calculated using uniform data from across the world. As a result, although this analysis is suitable for indicating the relative magnitudes in multiple countries, the results for an individual country may be less accurate than those of a vulnerability assessment carried out for the

Table 4.6.1 Countries with the 10 largest increases in flooded population

Country	Flooded population (million)
China	161.83
Bangladesh	107.59
Viet Nam	76.15
India	56.57
Indonesia	33.48
United States	24.35
Brazil	22.73
Egypt	19.46
Myanmar	17.89
Thailand	13.44

Table 4.6.2 Countries with the 10 largest increases in the relative flooded population

Country	Flooded population (%)
Bermuda	78
Saint Kitts and Nevis	50
Tonga	46
Antigua and Barbuda	44
Maldives	44
Turks and Caicos Islands	43
Kiribati	40
Suriname	39
Bahrain	38
Singapore	33

specific country. Furthermore, extremely small island countries, such as Tuvalu, cannot be represented by a latitude/longitude mesh with a spacing of 60 arc-seconds, and therefore are not included in the results.

Table 4.6.1 shows the countries with the 10 largest increases in the absolute number (using 2000 as a baseline) of people potentially affected by flooding. It is clear that countries containing mega-deltas and megacities, such as China, Bangladesh and Viet Nam, are greatly affected. Table 4.6.2 shows the countries with the 10 largest increases in relative population (using 2000 as a baseline) – found by dividing the increase in potential flooded population by the total population in the country.

This raises the ranking of island countries and regions with large proportions of affected population within the country, such as Bermuda, Saint Kitts and Nevis, Tonga, Antigua and Barbuda and the Maldives. Although it is sufficient to argue in terms of absolute numbers as a global problem, it is also important to investigate the relative number in terms of problems for each country.

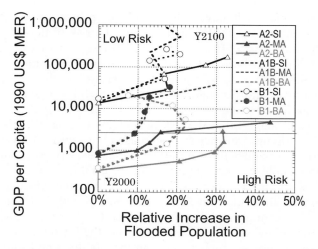

Figure 4.6.8 Relative increase in flooded population and GDP per capita, 2000–2100

Note: SI: Singapore, BA: Bangladesh, MA: Maldives.

Economic strength is important in terms of protective power against disasters – the ability to adapt in response to climate change. We will therefore discuss vulnerability by considering GDP per capita. The GDP per capita of Bermuda, Saint Kitts and Nevis and Antigua and Bermuda is extremely high. From among the most affected countries in Asia, the chosen examples were Bangladesh (BA), which suffers large absolute and relative impacts, the Maldives (MA), which has a large relative impact, and Singapore (SI), which has a strong economy combined with a high relative impact. Figure 4.6.8 shows the increase in the flooded population divided by the total population of the country on the horizontal axis, and the GDP per capita on the vertical axis.

The bottom right of the diagram indicates dangerous situations with relatively high impact and low economic strength that hinders responses, and the top left indicates safety. The value of 0 per cent on the horizontal axis is for 2000. Symbols indicate intervals of 25 years, and values for increase in GDP per capita through 2100 in these countries are found for each year by tracing a line from the bottom left of the diagram. Nicholls, Hoozemans and Marchand (1999) performed a vulnerability assessment by setting up a coastal protection scenario based on the assumption that countries with GDP per capita of US$600–2,400 are capable of mid-level protection, those at US$2,400–5,000 are capable of high-level protection and those with US$5,000 or more are capable of high-quality protection. In Figure 4.6.8, horizontal lines indicate the US$2,400 and US$5,000 levels.

Singapore has GDP per capita exceeding US$10,000 and is thought already to maintain protection capabilities. In the A2 scenario in

Bangladesh, which will have only mid-level protection by 2075, it is thought that during the twenty-first century the risk of flooding by storm surges will continue to affect more than 30 per cent of the population. For the Maldives, it was projected that sufficient adaptations must be made by 2075 to respond to sea-level rise. However, the results indicate that the Maldives and Bangladesh can begin high-level adaptations after 2075 in scenario A1 and after 2050 in scenario B1.

These results suggest that the risk of flooding in coastal regions, particularly in developing countries, will increase above current levels because of population growth before the effect of sea-level rise becomes significant. One example is the large number of casualties caused by Cyclone Sidr that struck Bangladesh in 2007. Therefore, the most appropriate adaptations are those that address population growth in the first half of the twenty-first century and deal with the sea-level rise in the second half of the century. However, because it may delay the introduction of adaptations to coastal disasters such as those in the Maldives and Bangladesh in scenario A2 described above, care is required in adopting scenarios that significantly limit economic growth in developing countries. From these points, the A1 scenario, which includes active policies to reduce differences between regions and promote technology exchange, and the B1 scenario, which includes policies to suppress fossil-fuel emissions along with the policies of A1, are thought to be appropriate. However, if population growth does not proceed according to this scenario, the risk of flood damage due to rising sea level is expected to increase by the end of the twenty-first century in coastal areas in Asia, Oceania and other locations, even in scenarios A1 and B1. These uncertainties must also be considered.

4-6-1-3 Conclusion

Increases in submerged/flooded areas and the affected population due to rising sea level and population growth, using the SRES scenario as the basic vulnerability of coastal regions throughout the world in the twenty-first century, were projected quantitatively on a 60 arc-seconds latitude/longitude mesh. The amount of sea-level rise differs with various greenhouse gas emission scenarios. In the A2 scenario, which is one of the worst, the areas submerged and flooded due to tropical cyclones around the world in the event of a 38 centimetre rise in sea levels by 2100 were projected as increases of approximately 230,000 and 180,000 km^2, respectively. The projected affected population increases to 470 and 600 million people, respectively. The highest numbers of the affected population are in mega-delta regions, and island countries have a high relative increase in affected population.

The increase in the affected population includes the effect of both sea-level rise and population growth. In the A2 scenario, population growth is the main factor, and the effect of sea-level rise becomes significant in the latter half of the twenty-first century. In such a situation, first of all, disaster prevention and management of coastal areas that can respond to population growth are required. Prevention and management that can also serve to adapt to the impact of sea-level rise would be ideal as "wise adaptation". If adaptations to global environmental changes are undertaken based on the strength of each individual country, the results of this study indicate quantitatively that economic growth in developing countries is essential, particularly in the latter half of the twenty-first century.

As seen from differences in population growth and sea-level rise between scenarios, there is uncertainty in the changes in the state of international society. Although the projected results were also uncertain regarding the size of the affected population, a negative impact appeared in the results of all scenarios that contain mitigation of global warming. Unless global warming can be prevented, adaptations must be considered along with mitigation. These response measures take many years from planning to implementation, and are therefore extremely expensive; for example, coastal protection programmes against the effects of the current climate have not yet fully achieved their goals, even in Japan. Global warming, which can become significant within one century, is thus a severe problem that cannot be avoided. Therefore, it is necessary to focus on adaptations to prevent additional vulnerabilities and negative impacts that appear during states of uncertainty, including providing the economic growth that enables necessary support while developing mitigations of global warming, even before obtaining accurate assessments.

4-6-2 Case study on assessment of inundation area induced by dual impacts of sea-level rise and land subsidence in the Chao Phraya delta

Some metropolises that are strongholds of politics, economies and living are located in huge deltas in Southeast Asian countries. Deltas such as the Chao Phraya, Red River and Mekong are called "mega-deltas". The IPCC (2007b) mentioned that mega-deltas will be vulnerable to natural disasters induced by global climate change, partly because they are located in very low lands in coastal regions and will be directly affected by sea-level rise due to global warming. What is more, land subsidence has taken place in most mega-deltas, and is also a factor in expanding flood damage. Thus it is important for sustainable development and adaptation

to global climate change to consider not only sea-level rise but also land subsidence in mega-deltas.

The purpose of this section is to assess the influence of the dual impacts of sea-level rise and land subsidence on the inundation area in the Chao Phraya delta. The situation of land subsidence in 2100 has been predicted using a method of reliable land subsidence mapping based on the observations of settlement proposed by Murakami, Yasuhara and Suzuki (2005) and Murakami et al. (2006). The future elevation model in the objective regions has been made based on the present elevation model and the predicted land subsidence using GIS. For investigating the influence of the dual impacts of both a 59 cm sea-level rise and land subsidence on the inundation area in the Chao Phraya delta, a hazard map of the inundation area has been created. The map shows that the inundation area caused by the dual impacts of sea-level rise and land subsidence will be approximately 1,000 km^2. When calculating the inundation area in mega-deltas it is thus important to consider not only sea-level rise but also land subsidence in the future.

4-6-2-1 The present situation of land subsidence

There are approximately 748 observation locations for monitoring settlements from 1996 to 2003 in the Chao Phraya delta (Figure 4.6.9).

We can understand the present situation of land subsidence in the region using the time-series records of settlements. A map of the distribution of land subsidence has been represented using reliable mapping combined with a spatial interpolation procedure based on geostatistics proposed by Murakami, Yasuhara and Suzuki (2005) and Murakami et al. (2006). The mapping method can show not only the distribution of expected settlements but also the distribution of estimated standard deviations based on the spatial correlation relationships of settlements. The interpolation method is based on the Kriging geostatistic, which is a spatial interpolation method, and assumes that an estimation at a location is expressed as the linear weighted summation of the observations. Figure 4.6.10 shows the interpolated result of the distribution of land subsidence in the region from 1996 to 2003.

The estimated settlements are drawn as contour lines and the estimated standard deviations are indicated as raster data. The map shows that severe land subsidence has taken place in Samut Prakarn, in the middle of Samut Sakhon and north of Pathum Thani.

4-6-2-2 The future situation of land subsidence

To investigate future land subsidence in the region, an observational prediction method for land subsidence proposed by Murakami, Yasuhara

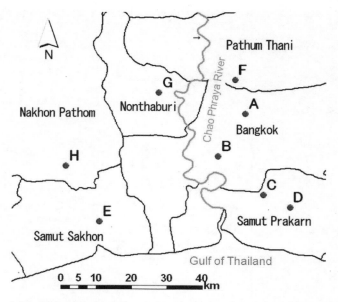

Figure 4.6.9 Observation locations of land subsidence in the Chao Phraya delta

and Suzuki (2005) has been used. The method is based on an assumption that an accumulated settlement subjected to seasonal changes of groundwater level can be expressed as the similar curve of Terzaghi's one-dimensional consolidation theory. An accumulated settlement S_i, after elapsed time t_i from the beginning of observation, can be predicted by the following equation:

$$S_i = S_{p0}\{1 - \exp(-C_R \cdot t_i)\} \tag{1}$$

where S_{p0} is residual settlement and C_R is the coefficient of settlement rate. Parameters which are S_{p0} and C_R in equation (1) can be determined by a back analysis using observations of settlements at a location. For investigating its applicability to future settlement prediction in the region, the method has been applied to eight representative locations (A to H) shown in Figure 4.6.9. Figure 4.6.11 shows the observed and predicted results of accumulated settlements in these locations. There is good agreement between observed and predicted results.

Future accumulated settlements at all the observation locations have been predicted using equation (1), and the future land subsidence has been represented using the proposed method for a reliable land subsidence mapping. Figure 4.6.12 shows a future situation of land subsidence that will take place from 2001 to 2100. In addition, the map shows the estimated standard deviation, which depends on both spatial interpolation error and future prediction.

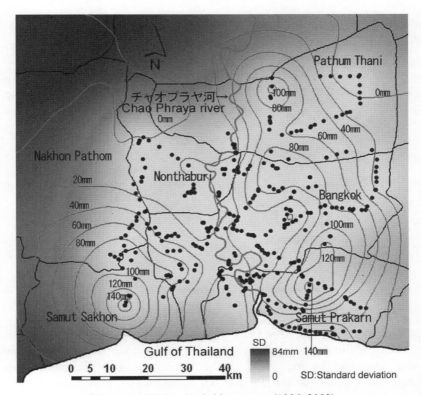

Figure 4.6.10 Land subsidence map (1996–2003)

According to the map, there are severe settlements in the middle east of Samut Prakan and the northern side of Samut Sakhon. Therefore, severe land subsidence will move towards the north in Samut Sakhon, and subsidence in the northern side of Pathum Thani in the present situation will decrease. Comparing the present land subsidence map with the future situation, the distribution of estimated standard deviation in the future map is larger than in the map of the present situation because the future standard deviation depends on both spatial interpolation error and future prediction. Therefore, it is important for investigating dual hazard due to sea-level rise and land subsidence to consider the estimation error caused by both spatial interpolation and future prediction.

4-6-2-3 Assessment of the influence of dual impacts of sea-level rise and land subsidence on inundation area

In order to assess the influence of dual impacts of sea-level rise due to global warming and land subsidence on the inundation area in the Chao

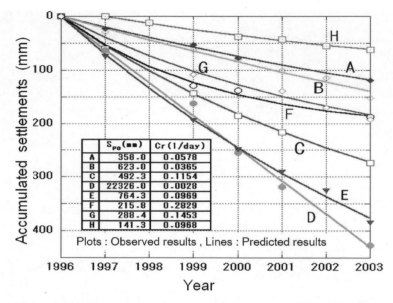

	S_{PO} (mm)	Cr (1/day)
A	358.0	0.0578
B	623.0	0.0365
C	492.3	0.1154
D	22326.0	0.0028
E	764.3	0.0969
F	215.8	0.2829
G	288.4	0.1453
H	141.3	0.0968

Plots : Observed results , Lines : Predicted results

Figure 4.6.11 Comparisons of observed settlements with predicted results

Phraya delta, GIS-aided spatial analysis has been performed on the basis of the predicted result of future land subsidence in 2100 shown in Figure 4.6.12. The inundation area is defined as the region which is below sea level. Ground level in the future situation was calculated from the present ground level in consideration of the future land subsidence. The severest sea-level rise due to global warming was assumed as 59 cm by the IPCC (2007a). Figure 4.6.13 shows calculated results of the area inundated due to sea-level rise in 2100.

Figure 4.6.13(a) shows inundation caused by sea-level rise alone: inundation areas are in coastal regions in Samut Sakhon, Bangkok and Samut Prakarn and the middle region of Bangkok. Figure 4.6.13(b) shows inundation caused by the dual impacts of sea-level rise and land subsidence. It is clearly indicated that inundation expands when considering future land subsidence. In particular, it widely expands in the middle of Samut Prakarn, in which severe land subsidence will take place. Figure 4.6.13(c) shows inundation regions due to sea-level rise and land subsidence plus estimation error caused by spatial interpolation and land subsidence prediction. The map indicates that the inundation region expands more than in Figure 4.6.13(b), without consideration of estimation error, and more than 70 per cent of Samut Prakarn will be flooded. The results show that it is important for estimating inundation regions in a future situation affected by global warming to consider not only sea-level rise but also land subsidence.

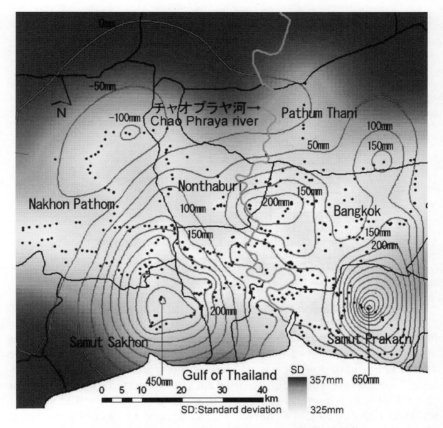

Figure 4.6.12 Future land subsidence map (2001–2100)

4-6-2-4 Conclusion

The influence of the dual impacts of sea-level rise due to global warming and land subsidence on inundation areas in the Chao Phraya mega-delta has been investigated using a method of reliable land subsidence mapping based on observations of settlements. Salient conclusions are as follows.

- Severe land subsidence takes place in the middle of Samut Prakarn and Samut Sakhon and the northern side of Pathum Thani. However, the severe land subsidence will move to the east in Samut Prakarn, to the north in Samut Sakhon and will become small in Pathum Thani by 2100.
- Inundation areas subjected to the dual impacts of sea-level rise and land subsidence are in coastal regions in Samut Sakhon, Bangkok and Samut Prakarn and the middle region of Bangkok. When considering estimation error caused by spatial interpolation and land subsidence

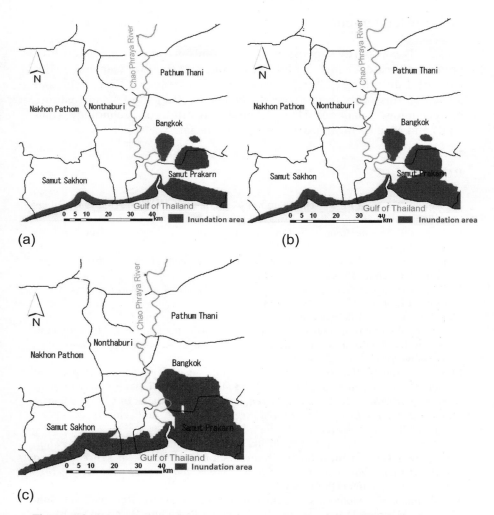

Figure 4.6.13 Inundation area caused by sea-level rise and land subsidence
(a) Sea-level rise alone
(b) Sea-level rise and land subsidence
(c) Sea-level rise, land subsidence and estimation error

predictions, the predicted result shows that more than 70 per cent of
Samut Prakarn will be inundated.

Therefore, it is necessary for sustainable development and adaptation
to the future situation affected by global warming in coastal regions subjected to severe land subsidence to take measures to mitigate inundation
damage in consideration of the dual impacts of sea-level rise and land
subsidence.

Acknowledgements

This study was partly supported by the Grant-in-Aid on Innovation Program of Climate Change Projection for the 21st Century (Japanese Ministry of Education, Culture, Science and Technology). Kind help and advice on this study from Professor Dennes T. Bergado (Asian Institute of Technology, Thailand), Dr Giao (Asian Institute of Technology, Thailand) and Mana Kitirat are also highly appreciated.

REFERENCES

Hoozemans, F. M. J., M. Marchand and H. A. Pennekamp (1993) *A Global Vulnerability Assessment, Sea-Level Rise*, 2nd edn. Delft: Delft Hydraulics.

IPCC (2000) *Special Report on Emission Scenarios*. Cambridge: Cambridge University Press.

IPCC (2007a) *Climate Change 2007: The Physical Science Basis*. Cambridge: Cambridge University Press.

IPCC (2007b) *Climate Change 2007: Impacts, Adaptation and Vulnerability*. Cambridge: Cambridge University Press.

Matsumoto, K., T. Takanezawa and M. Ooe (2000) "Ocean Tide Models Developed by Assimilating TOPEX/POSEIDON Altimeter Data into Hydrodynamical Model: A Global Model and a Regional Model Around Japan", *Journal of Oceanography* 56, pp. 567–581.

Mimura, N. (2000) "Distribution of Vulnerability and Adaptation in the Asia and Pacific Region", in *Global Change and Asia Pacific Coast – Proceedings of APN/SURVAS/LOICZ Joint Conference on Coastal Impacts of Climate Change and Adaptation in the Asia-Pacific Region*. Kobe: Asia Pacific Network for Global Change Research, pp. 21–26.

Murakami, S., K. Yasuhara and K. Suzuki (2005) "Reliable Land Subsidence Mapping by a Geostatistical Spatial Interpolation Procedure", in *Proceedings of 16th International Conference on Soil Mechanics and Geotechnical Engineering*, Vol. 4. Amsterdam: IOS Press, pp. 2829–2832.

Murakami, S., K. Yasuhara, K. Suzuki and H. Komine (2006) "Reliable Land Subsidence Mapping Using a Spatial Interpolation Procedure Based on Geostatistics", *Soil and Foundations* 46(2), pp. 123–134.

Nicholls, R. J., M. J. F. Hoozemans and M. Marchand (1999) "Increasing Flood Risk and Wetland Losses due to Global Sea-level Rise: Regional and Global Analyses", *Global Environmental Change* 9, Supplement 1, pp. S69–S87.

Nobuoka, H., N. Mimura and N. Fukuhara (2007) "Vulnerability Assessment for Sea-level Rise in the Asia and Pacific Region", in *Proceedings of Asian and Pacific Coasts (APAC) 2007*. Beijing: China Ocean Press, pp. 770–777.

Yukimoto, S. and A. Noda (2002) "Improvements of the Meteorological Research Institute Global Ocean-Atmosphere Coupled GCM (MRI-CGCM2) and Its Climate Sensitivity", in *CGER's Supercomputer Activity Reports*, Vol. 10. Tsukuba: CGER/NIES, pp. 37–44.

4-7

Adaptation and mitigation strategies in response to climate change

Makoto Tamura and Nobuo Mimura

4-7-1 Introduction

Historically speaking, there are two approaches to handling the issue of environmental change: one is to remove the causes of the change and the other is to adjust to the adverse effects. In the context of climate change, these responses are referred to as mitigation and adaptation measures, respectively. Figure 4.7.1 depicts a flowchart of climate change issues posed by greenhouse gas (GHG) emissions, including both impacts and countermeasures.

Mitigation strategies to reduce GHG emissions and their role in climate change include energy conservation, development of alternative energy and forest protection and afforestation programmes. In contrast, adaptation serves to adjust human and natural systems on the assumption of ongoing climate change, e.g. disaster prevention, changes in cultivated plant species and breeding new plant varieties. Figure 4.7.1 illustrates these as two cycles responding to climate change that must be properly combined to be fully effective.

Previous chapters have discussed climate change impacts on water, food, ecosystems and coastal areas. Such impacts will lead to socio-economic effects such as human migration, decreased crop yields, decline in the number of ski resorts and failure of infrastructure. It is clear that climate change affects multiple sectors, regions and countries; however, the degree of impact varies widely. Ironically, the most adverse and significant effects of climate change will probably be observed in developing

Climate change and global sustainability: A holistic approach, Sumi, Mimura and Masui (eds), United Nations University Press, 2011, ISBN 978-92-808-1181-0

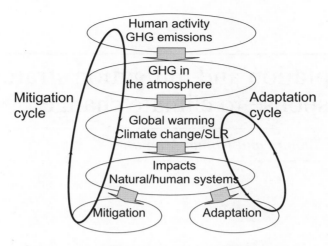

Figure 4.7.1 Response strategies to climate change

countries with low emission levels. For example, it is anticipated that these countries will experience serious damage due to floods and droughts.

In contrast, developed countries are considered to be relatively insensitive to the adverse impacts of climate change because their systems, such as infrastructure and prediction technologies as well as financial stability, have been developed for a long time and give them the means to minimize adverse impacts or insure against disasters. However, even developed countries cannot always avoid more violent physical events, such as torrential rainfall or severe drought, on a previously unimaginable scale. Hurricane Katrina in 2005 is representative of an event of such a large-scale impact; it destroyed protective levees and seriously damaged the city of New Orleans. Climate variability may exceed the design limits of any disaster prevention programme, and the exponential rise of health hazards due to thermal and other stresses can extensively challenge health systems. In recent years some Japanese studies have quantitatively reported the likelihood of increased risk of drought and torrential rain, loss of natural habitats such as beaches and forests, increase in regional variability of rice yields and more deaths caused by thermal stress and other factors. These adverse impacts cannot be ignored (Project Team for Comprehensive Projection of Climate Change Impacts, 2008: 96, 2009: 38; MOE, 2008: 70).

To date, responses to climate change have largely focused on reduction of GHG emissions. However, the major objective of countermeasures, as indicated under the UN Framework Convention on Climate Change, must be to ensure that global warming stays below a dangerous level. Even if the severest mitigation measures are implemented to reduce

GHGs accumulating in the atmosphere, it will be difficult to avoid the adverse impacts of climate change in the next few decades. Therefore, in addition to mitigation, adaptation measures will be a vital response to climate change; these include avoidance of local or short-term intensively adverse impacts on agriculture, local resources and ecosystems as well as the particularly vulnerable regions of many developing countries.

4-7-2 Mitigation strategies

Mitigation is a primary countermeasure to the effects of climate change. Figure 4.7.2 shows six stabilization scenarios for climate change. These are categorized by CO_2 emissions, concentration and average temperature. In scenario 1, which shows stabilization of climate at the lowest temperature, global CO_2 emissions would take a downward turn no later than 2015 and decrease by 50–85 per cent by 2050. Even in this best case, the average temperature is anticipated to rise by up to 2.4°C compared to that of the Industrial Revolution era. It would be very difficult to accomplish such a substantial reduction in CO_2 emissions. This is the most important reason why we must apply the concurrent use of mitigation and adaptation measures. In any case, countries throughout the world will have to establish their own targets for the total amount of GHG reduction and put them into practice.

Mitigation strategies are roughly divided into two categories: those that reduce sources of GHG and those that enhance sinks of GHG. Reduction in GHG emissions includes energy efficiency of supply and demand and use of technologies for reducing GHG emissions. Reduction from the supply aspect includes development and widespread use of alternative energy derived from non-fossil fuels, while reduction from the demand aspect includes energy conservation at various stages, such as production processes, transportation systems and domestic use. Enhancing sinks of GHG includes increasing absorption by ecosystems in areas such as afforestation, reafforestation, forest management and carbon capture storage (CCS) or sequestration. Afforestation and forest management can contribute to the conservation of ecosystems, but CCS is problematic because of the potential for adverse impacts on ecosystems.

Implementation of mitigation measures requires development of new technologies and innovative social systems. The ultimate measure is to construct a low-carbon society. To achieve this, it is necessary to promote energy and resource conservation and find sources of low-carbon energy supply from both technical and social perspectives. These responses are associated with efforts to minimize consumption of fossil-fuel energy and non-renewable resources.

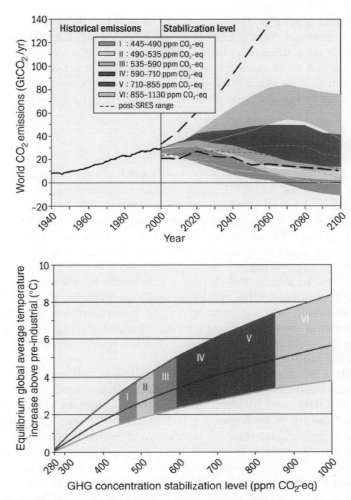

Figure 4.7.2 Stabilization scenario categories
Notes:
1. "Best estimate" climate sensitivity of 3°C (black line in middle of shaded area).
2. Upper bound of *likely* range of climate sensitivity of 4.5°C (line at top of shaded area).
3. Lower bound of *likely* range of climate sensitivity of 2°C (line at bottom of shaded area).
Source: IPCC (2007b).

International cooperation initiatives are also being pursued. The Kyoto Protocol proposed three flexible mechanisms: joint implementation, the clean development mechanism (CDM) and emissions trading. These

Table 4.7.1 Adaptation in natural and human systems

		Proactive	Reactive
Natural systems			Changes in phenology Changes in ecosystem composition Migration of plants/habitats
Human systems	Private	Purchase of insurance Construction of houses on stilts Redesign of oil rigs	Changes in farm practices Changes in insurance premiums Purchase of air conditioning
	Public	Early-warning systems New building codes, design standards Incentives for relocation	Compensatory payments, subsidies Enforcement of building codes Coastal care

Source: Klein, Nicholls and Mimura (1999); IPCC (2001).

mechanisms are regarded as mitigation measures that add economic in-centives to reduce emissions. Under the CDM, Japan has so far mainly promoted power generation projects and alternative chlorofluorocarbon (CFC) countermeasures for Asian countries. However, it will now focus on co-benefit projects that lead to energy conservation and pollution con-trol, resource conservation or waste reduction. The next challenge under a post-Kyoto Protocol that includes further promotion of this wide spec-trum of responses is to formulate an international framework that ad-dresses both mitigation and adaptation.

4-7-3 Adaptation strategies

In general, adaptation may be classified as reactive adaptation (respond-ing to an impact that has already occurred) or proactive adaptation (re-sponse in anticipation of an impact). Adaptation can also be referred to as either autonomous or deliberate. Table 4.7.1 illustrates a classification scheme for adaptation that can be applied to the natural environment and human society.

Planned adaptation is implemented based on clear political intentions, while autonomous adaptation is passive. In the course of history, human beings have always coped with changes in the natural environment in various ways. Humans undertake both proactive and reactive adaptation. However, they have typically conducted reactive adaptation to envir-onmental changes; for example, after natural disasters such as earth-quakes and volcanic eruptions or pandemic events, they often decided to

Table 4.7.2 Adaptation by sectors

	Technology options	Policy options	Social and economic options
Food	• Development of high-temperature-tolerant varieties • Shift in cultivation areas • Change in cultivation methods • Shift to aquaculture and development of aquaculture technologies • Information from promoters of agricultural improvement	• Development of mechanisms to support and advise on adaptation measures for elderly farmers • Adjustment of fishing seasons and fishing ground formation • Provision of information and human resources development	• Reconsideration of irrigation customs • Utilization of mutual aid systems (quick provision of damage information, and using this information in compensation claims)
Water use and water resources	• Introduction of raw water transmission and discharge control systems • Desalination of seawater • Use of treated sewage water, rainwater, etc. • Eutrophication control measures • Use of water-saving devices • Overall evaluation of sources of drinking water, and selection of suitable water purification processes	• Improvement of water supply (conversion from agricultural water to drinking water based on decrease in arable lands) • Restriction of deep groundwater pumping to control land subsidence • Raising awareness of water saving	• Intensification of farmland and reallocation of water rights • Introduction of mechanisms or regional flexible transfer of water during droughts • Indirect controls using economic instruments, such as a levy system in regulations for use of deep groundwater (to control land subsidence)

138

Natural ecosystems	• Designation and preservation of refuges • Establishing wildlife corridors • Conversion of artificial cedar forests to natural forests • Early detection and prevention of pine wilt • Installation of deer fences in alpine regions • Reduction in nutritive salts and other environmental load substances • Development of monitoring methods for each ecosystem	• Reconsideration and new designation of nature reserves, national parks, etc. • Regulation of artificial transplantation and fish release • Restrictions on tourist activities • Training of volunteers with knowledge and skills who are able to cooperate in monitoring • Raising awareness regarding reduction of treading impact on alpine flora, wetlands and protection of coral reefs	• Consensus-building among relevant entities regarding identification of and response to climate change impacts
Disaster prevention and large coastal cities	• Alterations in architectural styles • Maintenance and improvement of coastal protection facilities • Enhancing drainage systems • Development of super-levees with multiple functions • Effective utilization of existing facilities • Comprehensive sediment control in rivers and on coasts • Production and distribution of hazard maps • Provision of up-to-date information • Upgrading monitoring systems	• Changes and regulation of land use based on disaster prevention (i.e. relocation of housing, prohibitions and restrictions on construction in danger zones) • Integrated coastal zone management • Implementation of training and education for disaster prevention	• Establishment of voluntary organizations for disaster prevention • Establishment of a system of inundation insurance for residents • Establishment of funds and subsidies for post-disaster restoration

Table 4.7.2 (cont.)

	Technology options	Policy options	Social and economic options
Health	• Development of vaccines and new medicines • Removal of suitable conditions for emergence of disease • Suspending emissions of air pollutants • Production and distribution of healthcare guide manuals • Thorough surveillance of infectious diseases • Surveys on incidence and distribution of vectors	• Establishment of institutions and regulations for heatstroke prevention • Care for elderly households (i.e. utilization of care systems, and care provided by neighbourhood associations) • Capacity development for prevention planning for control of vector mosquitoes • Raising public awareness on healthcare	• Support for initiatives at workplaces and schools

Source: Modified from MOE (2008).

undertake measures to avoid recurrence of such severe damage. With regard to climate change, development of observation networks and climate models has made it possible to estimate future changes in climate, at least to some extent. This has brought opportunities to implement proactive adaptation to climate change. From a long-term perspective, it is obvious that proactive adaptation can reduce damage and countermeasure costs more effectively than reactive adaptation measures.

Climate change adaptation measures include the following functions (Hay and Mimura, 2006).

- *Avoiding or reducing the likelihood of an adverse event or condition*. This means taking preventive measures against anticipated effects, e.g. improving catchment management, thereby avoiding excessive runoff and hence flooding.
- *Reducing consequences*. This involves measures to diminish damages that have already occurred, e.g. ensuring healthy reef and mangrove systems, which act as buffers during a storm surge.
- *Redistributing or sharing the risk*. This includes measures to lessen the costs of damage by dispersing them among many people or over a longer period, e.g. insurance schemes.
- *Accepting risk*. This means doing nothing at least for a particular time, but includes the opportunity to learn from the experience.

Under a climate change adaptation strategy, these functions will vary according to the type of consequences. Table 4.7.2 classifies adaptation measures of some sectors into three options: technology, policy and socio-economic.

Most adaptation measures are not treated separately from conventional activities, such as change in farm practices in agriculture or construction of dykes for disaster management, but are additionally implemented according to the predicted consequences of climate change. Selection and prioritization of planned adaptation measures will also be important for implementation of these measures. Smith (1997) points out that the issues of flexibility and cost benefit should be considered during implementation of proactive measures, and that it is necessary to review constantly the time of action according to the impacts being experienced. The impacts of climate change can be considered from the perspective of the speed with which they occur, ranging from impacts gradually changing on a mid- to long-term scale to intensive events occurring in a sudden or local manner, known as extreme events. It is necessary to examine how a nation and its constituent regions should react to the impacts of climate change occurring over a relatively long term, based on various predictions, and consider strategies aimed for the future, such as land-use planning. On the other hand, real-time actions such as monitoring and early-warning systems must be implemented to counteract extreme events that

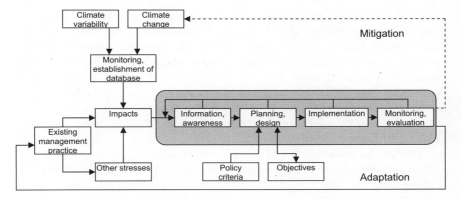

Figure 4.7.3 Adaptation planning
Source: Klein, Nicholls and Mimura (1999).

are difficult to predict by conventional forecasting, such as localized torrential rain and flooding.

The adaptation process should be implemented based on a sequence that includes impact estimation, policy planning, implementation and evaluation (Figure 4.7.3).

In order to ensure that the various adaptation measures are well integrated by examining their common and interacting characteristics, rather than treating each one separately, it is important to implement them in a flexible manner and continuously examine the adequacy of the actions. It will also be important to improve monitoring systems and advance prediction techniques. Most developing countries, however, lack the internal capacity to predict impacts. It is critical to overcome this deficiency through international cooperation and assist these developing countries in improving their adaptation capacities.

4-7-4 Interrelationship between mitigation and adaptation

It is often ineffective to implement adaptation or mitigation measures separately, while there may be significant beneficial synergies between the two responses. Table 4.7.3 shows a comparison between adaptation and mitigation measures.

It generally takes a long time for mitigation measures to take effect, but they can provide wide-ranging benefits. On the other hand, adaptation measures have a rather immediate effect, but tend to operate in limited areas. Although mitigation measures can be evaluated on the basis of GHG emissions, it is difficult to set similar baseline and result indicators for adaptation measures and properly evaluate their effectiveness. Both

Table 4.7.3 Characteristics of mitigation and adaptation

	Mitigation of climate change	Adaptation to climate change
Benefits	All systems	Selected systems
Scale	Global	Local to regional
Time span	Centuries	Years to centuries
Lead time	Decades	Immediate to decades
Effectiveness	Certain	Generally less certain
Ancillary benefits	Sometimes	Mostly
Polluter pays?	Typically yes	Not necessarily
Payer benefits	Only a little	Almost fully
Monitoring	Relatively easy	More difficult

Source: Fussel and Klein (2006).

measures have specific advantages and can be viewed as complementary to each other. To keep the negative impacts of climate change within a given scale, it will be necessary to take detailed countermeasures with a combination of mitigation and adaptation, foreseeing short-term and mid- to long-term targets of adverse impacts for each region.

In this context, it is helpful to prioritize mitigation and adaptation measures or consider responsive actions that can bring synergistic effects or co-benefits to other issues. Having a "portfolio" of both mitigation and adaptation measures can reduce vulnerabilities and risks associated with climate change. Furthermore, only limited resources, such as human resources, time and funds, are available to be allocated to these measures. By the same token, it is desirable not to take mutually contradictory actions when implementing mitigation and adaptation measures, except in emergencies.

Typical examples to illustrate the synergistic effects of mitigation and adaptation include programmes of afforestation and conservation of mangroves. Afforestation and forest conservation programmes stabilize carbon and enhance water storage capacity, thereby creating a buffer against flooding and drought and providing many synergistic benefits, such as preservation of ecosystems and their services. Other examples of synergies include household insulation using rainwater or wearing summer business attire ("cool biz" in Japan). Table 4.7.4 shows some more examples of the synergies.

On the other hand, there are actions that may increase GHG emissions or cause a contradiction or trade-off between mitigation and adaptation measures; these include excessive use of air conditioners, uncontrolled consumption of water for irrigation, desalination and use of water chillers in the fish culture industry to combat a rise in seawater temperature. Adaptation measures themselves often involve energy consumption, such as

Table 4.7.4 Examples of possible synergies between mitigation and adaptation

Sector	Water	Disaster risk management	Human health
Issue	Decreased water security	Selective attention to weather-related hazards introduces distortions into hazardscape reality	Increased incidence of water- and vector-borne diseases
Mitigation	Increase energy efficiency of water treatment and distribution systems	Land-use plans and other regulatory instruments prevent infrastructure from being located in high-risk areas	Reduce energy consumption by health facilities, based on results of energy audits
Adaptation	Increased rainwater harvesting at household and community levels	Integrate resistant design characteristics for geophysical hazards into "climate-proofing" measures; develop education/awareness programmes based on overall hazardscape	Strengthened quarantine regulations and border surveillance
Synergy	Decreased reliance on centralized water supply system	Enhance existing disaster management structures, systems, practices and processes at regional, national and community levels	Less use of healthcare facilities in business-as-usual scenario, reducing emissions even further

Source: Modified from ADB (2009).

temporary consumption of massive amounts of energy for infrastructure improvements or continuous consumption of energy by air conditioners to counteract higher temperatures due to climate change. These actions must be limited to emergencies with significant number of victims. Prediction techniques, vulnerability assessments and cost-benefit analyses for prioritizing appropriate interventions and finding an appropriate balance of mitigation and adaptation measures are keys to comprehensive understanding of the effects of mitigation and adaptation.

4-7-5 Adaptation and capacity development

Occurrence of adverse impacts and damage caused by climate change involves several factors. The first is large-scale external forces associated with climate change, such as increased temperature, sea-level rise and ex-

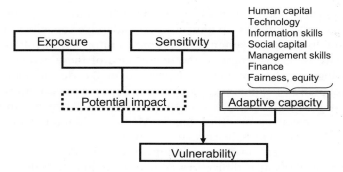

Figure 4.7.4 Vulnerability and adaptive capacity

treme weather events. The second factor is the sensitivity of natural and social systems, and the third factor is society's level of resilience or adaptive capacity. Figure 4.7.4 depicts the relationship between vulnerability, external forces, sensitivity and adaptive capacity.

It demonstrates that a society heavily affected by climate change has high vulnerability. Vulnerability can be described in various ways, but in this section it is defined as "the degree of susceptibility to external forces of a system and the scale of a capacity to convert the adverse effect and adapt to it or use it". Based on this definition, larger external forces and smaller resilience (adaptive capacity) can be considered to result in higher vulnerability. In other words, it becomes necessary to restrict external forces of climate change and increase society's adaptive capacity to lower the level of vulnerability.

Institutions taking the initiative in implementing adaptation measures are units of regions and communities. Consequently, the success or failure of adaptation measures in terms of lowering vulnerability depends on increasing the regions' adaptive capacity. In addition to external forces and sensitivity, adaptive capacity is one of the determinants of a society's vulnerability to climate change. Adaptive capacity refers to the abilities of natural and social systems to adapt to any environmental change. This component is reflected in resources, human resources, knowledge/recognition, information management, technologies, social systems, communities and risk management. Because of variations in this adaptive capacity, the adverse impacts of climate change are unevenly distributed across regions and societies (IPCC, 2007a).

Among other imperatives, developing countries with high vulnerability and serious adverse impacts of climate change will certainly need to increase their adaptive capacities. Their long-term targets would include the ability to use their own traditional experiences and knowledge about

natural disasters and to be able to implement monitoring and prediction techniques by themselves. To enhance these adaptive capacities, it is critical to establish a social system that promotes information collection and sharing and raise awareness of the importance of these activities. These methodologies are sometimes implemented in the development of regions. Adaptation is sometimes regarded as a means to accomplish development objectives, while development provides similar means to achieve adaptation objectives at other times (McGray, Hammill and Bradley, 2007: 57). In other words, because of the overlap between adaptation and regional development, increase in adaptive capacity depends on regional development paths. It is difficult to deliberate actions to reduce vulnerability to climate change and those promoting sustainable development while there are limited resources that can be allocated to both these action streams. Therefore, decision-makers have realized that "mainstreaming" or incorporating adaptation policies into existing socio-economic policies without distinguishing between climate change policies and, for example, national land and agriculture planning is a logical evolution of the preferred solution.

4-7-6 Adaptation and sustainability

As suggested by the preceding discussion, problems surrounding us are not limited to the adverse impacts of climate change. Human beings are facing multiple pressures that result from deterioration of biological resources, regional environmental pollution, changes in land use due to development, population growth and economic globalization.

Measures against climate change affect factors other than climate. It is also true that we have limited resources to respond to various challenges, including time, funding and human resources. Figure 4.7.5 shows a visual "roadmap" that can take us from adaptation and mitigation to sustainability.

Sustainability science aims to solve these problems and other issues simultaneously by developing various measures against climate change. For example, mitigation could contribute to formation of a resource-circulating society through co-benefits to improved air and water quality, sustainable forest management in developing countries, energy and resources conservation, and efficient and environmentally sound waste management. Adaptation is closely related to disaster prevention as well as land and agriculture planning, and can form part of an approach to create a safe and secure society ready to address the adverse impacts of future climate change. In other words, these measures, such as reduction

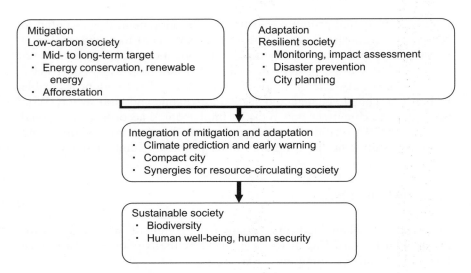

Figure 4.7.5 Adaptation and mitigation towards sustainability

of pressure on resources, management of environmental risks and improvement of adaptive capacities, lead in the same direction as creation of a sustainable society. This supports the incorporation of climate change policies into major existing socio-economic policies – the need to "mainstream" climate change policies.

Japan developed guidelines for "wise adaptation" that follow this model of integration (MOE, 2008). These guidelines emphasize the need for utilization of the latest results of regional vulnerability evaluation and monitoring; review and combination of various adaptation options; consideration of temperature ranges and margins that can respond to the adaptation measures from short- and long-term perspectives; appropriate incorporation of the measures into existing policies, such as disaster prevention planning; and more flexibility and preparedness of natural and socio-economic systems. Therefore, it is critical to move towards a low-carbon and resilient society that could serve as a framework for a future sustainable society.

4-7-7 Conclusion

Adaptation and mitigation are twin pillars in developing measures against climate change. These two categories of response represent the main strategies for improving social resilience to climate change, ensuring

human security and promoting sustainable development. It is essential to review and reconstruct our national policies on land use, environmental use and city/rural planning. In doing so, the ideal of a low-carbon and resilient society can be promoted so that it would help us to construct a sustainable society. Therefore, the high-level target is to adopt a flexible response to climate change and sustain a dynamic and vital society. Wise adaptation to climate change must be implemented according to regional realities, thereby resulting in change of regional and social modalities and possibly resulting in the solution of other problems simultaneously.

Acknowledgements

This section has benefited substantially from comments provided by Professor John Edward Hay. It was supported by the Nippon Life Insurance Foundation and the Sumitomo Foundation.

REFERENCES

ADB (2009) *Mainstreaming Climate Change in ADB's Operations. Climate Change Implementation Plan for the Pacific Islands Region, 2009–2015*. Manila: Asian Development Bank.

Fussel, Hans-Martin and Richard J. T. Klein (2006) "Climate Change Vulnerability Assessments: An Evolution of Conceptual Thinking", *Climatic Change* 75, pp. 301–329.

Hay, John and Nobuo Mimura (2006) "Supporting Climate Change Vulnerability and Adaptation Assessments in the Asia-Pacific Region: An Example of Sustainability Science", *Sustainability Science* 1, pp. 23–35.

IPCC (2001) *Climate Change 2001: Impacts, Adaptation and Vulnerability*. Cambridge: Cambridge University Press.

——— (2007a) *Climate Change 2007: Impacts, Adaptation and Vulnerability*. Cambridge: Cambridge University Press.

——— (2007b) *Climate Change 2007: Synthesis Report*. Cambridge: Cambridge University Press.

Klein, Richard J. T., Robert J. Nicholls and Nobuo Mimura (1999) "Coastal Adaptation to Climate Change: Can the IPCC Technical Guidelines Be Applied?", *Mitigation and Adaptation Strategies for Global Change* 4, pp. 239–252.

McGray, Heather, Anne Hammill and Rob Bradley (2007) *Weathering the Storm: Options for Framing Adaptation and Development*. Washington, DC: World Resource Institute.

MOE (2008) "Wise Adaptation to Climate Change – Report by the Committee on Climate Change Impacts and Adaptation Research", Global Environment Bureau, Ministry of Environment, Tokyo.

Project Team for Comprehensive Projection of Climate Change Impacts (2008) "Global Warming Impacts on Japan – Latest Scientific Findings", available at www.nies.go.jp/s4_impact/pdf/20080815report.pdf.

————— (2009) "Global Warming Impacts on Japan – Long-Term Climate Stabilization Levels and Impact Risk Assessment", available at www.nies.go.jp/s4_impact/pdf/20090612.pdf.

Smith, Joel B. (1997) "Setting Priorities for Adapting to Climate Change", *Global Environmental Change* 7, pp. 251–264.

5

Design climate policy

5-1

New international framework beyond the Kyoto Protocol

Hiroshi Hamasaki and Tatsuyoshi Saijo

5-1-1 Introduction

In February 2007 the UN Intergovernmental Panel on Climate Change (IPCC) observed that the average global temperature climbed 0.74°C in the 10 years from 1996 to 2005, and basically concluded that global warming is escalating due to human activity. If countermeasures are not taken, the panel warns that the temperature could climb a maximum of 6.4°C by the end of this century compared to the end of the twentieth century. With this in mind, discussion regarding the post–Kyoto Protocol international framework for the reduction of greenhouse gases after 2013 has become animated. In January 2007 the European Union independently declared that it would reduce greenhouse gases by at least 20 per cent by 2020 (compared to the level in 1990). In May 2007, looking ahead to the G8 summit to be held in Germany in June, Prime Minister Abe and the Japanese government proposed the strategy of "Cool Earth 50". Regarding the post-Kyoto framework, Abe proposed that all the major emitting countries, including the United States, China and India, aim to create a framework that will accomplish a 50 per cent global reduction by 2050. The details of this plan have not been produced, however, and what comes after the promised term of the Kyoto Protocol – in other words, the specific institutional design of the global framework after 2013 – remains unclear.

We begin by assessing the Kyoto-type framework, which sets emission targets to developed countries and no targets to developing countries,

Climate change and global sustainability: A holistic approach, Sumi, Mimura and Masui (eds), United Nations University Press, 2011, ISBN 978-92-808-1181-0

from economic and environmental perspectives by using a dynamic computable general equilibrium model. Secondly, we take the global emissions trading scheme (GETS) as an alternative to the Kyoto Protocol, and assess it from economic and environmental perspectives.

5-1-2 Methodology

This study uses the GTAP-E model (Burniaux and Truong, 2002), which is the standard GTAP model (Hertel, 1997) but with energy substitution incorporated into the basic production structure (see Figure 5.1.1). GTAP stands for Global Trade Analysis Project, and the GTAP model is a global computable general equilibrium (CGE) model developed at the Center for Global Trade Analysis, Purdue University, USA, for use in global trade analysis. With energy substitution incorporated, the modified GTAP-E model is often used for trade-environment analysis. Here we further modify the GTAP-E model to allow for the disaggregation of the electricity generation sector into various "technologies" such as "coal-fired", "gas-fired", "oil-fired", "hydro", "nuclear" and "others". Each technology is assumed to produce a particular type of product (coal-electricity – ELYCoal; gas-electricity – ELYGas, etc.) using relatively fixed input proportions, and we then combine the different electricity outputs using a constant-ratio-of-elasticity-of-substitution-homothetic (CRESH) production structure. This approach of disaggregating the production structure of an aggregate commodity such as electricity has been referred to as the "technology bundle" approach (see Figure 5.1.2) (Saijo and Hamasaki, 2009).

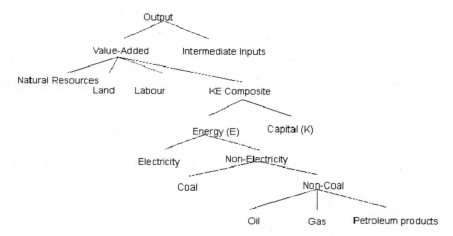

Figure 5.1.1 Standard GTAP-E production structure

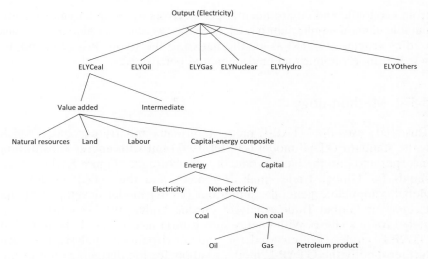

Figure 5.1.2 Production structure for electricity sector

This kind of a production tree is a convenient way of representing separable, constant return-to-scale technologies. Each group of equations refers to one of the branches in the production tree. For each branch, substitution among inputs within the nest follows directly from the constant elasticity of substitution form of the production function for that branch.

For example, the value-added nest in Figure 5.1.1 is described as follows:

$$qfe(i,j,r) = qva(j,r) - \sigma_{VA} * [pfe(i,j,r) - pva(j,r)]$$

where
$qfe(i,j,r)$: percentage change in quantity of endowment commodity i demanded by firms in sector j of region r
$qva(j,r)$: percentage change in quantity index of value added in firms of sector j in region r
σ_{VA}: substitution elasticities in value-added branch
$pfe(i,j,r)$: percentage change in demand price of endowment commodity i supplied to firms in sector j of region r
$pva(i,j,r)$: percentage change in price of value added in sector j of region r.

This study uses an aggregation of nine regions and 14 sectors based on the GTAP version 6 database. Details of the aggregation are presented in Table 5.1.1.

Table 5.1.1 Categorizations of regions and sectors

Regions	Sectors
China	Agriculture
India	Coal
Japan	Oil
USA	Gas
Canada	Petroleum products
EU15	Electricity
Russia	Iron and steel
Rest of Annex I	Non-ferrous metal
Rest of the world	Mineral products
	Paper, pulp and publishing
	Chemicals, rubber and plastic
	Other manufacturing
	Transport
	Service

5-1-3 Was Kyoto dead?

The most glaring weakness in the Kyoto Protocol is that China and India do not have quantitative emission targets and Russia's commitment is quite generous. In addition, the largest greenhouse gas contributor, the United States, has not ratified the protocol. The Kyoto Protocol imposes costs on sources in countries with commitment, but no costs on sources outside these industrialized countries. The difference in costs across countries can also cause emission leakage, which can further reduce the efficiency and environmental benefits of the protocol (Aldy and Stavins, 2007a). Leakage of emissions could come about by relocation of carbon-intensive industries from countries with emission commitments to non-participating countries, or by increased consumption of fossil fuels by non-participating countries in response to declines in world oil and coal prices. An authoritative survey concludes that "Leakage rates in the range 5 to 20 per cent are common" (IPCC, 2001). Article 3 of the UN-FCCC defines the principle of common but differentiated responsibilities (CBDR), but there is no generally agreed definition. Under the existing Kyoto Protocol, the principle of CBDR has been translated in practice into a set of specific, quantitative emission mitigation obligations for industrialized countries and no emission mitigation obligations for developing countries (Aldy and Stavins, 2007b). This analysis evaluates the Kyoto-type framework, which set GHG emission reduction targets for developed countries and no targets for developing countries.

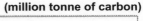

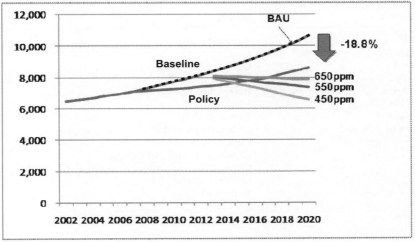

Figure 5.1.3 Global emissions

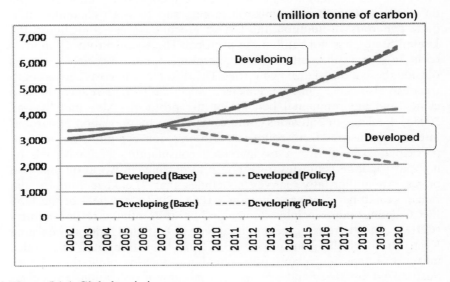

Figure 5.1.4 Global emissions
Note: The lower lines represent emissions of developed countries and the upper lines represent emissions of developing countries. Solid lines represent BAU and broken lines represent the Kyoto-type scenario.

Under the simulation, we assume that the Kyoto-type framework will be kept after 2012, the last year of the Kyoto Protocol, and Annex I countries will reduce their emissions by 40 per cent below the 1990 level in 2020, the toughest IPCC (2007) target for Annex I countries to stabilize carbon concentration at 450 ppm. Figure 5.1.3 shows deviation of global carbon emissions from the baseline and climate change stabilization scenarios of 450 ppm, 550 ppm and 650 ppm. Global emissions will decrease by 18.8 per cent below the BAU scenario in 2020 if developed countries reduce their emissions by 40 per cent below 1990 by 2020. However, the reductions are not enough to meet even the 650 ppm scenario.

Figure 5.1.4 shows emissions of developed and developing countries under the uncontrolled scenario and the Kyoto-type scenario. Under the BAU scenario, emissions of developing countries exceed developed countries in 2007. Under the simulation scenario, emissions from developed countries will deviate sharply from the baseline, but developing countries' emissions will increase compared to the baseline due to carbon leakages.

5-1-4   Global emissions trading scheme

Promoting participation may be the greatest challenge for the design of climate policy architecture. No policy architecture can be successful without the United States, Russia, China and India taking meaningful actions to slow their greenhouse gas emission growth and eventually reducing their emissions (Aldy and Stavins, 2007b). Developing countries will be the source of big increases in emissions in the coming years, according to the business-as-usual path. However, developing countries point out that it was industrialized countries that created the problem of global climate change, and developing countries should not be asked to limit their economic development to pay for it. To overcome these problems, Stern (2008) proposes international cap-and-trade systems as an alternative to the Kyoto Protocol for three reasons: managing risks of dangerous climate change by imposing an absolute limit on emissions; reducing the costs of action; and generating private sector financial flows to developing countries, which can be used for low-carbon development. In the simulations, a global emissions trading scheme (GETS) was introduced in 2013 with credible commitments to keep it in place over the long run, adjusting the rate as necessary to achieve the profile of global emissions depicted in Figure 5.1.5. There is no agreed-upon global emission path to stabilize climate change; hence we take den Elzen and Höhne's (2008) 450 ppm scenario, 25 per cent below 1990 in 2020.

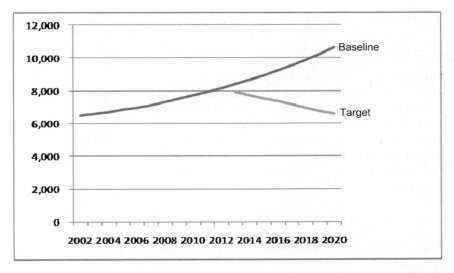

Figure 5.1.5 Global emission targets and paths, 2002–2020 (million tonnes of carbon)

The pattern of international transfers and the macroeconomic effect of cap and trade are highly sensitive to how emission rights are reallocated (IMF, 2008). In the simulations, we assume four types of initial allocation methods of emission rights. Each economy receives emission rights according to its population, GDP and a hybrid of population and GDP. In the hybrid of population and GDP, half of emission rights are allocated according to GDP and half according to population in each economy.

5-1-4-1 GETS per capita

This section describes key results of the global emissions trading scheme with per capita allocation. Under the scheme, every single person has a right to emit the same amount of carbon.

Firms change their technology, substituting away from carbon-intensive inputs and into capital and labour. Households change their consumption patterns from energy-intensive goods. The macroeconomic impacts of major economies are depicted in Figure 5.1.6. Changes of GDP depend on how intensively it uses carbon-intensive energy to make goods and services for the domestic market and exports. China is the least efficient in the use of energy. It is producing nine times more emissions per unit of output than Japan, seven times more than Western Europe, five times more than the United States and three times more than Eastern Europe, Russia and other emerging and developing economies (IMF, 2008). As a result, China will be highly affected in terms of GDP. The GDP loss of

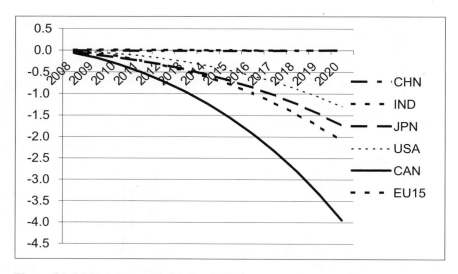

Figure 5.1.6 Macroeconomic impact (GDP)
Note: Percentage deviation from the baseline.

Table 5.1.2 International transfers under GETS (US$ million)

China	40,548
India	112,117
Japan	−16,228
USA	−125,378
Canada	−13,417
EU15	−58,121

Note: This table shows the net value of international payment for emission rights. A positive value denotes a receipt of transfers.

Japan will be lower than in other countries due to the country's high energy efficiency and high dependency on imported fuels.

Table 5.1.2 shows cumulative international transfers under GETS from 2013 to 2020. India is the biggest recipient, with transfers reaching US$112,117 million. India is a low-energy-efficient country, which means it can reduce its own emissions at a lower price compared to developed countries. In addition, India's per capita emission is much lower than the world average. In 2005 India's population was 16.8 per cent of the world total, but its emissions were 4.5 per cent. India can sell surplus emission rights to other countries. In the same year, China's population was 20.4 per cent of the world total and its emissions were 19.0 per cent. China's surplus emission rights are much lower than India's. As a result, international transfers of China were smaller than India.

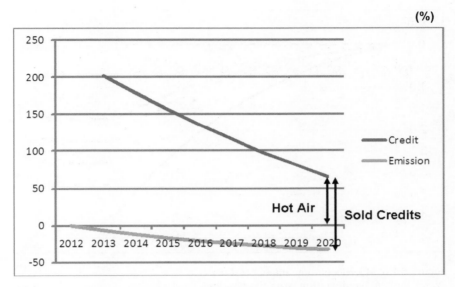

Figure 5.1.7 India's actual emissions and emission rights
Note: Cumulative deviations from the baseline.

Table 5.1.3 Comparison between Kyoto and GETS (%)

		Kyoto type	GETS
GDP	China	0.0	−2.5
	India	0.0	−1.2
	Japan	−1.7	−0.5
	USA	−1.3	−0.9
	Canada	−3.9	−1.7
	EU15	−2.1	−0.9
Emissions		−18.8	−38.4

Note: Cumulative deviation from the baseline.

Figure 5.1.7 shows India's actual emissions and allocated emission rights. The gap between allocated emissions and baseline represents hot air, and the gap between actual emissions and baseline represents actual reduced emissions in China. In other words, India is allocated more credits than it actually emits under the baseline scenario and it can sell the hot air to other countries. In addition, India has a lot of low-cost mitigation options, and under one carbon price it can sell emission reductions from the baseline as well.

Key results of the Kyoto type and GETS with per capita allocation are compared in Table 5.1.3. Except China and India, which have no binding target under the Kyoto type, GDP in the GETS scenario improves compared to the Kyoto-type scenario.

Table 5.1.4 International transfers under GETS (US$ million)

	Per capita	Per GDP	Hybrid
China	40,548	−119,674	−41,056
India	112,117	−44,858	32,559
Japan	−16,228	107,540	46,791
USA	−125,378	147,349	13,458
EU15	−58,121	130,233	37,805

Note: 2020 figures.

Table 5.1.5 GDP change (%)

	Per capita	Per GDP	Hybrid
China	−2.5	−2.5	−2.5
India	−1.2	−2.4	−1.9
Japan	−0.5	−0.5	−0.5
USA	−0.9	−0.8	−0.8
EU15	−0.9	−0.6	−0.8

Note: Cumulative deviations from the baseline.

If GETS is introduced, climate change can be stabilized without imposing heavy damage on each country's economy compared to the Kyoto-
type framework. GETS encourages both developed and developing
countries to price carbon emissions in the country. Developing countries
are projected to produce 82 per cent of emissions between 2002 and 2020.
Excluding developing countries from carbon mitigation activities is very
costly. GETS with per capita allocation increases additional financial flow
to developing countries, and developing countries can spend the budget
on mitigation and adaptation to climate change.

5-1-4-2 *Comparison of different allocations*

Table 5.1.4 shows differences of international transfers among different
allocations of emission rights. In per capita allocation, developing countries receive more credits than developed countries, because per capita
emission of developing countries is much lower than that of developed
countries. Hence, developed countries have to pay to buy credits from
developing countries. Conversely, in per GDP allocation, developing
countries have to pay to buy credits from developed countries, because
emission per unit of GDP of developing countries is more than that of
developed countries. In the hybrid, half the credits are allocated on a per
capita basis and the rest are based on per GDP.

   Table 5.1.5 represents GDP change. There are no significant differences
in GDP between the three allocation methods, but GDP in India is relatively sensitive to the allocation method of emission rights because the

amount of international transfer differs significantly depending on the allocation method.

5-1-5 Conclusion

The IPCC Fourth Assessment Report (2007) finds that human actions are "very likely" the cause of global warming – meaning a 90 per cent or greater probability – and stabilizing climate change is an emergency issue to be addressed by the international community. Under the existing Kyoto Protocol, the principle of CBDR has been translated in practice into a set of specific, quantitative emission mitigation obligations for industrialized countries and no emission mitigation obligations for developing countries. However, this modelling exercise shows that it is very costly to mitigate carbon emissions without involving developing countries, which will be a major source of global emission increases in the coming decades. If GETS is introduced, climate change can be stabilized without imposing heavy economic damage compared to the Kyoto framework. GETS encourages both developed and developing countries to price carbon emissions in the country. GETS with per capita allocation increases additional financial flow to developing countries, which can spend the budget on mitigation and adaptation to climate change.

REFERENCES

Aldy, Joseph and Robert N. Stavins (2007a) "Introduction: International Policy Architecture for Global Climate Change", in Joseph E. Aldy and Robert N. Stavins (eds) *Architectures for Agreement, Addressing Global Climate Change in the Post-Kyoto World*. Cambridge: Cambridge University Press, pp. 1–27.
——— (2007b) "Architectures for an International Global Climate Change Agreement: Lessons for the International Policy Community", in Joseph E. Aldy and Robert N. Stavins (eds) *Architectures for Agreement, Addressing Global Climate Change in the Post-Kyoto World*. Cambridge: Cambridge University Press, pp. 350–367.
Burniaux, Jean-Marc and Truong Phuoc Truong (2002) "GTAP-E: An Energy-Environmental Version of the GTAP Model", GTAP Technical Paper 16, Center for Global Trade Analysis, Purdue University.
den Elzen, Michel and Niklas Höhne (2008) "Reductions of Greenhouse Gas Emissions in Annex I and Non-Annex I Countries for Meeting Concentration Stabilisation Targets", *Climate Change* 91, pp. 249–274.
Hertel, Thomas (ed.) (1997) *Global Trade Analysis Modelling and Applications*. Cambridge: Cambridge University Press.
IMF (2008) *World Economic Outlook*, April. Washington, DC: IMF.

IPCC (2001) *Climate Change 2001*. Cambridge: Cambridge University Press.
——— (2007) *Climate Change 2007*. Cambridge: Cambridge University Press.
Saijo, Tatsuyoshi and Hiroshi Hamasaki (2009) "United Nations Emission Trading Scheme (UNETS): New International Framework beyond the Kyoto Protocol", paper presented at Fourth East Asian Symposium on Environmental and Natural Resource of Economics, Taipei, 2–3 March.
Stern, Nicholas (2008) "Key Elements of a Global Deal on Climate Change", London School of Economics and Political Science, London.

5-2

Emission reductions policy mix: Industrial sector greenhouse gas emission reductions

Seiji Ikkatai

5-2-1 Trends in industrial sector GHG reduction policies

Energy-oriented carbon dioxide (CO_2) emissions from the industrial sector in Japan as of fiscal year 2007 were approximately 471 million tonnes, accounting for 38.6 per cent of Japan's total energy-oriented CO_2 emissions (Ministry of Environment, undated). Overall, trends since 1990 (base year for the Kyoto Protocol) are flat or slightly declining (Figure 5.2.1).

Emissions from the residential and business sectors have tended to rise from the base year, and whereas the transport sector has tended to level off or decline in recent years, the trend is that of an increase from the base year. For these values, the greenhouse gas (GHG) emission components corresponding to the electricity supplied to each sector from fossil-fuel-fired power stations are calculated as emissions from that sector.

Looking at the overall trends in emissions from fiscal years 2005 to 2007 (the most recent years for which data are available), a trend is observed where emissions in 2006 are lower than those in the previous year, whereas a rise is seen in 2007. A major factor behind this is the fact that the winter of 2006 was the second warmest on record, and winter heating energy consumption in the residential and business sectors declined. Emissions from the industrial sector continued to grow in 2006 and 2007 as a result of an upward trend in the economy. Another reason why GHG emissions increased from 2006 to 2007 is the rise in CO_2 emission units

Climate change and global sustainability: A holistic approach, Sumi, Mimura and Masui (eds), United Nations University Press, 2011, ISBN 978-92-808-1181-0

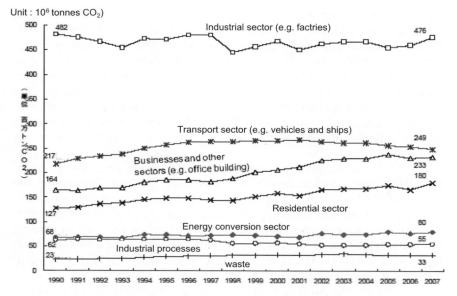

Figure 5.2.1 Trend of CO_2 emissions by sectors

due to back-up operations of fossil-fuel-fired power plants accompanying the shutdown of nuclear power plants after the Chubu earthquake.

In addition, the proportion of emissions from Japan's coal-fired power stations is growing, and this factor is contributing greatly to GHG emissions. Overall, total emissions in 2007 increased by 8.2 per cent compared with 1990 (based on preliminary data), which is a major divergence from the Kyoto Protocol reduction target of −6.0 per cent.

5-2-2 Status of GHG reduction measures in Japanese corporations

5-2-2-1 Reduction policies for the industrial sector

Accompanying the Kyoto Protocol coming into effect in February 2005, Japan developed a plan to achieve the protocol target based on the Law Concerning the Promotion of Measures to Cope with Global Warming. This plan details measures and policies for each sector, and in the case of the industrial sector, which possesses the highest share of emissions, it mandated "Steady promotion of measures headed by continued voluntary action plans" as "efforts by the industrial sector (manufacturing companies etc.)". In terms of reduction measures, many can be attributed to the

Keidanren Voluntary Action Plan on the Environment drawn up in 1997. This plan recommends "Entirely voluntary efforts in all industries conducted based on personal judgement without pressure from any quarter" (translated citation from the plan). Details of efforts are summarized as "Best efforts viewed as being at the very limit at the present time by each industry" (translated citation). On this account, the targets of the plan are varied. They include improving CO_2 emission and energy consumption units based on production volume and revenue, as well as reducing overall emission quantities and implementing other energy conservation measures.

Furthermore, measures to supplement this include a reporting system for GHG emissions from companies based on the Law Concerning the Promotion of Measures to Cope with Global Warming, and the promotion of energy conservation and improvement of energy efficiency of products as per a top-runner format in large factories based on the Law Regarding the Rationalization of Energy Use. A voluntary domestic emissions trading system based on tax incentives and subsidies that is also related to energy conservation has been set up.

In addition, the trial use of a domestic integrated market related to emissions trading, including the aforementioned voluntary domestic emissions trading system, started in 2008 under the premise of voluntary participation.

5-2-2-2   Reduction measures by the industrial sector

A research team from the Research Center for Advanced Policy Studies at the Institute of Economic Research, Kyoto University (Kyoto, Japan), conducted questionnaire surveys and then follow-up interviews based on the results of these surveys in 2005 and 2006 regarding the extent to which Japanese corporations have set targets and are implementing GHG reduction measures, and what concrete measures are being implemented by companies that are carrying out reduction measures (Research Center for Advanced Policy Studies, 2007).

The questionnaire survey was carried out in fiscal year 2005, with questionnaires being sent to approximately 1,200 companies (including small and medium-scale enterprises) in Kobe and Fukuyama. From these, replies were received from 265 companies (a valid response rate of 22.4 per cent). In fiscal year 2006 questionnaires were sent to all the companies listed on the Tokyo Stock Exchange and the Osaka Stock Exchange (about 2,400 companies); replies were received from 589 companies (a valid response rate of 24.1 per cent). The results are described below.

First, the ratio of companies which answered that they possessed GHG reduction targets and were systematically carrying out GHG reductions was approximately 20 per cent among the small and medium-scale enter-

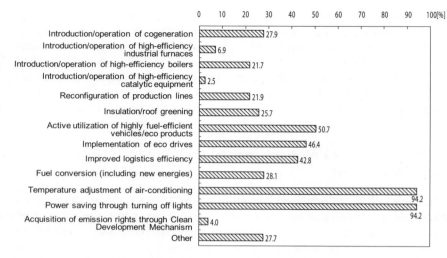

Figure 5.2.2 Nature of GHG reduction measures undertaken in fiscal year 2005

prises in the 2005 survey, whereas the ratio was approximately 58 per cent in the 2006 survey that covered companies listed on the Tokyo and Osaka Stock Exchanges. This suggested that relatively larger companies tended to carry out reductions. Next, companies which answered that they were carrying out measures in the 2006 survey were asked about the nature of GHG reduction measures they implemented in fiscal year 2005. The results are shown in Figure 5.2.2, and reveal a higher degree of implementation of measures that did not require capital investment (e.g. adjustment of air-conditioning temperature) compared with measures that did.

Of the companies in the 2006 survey which answered that they possessed targets, 32 per cent said they had absolute values for their reduction targets and 51 per cent said they had unit requirement targets. From these results, a structure is apparent in which GHG emissions tend to rise in line with increased economic activity. In addition, the proportion of companies which answered that they were calculating the cost incurred in reducing emissions of GHGs by one tonne was approximately 4.5 per cent in the 2005 survey, whereas it was 25.5 per cent in the 2006 survey. But while relatively larger companies tended to calculate such costs, of the group of companies listed on the Tokyo and Osaka Stock Exchanges, which represent the Japanese business world, no more than one in four companies were adopting such actions.

Taking into consideration the results of these questionnaire surveys, interview surveys were conducted in fiscal years 2005 and 2006 in 17 companies that were judged to be carrying out reduction measures more actively than others. Even for companies which answered that they were

calculating reduction costs, the methods adopted were varied, and virtually no companies were identified to be calculating marginal reduction costs as defined by economics. In addition, although energy conservation measures enabling costs to be recovered within a certain period (around one to three years) were being carried out, measures requiring extended periods to recover costs (e.g. installation of solar power generation equipment) were not being actively implemented to any great extent.

5-2-3 Analysis of motives behind GHG reduction in Japanese corporations

The research team analysed the motives for GHG reductions based on the 2006 questionnaire survey (ibid.). First, seven hypotheses were presented as motives for GHG reduction: achieving voluntary targets, cost reduction, incentive utilization, response to administrative rules such as the Law Concerning the Rational Use of Energy (Energy Conservation Law), client retention, pre-emptive response to environmental regulations and corporate social responsibility (Anton, Deltas and Khanna, 2004; Arimura, Hibiki and Katayama, 2007; Henriques and Sadorsky, 1996; Khanna, 2001). We attempted quantitative analysis in terms of correlation with reduction activities conducted by companies. Measures raised as reduction activities were introduction of environmental management systems, environmental reports and environmental accounting; setting up of voluntary company targets for emission reductions; and introduction of forward-looking efforts for counting GHG emissions, counting the costs related to reducing GHG emissions and calculating and elucidating marginal reduction costs. The findings are shown in Table 5.2.1. Motives that had a strong correlation with these reduction activities were achieving voluntary targets, incentive utilization, response to administrative rules such as the Energy Conservation Law and pre-emptive response to environmental regulations. The two motives of cost reduction and implementation of corporate social responsibility had almost no correlation with efforts related to GHG reduction.

This research showed that motives such as achieving voluntary targets within individual corporate groups, incentives from administrative and financial organizations, response to administrative rules and pre-emptive responses in anticipation of future environmental restrictions had a stronger correlation with GHG reduction activities compared with motives such as implementing corporate social responsibility and cost reduction. In particular, pre-emptive responses in anticipation of future environmental restrictions had a strong correlation with GHG reduction activities. This finding signifies that forecasts by companies of future poli-

Table 5.2.1 Correlation between reduction activities and reduction motives

Motive / Interest/activity	Achieving voluntary targets	Cost reduction	Incentive utilization	Response to administrative issues such as Energy Conservation Law	Retaining clients	Pre-emptive response to environmental regulations	Corporate social responsibility
Introduction of environmental management systems				X	X		
Introduction of environmental reports							
Introduction of environmental accounting	X		X	X		X	
Setting up of voluntary company targets for emission reductions	X			X			
Introduction of forward-looking efforts for counting GHG emissions	X			X			
Introduction of forward-looking efforts for counting the costs related to reducing GHG emissions	X						
Introduction of forward-looking efforts for calculating and elucidating marginal reduction costs	X		X			X	

Note: X means the correlation (in terms of marginal effect) was significantly positive in each estimation.

cies may act as strong motives for GHG reduction, and that the strength of signals put out by the government regarding future policies has a major influence on reduction activities in companies.

From this research, we can determine the general direction required so that Japanese companies further increase their GHG reduction activities in the future. First, companies should set more stringent voluntary targets, but this may prove difficult from the perspective of the original nature of "voluntary targets". Second, existing regulations and incentives should be stepped up and augmented. However, regulations in force at present, headed by the Energy Conservation Law, do not necessarily incorporate clauses for GHG reductions based on absolute values. Furthermore, since incentives have budgetary limitations, substantial reductions cannot be anticipated through these alone. Finally, the government should define a clear policy for introduction of a system with legal force over the long term. This research has not clearly indicated the form such a legal system should adopt, but in concrete terms climate change policies such as a carbon tax or capped emissions trading could be considered.

One of the important conclusions obtained from this research is that there are limitations in basing GHG reductions solely on corporate internal motives such as cost reduction and implementation of corporate social responsibility.

5-2-4 Analysis of GHG reduction costs in Japanese corporations

Let us now look at the extent to which Japanese corporations are incurring costs in reductions of GHGs. To elucidate this reality, in fiscal year 2007 the survey team from Kyoto University collated approximately 1,000 panel datasets related to GHG reduction quantities and costs for the period 1999–2006 from environmental reports and financial statements announced publicly by 17 industries, including food processing and steel making (Research Center for Advanced Policy Studies, 2008). To ensure data coherence, the companies' analyses were limited to those using the Environmental Accounting Guidelines from the Ministry of Environment.

In addition, a formula estimated for the "reduction–cost function", approximated as a quadratic curve with convexity at the bottom, was tested as a theoretical model. The rationale was that for companies, if energy-conserving equipment such as high-efficiency boilers is installed from the start, the costs of reduction after subtracting savings such as fuel costs are negative; however, such measures are later expanded with greater reduction targets and reduction costs gradually revert to being positive.

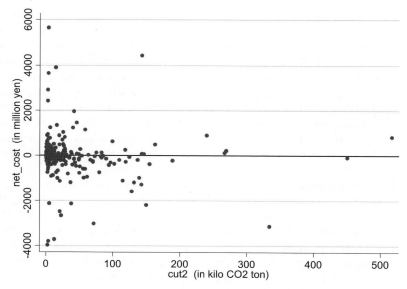

Figure 5.2.3 Scatter diagram showing GHG reduction cost

Analyses of corporate public data for each company verified the statistical significance of approximating the relationships between reduction costs and actual reduction quantities as a quadratic curve with convexity at the bottom. Based on this analysis, the mean marginal reduction cost for all industry types obtained from all panel data was approximately ¥–6,800. This shows that, presently at least, introduction of energy conservation equipment in many companies to reduce GHGs is not incurring expense but rather is generating profits. In the case of Japan, the findings strongly suggest that there is significant scope in terms of energy conservation measures that generate profits. Actual GHG reduction quantities (values after revenue and fixed asset balance growth rate adjustments) and GHG reduction cost data after subtracting the energy conservation merits obtained in the survey are plotted in the scatter diagram shown in Figure 5.2.3.

5-2-5 Issues regarding reduction measures in the Japanese industrial sector

Taking into consideration the survey findings discussed above, issues regarding GHG reduction measures in Japan's industrial sector are detailed in the following sections.

5-2-5-1 Ideal method for target setting

As mentioned previously, reduction targets in Japan's industrial sector are essentially dependent on the industry's voluntary target settings. Individual industries and companies establish their future outlooks and set voluntary targets accordingly. In general, it is difficult to expect these targets to be in accordance with scientifically required reductions derived from the progress in climate change. In addition, it is difficult to expect that these targets will conform to the Kyoto Protocol and mid-term targets or be set to balance with other sectors such as residential and transport.

A further problem is that most of these targets are reduction values based on unit requirements rather than absolute values. Consequently, even if these per-unit targets are achieved, it is highly possible that GHG emissions will increase. In the economic recovery period starting in 2005, despite a decline in the residential sector emission quantity, industrial sector emissions increased. In addition, since target setting is voluntary, there is a limitation in that even if the targets are not achieved, a company is not subject to legal penalties.

It is clear from the IPCC (2007) Fourth Assessment Report that there is an extremely urgent need for "developed" countries to reduce their GHG emissions substantially in the future. From this perspective, the current method of setting targets is clearly inappropriate, and there is a need to switch to target setting that takes into consideration the needs of natural science and ensures that targets are met with certainty.

5-2-5-2 Reduction methods

As is the case with target setting, reduction methods are for the most part left to the voluntary judgement of companies, and apart from the emissions trading system currently being introduced in Tokyo, overall reduction methods at the national and regional public body levels are not being applied. For this reason, put in the best possible terms, companies are adopting various methods most suited to their respective situations, including doing nothing. Put in the worst possible terms, the situation is that methods that are unrelated to and inconsistent with other companies and industries are being adopted and implemented.

5-2-5-3 Means of applying reduction costs

Viewing the circumstances mentioned above from an economic perspective, it can be deduced that the GHG marginal reduction costs for individual companies vary and the situation is inconsistent. In general, this may enable lower GHG reduction costs for society as a whole to achieve

a specific quantity of reductions, but it signifies that the system is not highly efficient when it comes to cost versus effect. As mentioned previously, there is scope for generating profits through energy conservation depending on the company, but there are numerous examples whereby efforts have not been made to achieve such major reductions.

One cause of such a situation is that the reduction obligations placed on countries by the Kyoto Protocol have not been made compulsory for individual companies and citizens. For example, in the European Union individual member countries have been allocated a –8 per cent reduction obligation under the Kyoto Protocol, and these obligations have in turn been handed down to companies and citizens in member states via systems such as the EU Emissions Trading System cap and carbon taxes. In contrast, for Japan to meet its Kyoto Protocol target, the country must utilize its own financial resources to purchase emission permits from foreign countries if it does not meet the obligation in the end. Individual companies and citizens have no legal obligations. Needless to say, companies can purchase emission rights from overseas on a voluntary basis and allocate this to the national depreciation account, thereby counting this as part of Japan's reduction contribution. However, this remains a voluntary deed and not a legal obligation.

5-2-5-4 National economic issues

Based on the circumstances discussed above, a major problem is unfolding. Because a framework has not been built in Japan for GHG reduction measures that boast high effects versus costs, even though there is scope to reduce GHG using methods incurring less cost, this is not being executed. Some researchers fear that, as a result, the Japanese government will have no choice but to achieve its Kyoto Protocol target by purchasing emission rights from foreign countries using taxpayers' money. In general, with a domestic carbon tax and emissions trading system, the tax revenue and trading costs remain within the country: the tax revenue is spent and the emission purchase costs in trading end up as revenue for the counterparty. Incentives related to technological development and energy conservation work well, and the overall effect on the national economy is considered slight because positive and negative aspects cancel each other out. This contrasts with buying emission rights from foreign countries, where the purchasing power ends up being transferred offshore.

5-2-5-5 Issues regarding international competitiveness

Another major problem is the potential for a country's means of GHG reduction to link directly with issues associated with future economic

international competitiveness. On the assumption that developed countries will cut their emissions by 60–80 per cent by 2050, global climate change measures initially will likely proceed in the direction of halving GHG emissions globally by 2050, subsequently stabilizing climate change. With existing technologies, business styles, consumption patterns and lifestyles, this will lead to a substantial change in the structure of industry and consumption, and cause a transition to a social economy. The role of the socio-economic system is extremely large in achieving such a swift transition to a low-carbon social economy.

The existence of a new socio-economic system that incorporates economic incentives for the transition to a low-carbon social economy has major advantages from the aspects of technological innovation, business style and lifestyle, which also leads to international competitiveness. In contrast, a society in which existing policies continue may lose its competitiveness. In an era when the economy changes greatly in such a way, the corresponding cost structure may also vary greatly. The consequences cannot be accurately predicted by traditional cost-versus-effect analysis, and hence this situation must be monitored closely.

5-2-6 Emission reduction strategy changes in Europe and the United States

The abovementioned approach is reflected in the changes occurring in emission reduction strategies in the European Union and the United States. For example, the EU climate change and energy policy package decided in 2009 (coming into effect in 2013) has three strategy targets: tackling climate change issues, stepping up EU energy security and stepping up international competitiveness of the EU economy. By introducing proactive climate change policies headed by the EU Emissions Trading System, and by putting pressure on companies to reduce emissions through technological innovation and creation of new business models for a quick transition to a low-carbon social economy, the European Union is adopting international leadership directed at solving climate change issues while simultaneously trying to preserve its international competitiveness in the medium to long term (Ministry of Environment, British Embassy in Japan, 2007).

Until now, the United States has withdrawn from the Kyoto Protocol because it views climate change measures as having an adverse effect on its economy. However, with the inauguration of the Obama administration, the United States is accelerating deliberations regarding introduction of an EU-style emissions trading system at the federal level under the assumption of a return to the international post–Kyoto Protocol framework

starting in 2013. This major transition in mindset is supported by the outlook that, as with the European Union, a proactive climate change policy is an extremely important component in development of a country's economy (Ikkatai, Ishikawa and Ohori, 2007).

5-2-7 Direction of emissions reduction policy mix in the industrial sector

Taking into account considerations thus far, the fundamental direction of policy desirable for emission reductions in the industrial sector is that clear long-term reduction targets should be set; to achieve these targets, reduction methods that utilize market mechanisms should be introduced as a central component in combination with other supplementary policies; and the policy should be designed such that environmental preservation and economic development are aligned.

The heart of this policy is the mindset of attaching a market price to GHG emissions. More than anything, securing company profits and surviving in the market are the absolute priority for management in the industrial sector. For this reason, through setting stringent targets over the long term and capped emissions trading and carbon taxes, the GHG emissions situation of an individual company is directly linked to its profitability, and this will become the greatest incentive to modify the company's actions. Creating such an objective situation will not be possible merely through voluntary actions on the part of the industrial sector. Rather, a political decision is required based on agreement at the citizen level.

Next, a technological strategy is required so that these incentives give rise to innovative technologies and business models in companies. The fundamental direction of the strategy would be a transition to extremely reliable technologies like those found in ecosystems that are highly efficient, do not generate waste products and are sustainable. In this process, how utilization of carbon-capture and sequestration technology and nuclear power technology should be positioned and assessed will probably need to be decided.

As explained above, the market will clarify the future long-term costs of GHG emissions. In addition, once the direction of technological development has been clarified, Japan's industrial sector will be required to overcome major challenges. This will not be easy, and in some cases certain industries may have to exit the market. However, despite post–Second World War Japan being severely handicapped compared with Western countries, through unceasing technological development it was able to generate products that could compete in global markets from the

perspectives of quality and cost. When one recalls Japan's intellectual vitality in this respect, the country can be thought to be more than capable of meeting these challenges. When a major change in the social economy is required, private sector-free conceptions and challenges should be utilized to the greatest extent possible in the market and, if anything, government guidance through subsidies should be limited to supplementary policies.

The author firmly believes that when such challenges are overcome, Japan will have contributed to solving climate change issues while simultaneously the Japanese economy will have survived and Japan will come to occupy an honoured position in the global community through propagation of innovative technologies and business models (as well as lifestyles) around the world.

REFERENCES

Anton, W. R. Q., G. Deltas and M. Khanna (2004) "Incentives for Environmental Self-Regulation and Implications for Environmental Performance", *Journal of Environmental Economics and Management* 48(1), pp. 632–654.

Arimura, T. H., A. Hibiki and H. Katayama (2007) "Is a Voluntary Approach an Effective Environmental Policy Instrument? A Case for Environmental Management Systems", Resource for the Future Discussion Paper 07–31, available at http://papers.ssrn.com/sol3/papers.cfm?abstract_id=1001325.

Henriques, I. and P. Sadorsky (1996) "The Determinant of an Environmentally Responsive Firm: An Empirical Approach", *Journal of Environmental Economics and Management* 30(3), pp. 381–395.

Ikkatai, Seiji, Daisuke Ishikawa and Shuichi Ohori (2007) "The Effects of EU-ETS on Companies: Research by Interviews with Some European Companies", *Kikan Kankyo Kenkyu* 86-90(144), available at http://ideas.repec.org/n/nep-env/2007-04-09.html.

IPCC (2007) *Climate Change 2007*. Cambridge: Cambridge University Press.

Khanna, M. (2001) "Non-mandatory Approaches to Environmental Protection", *Journal of Economic Surveys* 15(3), pp. 291–324.

Ministry of Environment (undated) "Greenhouse Gas Emissions", available at www.env.go.jp/earth/ondanka/ghg/index.html (in Japanese).

Ministry of Environment, British Embassy in Japan (2007) "The Economics of Climate Change: Executive Summary", trans. AIM Team, National Institute for Environmental Studies, Tokyo.

Research Center for Advanced Policy Studies (2007) "Research Report on Economic Aspects of Fiscal Year 2006 Global Warming Countermeasures", Institute of Economic Research, Kyoto University.

——— (2008) "Research Report on Economic Aspects of Fiscal Year 2007 Global Warming Countermeasures", Institute of Economic Research, Kyoto University.

FURTHER READING

Baumol, W. and W. Oates (1988) *The Theory of Environmental Policy*. Cambridge: Cambridge University Press.

Central Environmental Council Global Environment Committee, Ministry of Environment (2001) "Interim Sub-committee Report on Target Achievement Scenarios", Ministry of Environment, Tokyo.

Environmental Agency (2004) "1995 Environmental White Paper Synopsis", Ministry of Finance Printing Bureau, Tokyo.

Ikkatai, Seiji (2008) *Japan's Options in a Low-carbon Era*. Tokyo: Iwanami Shoten.

IPCC (2001) *Climate Change 2001: Mitigation*. Cambridge: Cambridge University Press.

Matsushita, Kazuo (2007) *Recommendations for Environmental Policy*. Tokyo: Maruzen.

Takamura, Yukari and Yasuko Kameyama (eds) (2005) *Future of Global Warming Negotiations*. Hokkaido: Daigaku Tosho.

5-3

Shell energy scenarios to 2050

Shell International BV

5-3-1 Introduction

To help think about the future of energy, Shell has developed two scenarios that describe alternative ways it may develop. In the first scenario, called "Scramble", policy-makers pay little attention to more efficient energy use until supplies are tight. Likewise, greenhouse gas emissions are not seriously addressed until there are major climate shocks. In the second scenario, "Blueprints", growing local actions begin to address the challenges of economic development, energy security and environmental pollution. A price is applied to a critical mass of emissions, giving a huge stimulus to the development of clean-energy technologies such as carbon dioxide capture and storage, and energy efficiency measures. The result is far lower carbon dioxide emissions. Shell's chief executive, Jeroen van der Veer, said in 2008:

> We are determined to provide energy in responsible ways and serve our customers and investors as effectively as we can. Both these scenarios help us do that by testing our strategy against a range of possible developments over the long term. However, in our view, the Blueprints outcomes offer the best hope for a sustainable future, whether or not they arise exactly in the way we describe. We are convinced they are possible with the right combination of policy, technology and commitment from governments, industry and society globally. However, achieving them will not be easy, and time is short. We urgently need clear thinking, huge investment and effective leadership. Whatever your role in this, we hope these scenarios will help you understand better the choices you face.

Climate change and global sustainability: A holistic approach, Sumi, Mimura and Masui (eds), United Nations University Press, 2011, ISBN 978-92-808-1181-0

5-3-2 An era of revolutionary transitions

5-3-2-1 Step-change in energy use

Developing nations, including population giants China and India, are entering their most energy-intensive phase of economic growth as they industrialize, build infrastructure and increase their use of transportation. Demand pressures will stimulate alternative supply and more efficiency in energy use, but these alone may not be enough to offset growing demand tensions completely. Disappointing the aspirations of millions by adopting policies that may slow economic growth is not an answer, either, or not one that is politically feasible.

5-3-2-2 Supply will struggle to keep pace

By 2015 growth in the production of easily accessible oil and gas will not match the projected rate of demand. While abundant coal exists in many parts of the world, transportation difficulties and environmental degradation ultimately pose limits to its use. Meanwhile, alternative energy sources such as biofuels may become a much more significant part of the energy mix, but there is no "silver bullet" that will completely resolve supply–demand tensions.

5-3-2-3 Environmental stresses are increasing

Even if it were possible for fossil fuels to maintain their current share of the energy mix and respond to increased demand, CO_2 emissions would then be on a pathway that could severely threaten human well-being. Even with the moderation of fossil-fuel use and effective CO_2 management, the path forward is still highly challenging. Remaining within desirable levels of CO_2 concentration in the atmosphere will become increasingly difficult.

5-3-2-4 Preparing for the future

When all three of the most powerful drivers of our current energy world – demand, supply and effects on the environment – are set to undergo significant change, we face an era of revolutionary transitions and considerable turbulence. In addition, while prices and technology will drive some of these transitions, political and social choices will be critical. Those choices depend on how alert we are to the transitions as they happen, especially because for a decade or so we may be distracted by what appears to be healthy development. However, underneath this

"business-as-usual" world, the transitions are already beginning: governments and companies are positioning for longer-term alternatives; regulatory frameworks are being debated; as there will be no silver bullets, new technology combinations are under development such as intermittent renewable sources being integrated into existing power supply systems; and new infrastructures, such as carbon dioxide capture and storage (CCS), are required and older inefficient ones need to be decommissioned.

Given that profound change is inevitable, how will it happen? Will national governments simply scramble to secure their own energy supplies? Alternatively, will new blueprints emerge from coalitions between various levels of societies and government, ranging from the local to the international, that begin to add up to a new energy framework?

5-3-3 Scramble

Scramble reflects a focus on national energy security. Immediate pressures drive decision-makers, especially the need to secure energy supply in the near future for themselves and their allies. National governmental attention naturally falls on the supply-side levers readily available, including the negotiation of bilateral agreements and incentives for local resource development. Growth in coal and biofuels becomes particularly significant.

Despite increasing rhetoric, action to address climate change and encourage energy efficiency is pushed into the future, leading to largely sequential attention to supply, demand and climate stresses. Demand-side policy is not pursued meaningfully until supply limitations are acute. Likewise, environmental policy is not seriously addressed until major climate events stimulate political responses.

Events drive late, but severe, responses to emerging pressures that result in energy price spikes and volatility. This leads to a temporary slowdown within an overall story of strong economic growth.

Although the rate of growth of atmospheric CO_2 has been moderated by the end of the period, the concentration is on a path to a long-term level well above 550 ppm. An increasing fraction of economic activity and innovation is ultimately directed towards preparing for the impact of climate change.

5-3-3-1 Fear and security

National governments, the principal actors in Scramble, focus their energy policies on supply levers because curbing the growth of energy demand – and hence economic growth – is simply too unpopular for politicians to undertake. A lack of international cooperation means that individual

countries are unwilling to act unilaterally in a way that will damage their own economic growth. The result is a relatively uncoordinated range of national mandates and incentives for developing indigenous energy supplies where available, including coal, heavy oils, biofuels and other renewables, which leads to a patchwork of local standards and technologies.

At the international level, Scramble is a world of bilateral government deals between energy producers and energy consumers, with national governments competing with each other for favourable terms of supply or access by their energy companies. There is a strong element of rivalry between consumer governments, but they align with each other where their interests coincide. In this scenario, national energy companies play key intermediary roles, but themselves become increasingly mired in political machinations. Globalization exacerbates the tensions within and between nations, and distracts policy-makers from the need to take action and build international coalitions to face the challenges of energy and climate change.

Although business cycle variations continue, energy prices are generally strong. This is not only because of the intrinsic pressures on supply but also because OPEC has learned from the price increases since 2004 that the world can absorb higher energy prices relatively easily. In the economic interests of its members, therefore, OPEC manages oil supply to minimize any incipient price weakness.

With strong prices and lagging supply, "favourable terms" for importing nations increasingly means just some assurance of uninterrupted supply.

In Scramble, major resource holders are increasingly the rule-makers rather than the rule-takers. They use their growing prominence in the world to influence international policies, particularly when it comes to matters they insist are internal, such as human rights and democratic governance. Nations which have hammered out "favourable" deals with oil-producing nations do not want to rock the energy boat they have just managed to board, resulting in a world in which international relations are mainly a race to ensure continuing prosperity, not the building of a more sustainable international community.

There are enormous disparities in the economic and energy performances of different countries. Developing nations scramble to procure the energy necessary to climb the economic ladder, while wealthy nations struggle to adapt their energy consumption patterns to maintain their existing lifestyles.

5-3-3-2 *Flight into coal*

In the face of growing energy concerns, political and market forces favour the development of coal as a widely available, low-cost energy option. Partly in response to public pressures for "energy independence"

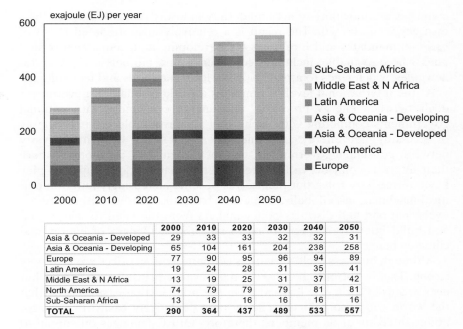

Figure 5.3.1 Final energy consumption by region in Scramble
Note: Please see page 312 for a colour version of this figure.

and partly because coal provides a local source of employment, government policies in several of the largest economies encourage this indigenous resource. Between 2000 and 2025 the global coal industry doubles in size, and by 2050 it will be two-and-a-half times as large.

However, coal has its own problems, which environmental pressure groups do not hesitate to point out. In the United States and other high-income countries, the building of each new coal plant creates a battleground of protest and resistance. In China, local environmental degradation provokes pockets of unrest, and the Chinese rail system struggles to transport large quantities of coal across the country – necessitating significant and costly improvements to the country's railway infrastructure, as well as coal imports from Australia, Indonesia and elsewhere. Perceived changes in world climate are attributed to the growing coal industry in China and the United States. Despite widespread protests against coal, governments – fearful of the potential damage to economic growth – are slow to establish meaningful greenhouse gas management schemes through carbon taxation, carbon trading and efficiency mandates.

First coal, then biofuels followed by renewable energy, are sequential supply responses to the increasing energy demand. However, no single or easy solution to the energy challenge exists. Government-driven effi-

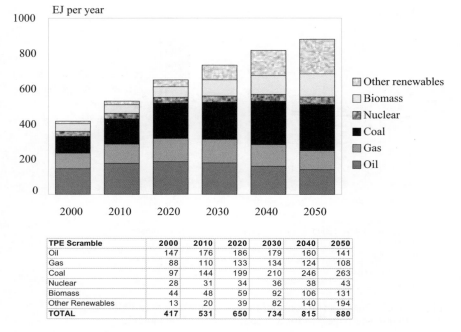

Figure 5.3.2 Primary energy by source in Scramble
Note: Please see page 312 for a colour version of this figure.

TPE Scramble	2000	2010	2020	2030	2040	2050
Oil	147	176	186	179	160	141
Gas	88	110	133	134	124	108
Coal	97	144	199	210	246	263
Nuclear	28	31	34	36	38	43
Biomass	44	48	59	92	106	131
Other Renewables	13	20	39	82	140	194
TOTAL	417	531	650	734	815	880

ciency measures are introduced when stresses become too high for the market to cope with. Final energy consumption by region and primary energy by source in Scramble are shown in Figures 5.3.1 and 5.3.2, respectively.

5-3-3-3 The next green revolution

Large agricultural lobbies are already powerful in developed nations, and a huge push for biofuels develops early in this scenario. This helps meet the rapid growth in demand for liquid transport fuels, but also leads to unintended consequences. First-generation biofuels compete with food production, driving up world market prices, especially in those countries that use maize as a staple. In addition, regions with insufficient production potential, such as the European Union, import the shortfall and so indirectly encourage poorer nations to destroy large sections of rainforests and habitats in order to grow palm oil and sugar-cane. The result of these land-use changes is that significant quantities of CO_2 stored in the soil are released.

   The reaction to these unintended consequences plays its part in helping to establish second-generation biofuels by 2020 – those that use the

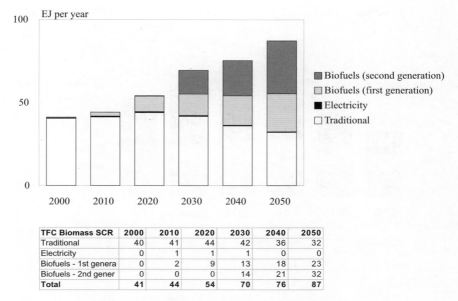

TFC Biomass SCR	2000	2010	2020	2030	2040	2050
Traditional	40	41	44	42	36	32
Electricity	0	1	1	1	0	0
Biofuels - 1st genera	0	2	9	13	18	23
Biofuels - 2nd gener	0	0	0	14	21	32
Total	41	44	54	70	76	87

Figure 5.3.3 Final energy consumption of biomass in Scramble
Note: Please see page 313 for a colour version of this figure.

woody parts of plants, including waste products such as stalks and leaves from plants grown for food production. Certification systems also emerge to promote sustainability of both first- and second-generation biofuels. A key advantage of second-generation biofuels is that energy yields are much higher, particularly outside the tropical regions. Most OECD countries, being in temperate regions, encourage and eagerly embrace economic routes to second-generation biofuels.

Biomass will represent around 15 per cent of primary energy by 2050. Biofuels become a significant part of this, in particular helping to diversify the supply of transport fuel. However, with accelerating demand, fossil fuels remain an important part of the energy mix. Final energy consumption of biomass, including biofuels, is shown in Figure 5.3.3.

5-3-3-4 Solutions are rarely without drawbacks

How unconventional oil from oil sands, shale and coal is developed provides a typical Scramble example of solutions being introduced with immediate benefits to energy security but some later negative consequences. Throughout the 2010s, investors will pour more capital into unconventional oil projects that make an important contribution to addressing supply pressures. Nevertheless, these attract increasing opposition from

powerful water and climate lobbies that oppose the environmental foot-print of additional developments. This ultimately provokes a political backlash that challenges even the best-managed projects.

As supply-side actions eventually prove insufficient or unpopular in addressing growing demand pressures, governments finally take steps to moderate energy demand. However, because pressures have already built up to a critical level, their actions are often ill-considered, politically driven knee-jerk responses to local pressures, with unintended consequences.

In Scramble, a typical three-step pattern begins to emerge: first, nations deal with signs of tightening supply by a flight into coal and heavier hydrocarbons and biofuels; then, when the growth in coal, oil and gas can no longer be maintained, an overall supply crisis occurs; and finally, governments react with draconian measures such as steep and sudden domestic price rises or severe restrictions on personal mobility with accompanying disruptions in value chains and significant economic dislocations. By 2020 the repetition of this volatile three-step pattern in many areas of the energy economy results in a temporary global economic slowdown.

5-3-3-5 The bumpy road to climate change

The focus on maintaining economic growth, especially in emerging economies, leaves the climate change agenda largely disregarded. The emerging economic pressures of energy supply and demand tensions make it even more difficult for politicians to act until they are forced to, despite their ongoing rhetoric of concern. Addressing climate change is perceived as an additional economic pressure. Given the type of response required, nobody is prepared to risk being the first to act. Eventually, this lack of action creates fertile conditions for politically opportunistic blame for extreme weather events and supply crunches and triggers knee-jerk, politically driven responses. These are not only late, but often too small to make a difference on the demand side.

5-3-3-6 Necessity – The mother of invention

The declining share of hydrocarbon fuels in the overall energy mix, the growing contribution from alternative energy sources and greater energy efficiency all moderate the rate of growth of CO_2 in the atmosphere. However, the subsequent restoration of economic growth means that vigorous energy consumption resumes with its accompanying rebound in CO_2 emissions, and concentrations are already high. A consensus develops around the need for a new international approach to energy security and climate change mitigation; however, the world is 20 years behind

where it would have been had it set up such a system by 2015. Economic growth continues to deliver increasing prosperity to many, but market responses to greenhouse gas challenges have been delayed by the absence of regulatory certainty and international agreements. An increasing amount of economic activity and innovation is directed towards preparing for the impact of climate change. Having avoided some hard choices early on, nations now recognize they are likely to face expensive consequences beyond 2050.

5-3-4 Blueprints

Blueprints describes the dynamics behind new coalitions of interests. These do not necessarily reflect uniform objectives, but build on a combination of supply concerns, environmental interests and associated entrepreneurial opportunities. It is a world where broader fears about lifestyle and economic prospects forge new alliances that promote action in both developed and developing nations. This leads to the emergence of a critical mass of parallel responses to supply, demand and climate stresses, and hence the relative promptness of some of those responses.

This is not driven by global altruism. Initiatives first take root locally as individual cities or regions take the lead. These become progressively linked as national governments are forced to harmonize resulting patchworks of measures and take advantage of the opportunities afforded by these emerging political initiatives. Indeed, even the prospect of a patchwork of different policies drives businesses to lobby for regulatory clarity.

As a result, effective market-driven demand-side efficiency measures emerge more quickly, and market-driven CO_2 management practices spread. Carbon trading markets become more efficient, and CO_2 prices strengthen early. Energy efficiency improvements and the emergence of mass-market electric vehicles are accelerated. The rate of growth of atmospheric CO_2 is constrained, leading to a more sustainable environmental pathway.

5-3-4-1 Starting at the grassroots

While international bodies argue over what environmental policies should be and which policies are feasible, and many national governments worry about energy security, new coalitions emerge to take action. Some bring together companies from different industries with a common energy interest. Others involve coalitions of cities or regions, which begin to take their destinies into their own hands and create their own blueprints for their energy futures. Individuals effectively begin to delegate responsibility for the complexities of the energy system to a broader

range of institutions besides national governments. Cash, votes and legitimacy reward the successful.

As more consumers and investors realize that change is not necessarily painful but can be attractive, the fear of change is moderated and ever more substantial actions become politically possible. These actions, including taxes and incentives in relation to energy and CO_2 emissions, are taken early on. The result is that although the world of Blueprints has its share of profound transitions and political turbulence, global economic activity remains vigorous and shifts significantly towards a less energy-intensive path.

Perceptions begin to shift about the dilemma that continued economic growth contributes to climate change. Alongside the quest for economic betterment, air quality and local environmental concerns, rather than climate change or green entrepreneurship, initially impel action in countries such as China, India and Indonesia. Gradually, however, people make the connection between irregular local climate behaviour and the broader implications of climate change, including threats to water supplies and coastal regions. In addition, successful regions in the developing world stimulate their local economy by attracting investments in clean facilities made possible by the clean development provisions of the international treaties that replace the Kyoto Protocol, which expires in 2012. These allow industrialized countries to invest in emission reduction projects in developing countries as an alternative to more costly projects at home.

The key enabler of these energy system blueprints is the introduction of a CO_2 pricing mechanism using a carbon emissions trading scheme that begins in the European Union and is progressively adopted by other countries, including the United States and, later, China. This trading regime gives a boost to new industries emerging around clean alternative and renewable fuels, and carbon capture and storage. In addition, carbon credits boost income, particularly for those investing in renewable energy, and reduce investment uncertainties.

5-3-4-2 Paths to alignment

This critical mass of participation in international frameworks does not stem from an outbreak of global altruism. Instead, the new initiatives at the regional and national levels create incentives for broader change, partly in response to pressure from multinationals. Companies argue strongly for clear, harmonized international policies as a way of avoiding the inefficiencies and uncertainties that result from a patchwork of local and national standards and regulations.

The United States responds to both public and industry pressure by taking significant steps to foster greater fuel efficiency through three new initiatives: well-to-wheels carbon assessments of fuels sold; a gradual rise

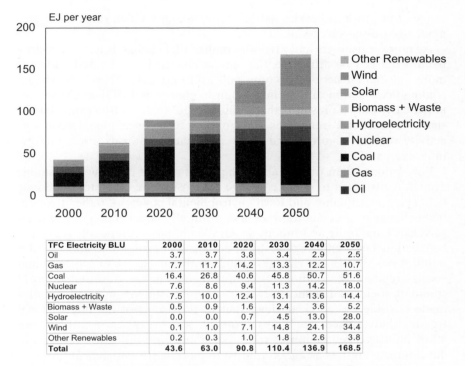

TFC Electricity BLU	2000	2010	2020	2030	2040	2050
Oil	3.7	3.7	3.8	3.4	2.9	2.5
Gas	7.7	11.7	14.2	13.3	12.2	10.7
Coal	16.4	26.8	40.6	45.8	50.7	51.6
Nuclear	7.6	8.6	9.4	11.3	14.2	18.0
Hydroelectricity	7.5	10.0	12.4	13.1	13.6	14.4
Biomass + Waste	0.5	0.9	1.6	2.4	3.6	5.2
Solar	0.0	0.0	0.7	4.5	13.0	28.0
Wind	0.1	1.0	7.1	14.8	24.1	34.4
Other Renewables	0.2	0.3	1.0	1.8	2.6	3.8
Total	**43.6**	**63.0**	**90.8**	**110.4**	**136.9**	**168.5**

Figure 5.3.4 Final energy consumption of electricity in Blueprints
Note: Please see page 313 for a colour version of this figure.

in the US Corporate Average Fuel Economy (CAFE) standards, which lay down minimum fuel economy standards for cars to reach European levels of 2007 by 2020; and taxes on the sale of less fuel-efficient vehicles to encourage the purchase of more fuel-efficient cars. Europe, meanwhile, imposes stricter CO_2 emission allowances rather than adding to the already significant fuel taxes, and sets aggressive emission reduction targets.

The Chinese and Indian governments attempt to balance the intense domestic and international political pressures to sustain economic growth as well as respond to concerns about climate change and energy efficiency. In return for their participation in international frameworks, they secure agreements that will facilitate technology transfer and investment in energy-efficient plants. They also receive assurances that a substantial proportion of the future revenues raised through international auctioning of emission permits will be channelled to nations on a per capita basis. Behind the scenes, all parties anticipate that such agreements will ultimately benefit all, through the increasing openness of China and India to international markets and investment.

These developments bring increasing alignment between the US, Chinese, Indian, Japanese and European approaches to CO_2 management. From 2012 a critical mass of nations participate in meaningful emissions trading schemes, stimulating innovation and investment in new energy technologies and paving the way to CO_2 capture and underground storage after 2020.

In Blueprints, developing economies climb the energy ladder, but overall the journeys of both the developed and developing economies follow less energy-intensive paths. Figure 5.3.4 shows the energy ladders to 2050.

5-3-4-3 Developments benefit the energy poor

In Blueprints, the disorderly but early development of innovative solutions and adoption of proven practices from the grassroots benefit low-income nations as well. Initially, this stems from the dynamics of the oil market: OPEC raises oil production to maintain lower prices and defer the development of more costly substitutes. Benefits also begin to emerge from accelerated growth in distributed power generation from wind and solar energy.

Government mandates for vehicles with significantly reduced and zero emissions, fiscal incentives to support the build-up of mass production and ever more wind and solar power stimulate a surge in electric transport powered by battery, fuel-cell or hybrid technologies. High overall efficiency of electric cars reduces demand in the transport sector and changes the fuel mix. In Blueprints, the more efficient end use of electricity and the resulting slower growth in primary energy demand mean that the former energy-poor enjoy an additional boost in their standard of living made possible by the resulting affordable energy prices.

5-3-4-4 Both disaggregation and integration

By 2050 one of the key revolutionary transitions observable in Blueprints is that economic growth no longer mainly relies on an increase in the use of fossil fuels. It is increasingly a world of electrons rather than molecules. Electric vehicles are becoming the norm in the transport sector because of their attractiveness to consumers and cost-effectiveness once governments have incentivized the build-up to mass production. Power generation from renewable energy sources is growing rapidly, while utilities that still rely on coal and gas are required to implement strict carbon abatement technologies. In the developed world, almost 90 per cent of all coal- and gas-fired power stations in the OECD and 50 per cent in the non-OECD world have been equipped with CCS technologies by 2050. This reduces overall CO_2 emissions by 15–20 per cent compared to what

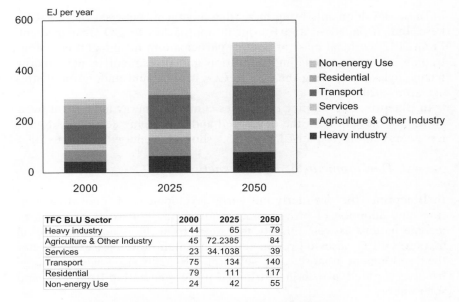

TFC BLU Sector	2000	2025	2050
Heavy industry	44	65	79
Agriculture & Other Industry	45	72.2385	84
Services	23	34.1038	39
Transport	75	134	140
Residential	79	111	117
Non-energy Use	24	42	55

Figure 5.3.5 Final energy consumption by sector in Blueprints
Note: Please see page 314 for a colour version of this figure.

they would have been without CCS. New financial, insurance and trading markets are already emerging that help finance the major investments necessary to build this new infrastructure. Europe's lack of indigenous fossil fuels does not place it at a disadvantage, thanks to the emergence of these new renewable technologies. It does well economically in spite of its shrinking population and the fact that capital stock was replaced earlier to meet tightening efficiency requirements.

In Blueprints, a second, more profound transition occurs at the political level, where there is increased synergy between national policies and those undertaken at the subnational and international levels. Although details may differ from nation to nation, international organizations concerned with the environment, global economic health and energy increasingly agree on feasibility. This makes "big-picture" action more possible than ever. Unlikely partnerships begin to form across political divides. Cities across the world continue to share experience and create broader partnerships. The C-40 group of leading cities, which continue to grow in number, identifies best practices in urban development, and eventually rural areas begin to join these coalitions – in part to avoid becoming the dumping grounds for old technologies.

Reducing CO_2 emissions through electrification triggers strong growth in the power sector and pulls in renewable energies. By 2050 over 60 per cent of electricity is generated by non-fossil sources (Figure 5.3.5). CCS

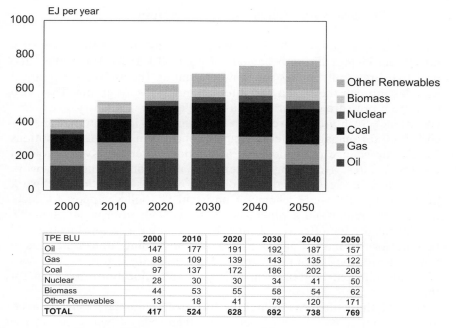

TPE BLU	2000	2010	2020	2030	2040	2050
Oil	147	177	191	192	187	157
Gas	88	109	139	143	135	122
Coal	97	137	172	186	202	208
Nuclear	28	30	30	34	41	50
Biomass	44	53	55	58	54	62
Other Renewables	13	18	41	79	120	171
TOTAL	**417**	**524**	**628**	**692**	**738**	**769**

Figure 5.3.6 Primary energy by source in Blueprints
Note: Please see page 314 for a colour version of this figure.

can make an important contribution to reduce emissions, but it is not a silver bullet.

This is a world of steady economic development and global economic integration. Yet the grassroots pressures and growing transparency that characterize Blueprints also put relentless pressure on governments to become more accountable in both democratic and authoritarian countries. In some cases this facilitates orderly transitions. However, the accelerated pace of technological and regulatory change in this scenario adds additional stresses, and the more rigid societies and political regimes struggle to adapt. Tensions between urban and rural communities increase and there is dramatic political change in several countries, particularly where governance is poor. Unless they have acted and invested wisely, this affects even the wealthier energy-exporting nations when exports and revenues eventually begin to decline. This is a world of increasing global alignment coupled with ongoing, widely distributed political turbulence. However, this is turbulence that has progressively less impact on the functioning of the global energy system.

Meaningful CO_2 pricing stimulates energy efficiency and electrification of the energy system, reducing the demand on conventional hydrocarbon resources (Figure 5.3.6).

5-3-4-5 Blueprints for climate change responses

Agreements on how to address climate concerns are not the result of a miraculous change in the behaviour of political leaders. They reflect the way that grassroots values are now imprinting themselves on political agendas through the media and international pressure groups. They also stem from pressure exerted by industries eager for regulatory clarity and consistency. Such pressure results in breakthroughs in an international architecture for managing energy security concerns in parallel with options for climate change mitigation and adaptation. After the Kyoto Protocol expires in 2012, a meaningful international carbon trading framework with robust verification and accreditation emerges from the patchwork of regional and city-city schemes. Consistent US policy support for technology investment and deployment pays dividends in providing tangible breakthroughs for effective change. More reliable energy statistics and better-informed market analysis allow carbon trading futures markets to reflect clearer long-term price signals. Because of these frameworks, markets can anticipate tightness in CO_2 emission allocations and plan for them.

By 2055 the United States and the European Union are using an average of 33 per cent less energy per capita than today. Chinese energy use has also peaked. India is still climbing its energy ladder, but as a relative latecomer it has to be resourceful in following a lower energy-intensive development path. The political and bureaucratic effort to harmonize and align energy policies is difficult and requires a great deal of up-front investment; however, in Blueprints, in a critical mass of countries people support national leaders who promise not only energy security but also a sustainable future.

Acknowledgements

This is an abridged version, reprinted by permission, taken from Shell International BV (2008) "Chart Data for the Year 2000 derived from Energy Balances of OECD Countries © OECD/IEA 2006 and Energy Balances of Non-OECD Countries © OECD/IEA 2006". For the full text see www.shell.com/scenarios.

5-4

Climate policy and international development cooperation

Shunji Matsuoka

5-4-1 Climate change and developing countries

5-4-1-1 Introduction

This chapter discusses what climate change really means for international development cooperation between developed and developing countries. The research question can be divided into three subquestions.
- How does climate change impact on developing countries?
- What is the cost benefit of climate policy for developing countries?
- What does climate change mean in terms of reform of development policy and international development cooperation?

The chapter describes these three subquestions and their answers in a step-by-step manner. First, it provides a brief sketch regarding the climate change impacts on developing countries.

Understanding the scientific evidence on climate change is a starting point for understanding developing countries' sustainable development issues of the twenty-first century. There is a vast amount of scientific literature on the subject. Here we focus on the consensus sent out by the Stern Review (Stern, 2006, 2007), the Intergovernmental Panel on Climate Change Fourth Assessment Report (IPCC AR4) and the UN Development Programme *Human Development Report* (UNDP, 2007), among others.

Our starting point is the growing consensus among climate scientists on the threshold marker for dangerous climate change. A consensus

Climate change and global sustainability: A holistic approach, Sumi, Mimura and Masui (eds), *United Nations University Press, 2011, ISBN 978-92-808-1181-0*

agreed at the L'Aquila G8 Summit in July 2009 identifies 2°C as a reasonable upper limit (Ministry of Foreign Affairs, Japan, 2009). Beyond this point, the future risks of catastrophic climate change will rise sharply.

We know that the world already suffers from climate change and that the average global temperature has increased by around 0.7°C since the advent of the industrial era (IPCC, 2007a). We know also that the trend is accelerating: average global mean temperature is rising at 0.2°C every decade. Based upon the present trends, the average temperature in the late twenty-first century will be over 2°C higher compared to the pre-industrial era.

5-4-1-2 Climate risk multipliers and developing countries

If the temperature increases by more than 2°C, five specific risk multipliers for human development reversals can be identified (UNDP, 2007: 27–31; IPCC, 2007a, 2007b, 2007d). These five multipliers impact more seriously on developing than developed countries. This is because developed countries have a more or less certain level of adaptive capacity to climate change, while developing countries do not have enough capacity to adapt. Furthermore, these five drivers for major human development reversal cannot be viewed in isolation. They will interact with each other and with pre-existing human development problems, creating powerful downward spirals. The UNDP (2007: 83) called it "low human development traps". We have to identify risk and vulnerability in order to understand low human development traps in developing countries.

Reduced agricultural productivity

Around three-quarters of the world's population living on less than US$1 a day depend directly on agriculture. Projected revenue losses for dryland areas in sub-Saharan Africa will amount to 26 per cent by 2060, with total revenue losses of US$26 billion (in constant 2003 terms), in excess of bilateral aid transfers to the region. Through its impact on agriculture and food security, climate change could leave an additional 600 million people facing acute malnutrition by the 2080s, over and above the level in a no-climate-change scenario.

Heightened water insecurity

Exceeding the 2°C threshold will fundamentally change the distribution of the world's water resources. By 2080 climate change could increase the number of people facing water scarcity around the world by 1.8 billion. Most of those people live in developing countries.

Increased exposure to coastal flooding and extreme weather events

The IPCC forecasts an increase in extreme weather events. Droughts and floods are already the main drivers of a steady increase in climate-related disasters. On average around 262 million people were affected by such disasters each year between 2000 and 2004, with over 98 per cent of them living in developing countries. Rising sea levels and more intense tropical storm activity could increase the number of people experiencing coastal flooding by 180–230 million.

The collapse of ecosystems

All predicted species extinction rates accelerate beyond the 2°C threshold, with 3°C marking the point at which 20–30 per cent of species would be at "high risk" of extinction. Coral reef systems, already in decline, would suffer extensive "bleaching", leading to the transformation of marine ecologies, with large losses of biodiversity and ecosystem services. This would adversely affect hundreds of millions of people dependent upon fish for their livelihoods and nutrition.

Increased health risks

Climate change will impact on human health on many levels. Globally, an additional 220–400 million people could be at increased risk of malaria. Exposure rates for sub-Saharan Africa, which accounts for around 90 per cent of deaths, are projected to increase by 16–28 per cent.

5-4-1-3 Risk and vulnerability in developing countries

Climate change risk in developing countries is different from that in developed countries. For the period 2000–2004, on an average annual basis, one in 19 people living in the developing world were affected by a climate disaster. The comparable figure for OECD countries was one in 1,500 affected – a risk differential of 79 (ibid.: 71).

Developing countries are at a double disadvantage in this area: they are located in tropical areas which stand to experience some of the most severe early impacts from climate change; and agriculture – the sector most immediately affected – plays a far greater social and economic role.

Moreover, not only risk but also vulnerability are important for climate impact on developing countries. Risk affects individuals, families and communities. Vulnerability is different from risk. Vulnerability is individual or social capacity to manage such hazards without suffering a long-term, potentially irreversible, loss of well-being. For example, sea-level-rise risk is the same for Japan and other Asian coastal countries,

but they do not share the same vulnerabilities. Income level and social capacity to adapt to climate risks are quite different among various countries.

Developing countries and their poorest citizens are most vulnerable to climate change. The following are among the factors which create a predisposition for the conversion of risk into vulnerability (ibid.: 70–72).

- *Poverty and low human development.* High concentrations of poverty among populations exposed to climate risk are a source of vulnerability. The 2.6 billion people – 40 per cent of the world's population – living on less than US$2 a day are intrinsically vulnerable because they have fewer resources with which to manage risks.
- *Disparities in human development.* Inequalities within countries are another marker for vulnerability to climate shocks. One recent quantitative assessment of the human impacts of disasters found that countries with high levels of income inequality experience the effects of climate disasters more profoundly than more equal societies (Roberts and Parks, 2007).
- *Lack of climate defence infrastructure.* Infrastructural disparities help to explain why similar climate impacts produce very different outcomes.
- *Limited access to insurance.* Insurance can play an important role in enabling people to manage climate risks without having to reduce consumption or run down their assets. Private markets and public policy can play a role. Households in rich countries have access to private insurance to protect themselves against climate-related losses; most poor households in developing countries do not. Social insurance is another buffer against vulnerability.

Next, we will touch on the cost benefit of climate policy and the economic impact on developing countries by climate change based upon the Stern Review.

5-4-2 Cost-benefit analysis of climate policy and developing countries

The human and ecological costs of dangerous climate change cannot readily be captured in simple cost-benefit analysis. However, such analysis will assist us in understanding the feasibility and/or rationale of the early implementation of climate policy.

The Stern Review on the economics of climate change commissioned by the UK government provided a strong response using cost-benefit analysis based on long-run economic modelling (Stern, 2007).

5-4-2-1 The Stern Review

Based on the discussion about climate change at the G8 Gleneagles Summit on 6–8 July 2005, UK Chancellor of the Exchequer Gordon Brown made a request to Nicholas Stern, the formal chief economist of the World Bank, to analyse the economic risk evaluation of climate change and economic efficiency of policy options in July the same year.

Stern thus, at the end of October 2006, examined the risk of climate change and calculated various climate policies' cost and benefit. He then published his review with the results from the study, concluding that early state action and also strong CO_2 reduction policy enforcement on greenhouse gases (GHGs) are the most efficient. The Stern Review is the first and most comprehensive cost-benefit analysis of climate policy.

5-4-2-2 Long-term target of GHG concentration

In the Stern Review, on appropriation of climate policy, common understanding about a long-term stabilization target is important, based on scientific predictions about various climate change issues. For example, a GHG emissions target in the range of 450–550 ppm (355–455 ppm in terms of CO_2) strikes a balance between stability and cost: anything higher would substantially increase the risks of very harmful impacts while reducing the expected costs of mitigation by comparatively little (Stern, 2006: 17). Density of GHGs at 450–550 ppm is predicted to cause a temperature increase of 2–3°C.

5-4-2-3 Cost of inaction

The Stern Review discusses the cost of inaction (ibid.: 8–10):

> Integrated assessment models provide a tool for estimating the total impact on the economy; our estimates suggest that this is likely to be higher than previously suggested ...

> Most formal modelling in the past has used as a starting point a scenario of 2°C–3°C global warming. In this temperature range, the cost of climate change could be equivalent to a permanent loss of around 0%–3% in global world output, compared with what could have been achieved in a world without climate change ...

> However, those earlier models were too optimistic about global warming: more recent evidence indicates that temperature changes resulting from BAU trends in emissions may exceed 2°C–3°C by the end of this century. This increases the

likelihood of a wider range of impacts than previously considered. Many of these impacts, such as abrupt and large-scale climate change, are more difficult to quantify. With 5°C–6°C global warming – which is a real possibility for the next century – existing models that include the risk of abrupt and large-scale climate change estimate an average 5%–10% loss in global GDP, with poor countries suffering costs in excess of 10% of GDP . . .

First, including direct impacts on the environment and human health (sometimes called "non-market" impacts) increases our estimate of the total cost of climate change on this path from 5% to 11% of global per-capita consumption. There are difficult analytical and ethical issues of measurement here. The methods used in this model are fairly conservative in the value they assign to these impacts.

Second, some recent scientific evidence indicates that the climate system may be more responsive to greenhouse-gas emissions than previously thought, for example, because of the existence of amplifying feedbacks such as the release of methane and weakening of carbon sinks. Our estimates, based on modelling a limited increase in this responsiveness, indicate that the potential scale of the climate response could increase the cost of climate change on the business as usual (BAU) path from 5% to 7% of global consumption, or from 11% to 14% if the non-market impacts described above are included.

Third, a disproportionate share of the climate-change burden falls on poor regions of the world. If we weigh this unequal burden appropriately, the estimated global cost of climate change at 5°C–6°C global warming could be more than one-quarter higher than without such weights.

It concludes: "Putting these additional factors together would increase the total cost of BAU climate change to the equivalent of around a 20% reduction in consumption per head, now and into the future" (ibid.: 10).

The report discusses the cost of action when the policy is to stabilize GHG emissions at 550 ppm:

Estimating the costs of these changes can be done in two ways. One is to look at the resource costs of measures, including the introduction of low-carbon technologies and changes in land use, compared with the costs of the BAU alternative. This provides an upper bound on costs.

The second is to use macroeconomic models to explore the system-wide effects of the transition to a low-carbon energy economy. These can be useful in tracking the dynamic interactions of different factors over time, including the response of economies to changes in prices. (Ibid.: 12–13)

In conclusion: "Resource cost estimates suggest that an upper bound for the expected annual cost of emissions reductions consistent with a

trajectory leading to stabilization at 550 ppm is likely to be around 1% of GDP by 2050" (ibid.: 13).

This "cost of action" of 1 per cent of GDP is much quoted; however, it was calculated using the bottom-up approach, estimated with a range from –1 per cent (net gains) to +3.5 per cent of GDP. Using a macroeconomic model, the costs of stabilization at 500–550 ppm were centred on 1 per cent of GDP by 2050, with a range of –2 to +5 per cent of GDP. It is necessary to note the point that the highest numerical value is 1 per cent.

In addition, there are some important prerequisites in cost estimations in the Stern Review. First, much early research used 2–3 per cent, but the social discount rate (SDR) in the Stern Review uses 0.1 per cent. Reflecting the fact that the review is estimating long-term cost over 200 years, the 0.1 per cent setting of the SDR is advocated by mainstream economic scholars like Tol (2006) and Nordhaus (2007).

A high SDR means one can greatly discount the damage that perhaps can occur in the future; on the other hand, a low SDR means estimating future damage cost without significant discount, and this connects largely to estimating the cost of climate change. In addition, when the SDR is low, the benefit to future generations of early action on climate change is measured highly. Thus, including the ethical viewpoint of future generations, a relatively low SDR of 0.1 per cent is set in the Stern Review.

Second, the range of damage is widened (from the previous 100 years to 200 years), and the emphasis is on the non-market section such as damage to health.

It is necessary to note the results are based on prerequisites such as the estimated value of the total cost of BAU climate change compared to around a 20 per cent reduction in consumption per head, now and into the future (Stern, 2006: 14).

5-4-2-4 Benefit of action

The benefit of action can be gained when executing policy:

> Comparing the social costs of carbon on a BAU trajectory and on a path towards stabilization at 550 ppm, we estimate the excess of benefits over costs, in net present value terms, from implementing strong mitigation policies this year, shifting the world onto the better path: the net benefits would be of the order of $2.5 trillion.

> The current evidence suggests aiming for stabilization somewhere within the range 450–550 ppm. The ultimate concentration of greenhouse gases determines the trajectory for estimates of the social cost of carbon; these also reflect the particular ethical judgments and approach to the treatment of uncertainty embodied in the modelling. Preliminary work for this Review suggests that, if

the target were between 450–550 ppm, then the social cost of carbon would start in the region of \$25–30 per tonne of CO_2 – around one third of the level if the world stays with BAU. (Ibid.: 17)

In this way, the Stern Review shows that stabilizing GHG concentration at 450–550 ppm is a more necessary and efficient strategy, rather than selecting climate policy at an early stage.

5-4-2-5 Evaluation of Stern's cost-benefit analysis

Why did Stern deviate from the structure used in mainstream economics? The report title suggests that an effective climate policy is the desired outcome, as there is no other choice. Although not specified by the Stern Review, the basic forecasting technique is not used, but rather a backcasting method. Perhaps the influence and damage of climate variation, which have become clear in developing countries above all, as well as diverse scientific knowledge about variation in climate, led Stern to view mainstream economics and the forecasting method as fundamentally limited.

When the Stern Review is read from such a point of view, the importance of creating mutual understanding about a stabilization target is emphasized, as well as setting a target for long-term greenhouse gas emissions and assigning the correct value to the influential damage of variation in climate.

Setting long-term targets according to the "precautionary principle" is a means to damage limitation. There is a need to move from a high-carbon society to a low-carbon society by making the backcast the target setting. It is equally important to achieve effectiveness and combined efficiency by putting the various policy measures (command and control, market-based instruments and voluntary approaches) into effect.

5-4-2-6 Developing countries in the Stern Review

The Stern Review first pointed out the risk that climate change will cause food shortage in Africa, flooding in Southeast and South Asia and desertification/dryness in the Amazon. The report states that the impacts of climate change are not evenly distributed. The poorest countries and people will suffer earliest and most; the problem of the climate change risks peculiar to developing countries is emphasized. In addition, if and when the damage appears it will be too late to reverse the process. Thus we are forced to look a long way ahead (ibid.: 7).

Climate change is a grave threat to the developing world and a major obstacle to continued poverty reduction across its many dimensions. First, developing regions are at a geographic disadvantage: they are already warmer, on average,

than developed regions, and they also suffer from high rainfall variability. As a result, further global warming will bring poor countries high costs and few benefits. Second, developing countries – in particular the poorest – are heavily dependent on agriculture, the most climate-sensitive of all economic sectors, and suffer from inadequate health provision and low-quality public services. Third, their low incomes and vulnerabilities make adaptation to climate change particularly difficult. (Ibid.)

For many of these developing countries, the risk possibilities of climate change are higher than the risks associated with natural geography or social economy. From this point of view, the ability for advanced countries to support developing countries by the formation of international climate policy is crucial.

According to the Stern Review: "Adaptation policy is crucial for dealing with the unavoidable impacts of climate change, but it has been under-emphasised in many countries" (ibid.: 21). Furthermore, the challenge of adaptation will be particularly acute in developing countries, where greater vulnerability and poverty will limit the capacity to act. As in developed countries, the costs are difficult to estimate, but are likely to run into tens of billions of dollars. But "Adaptation is the only response available for the impacts that will occur over the next several decades before mitigation measures can have an effect ... Unlike mitigation, adaptation will in most cases provide local benefits, realized without long lead times" (ibid.).

Therefore, adaptation efforts in developing countries must be accelerated and supported, including through international development assistance. Creating a broadly similar carbon price signal around the world, and using carbon finance to accelerate action in developing countries, are urgent priorities for international co-operation ... Scaling up flows of carbon finance to developing countries to support effective policies and programmes for reducing emissions would accelerate the transition to a low-carbon economy. (Ibid.: 23–24).

The Stern Review therefore proposes the foundation of a carbon finance mechanism by setting the international carbon price according to the expansion in an emissions trading system. Furthermore, the report points out "Curbing deforestation is a highly cost-effective way of reducing greenhouse gas emissions", and especially important for developing countries.

5-4-3 Climate policy and international development cooperation

Based on the analysis in the Stern Review, IPCC AR4 and the UNDP *HDR*, climate change risks have an influence on the whole global society.

Physiographic factors, such as many developing countries being in tropical regions, combine with the industrial factor (dependency on agriculture) and social economic factors, such as low income and the high income disparity in developing countries in particular, to make these countries fragile (vulnerability).

For these fragile developing countries, the risk of climate change causing them to fall into low human development traps increases, and it can make it difficult for developing countries which are close to achieving the Millennium Development Goals (MDGs) actually to achieve them.

The Stern Review, referring to the cost of climate change policy, acknowledges the need for the policy to be implemented as soon as possible, and the responsibility of developed nations (common but differentiated responsibilities in the UNFCCC) to assist developing countries to reduce GHG emissions and adapt to climate change. More than half of the world's present CO_2 discharge derives from developing countries, and restraint and reduction of CO_2 discharges in developing countries are vital.

If the effects of climate change, which are already becoming clear, are not addressed, socio-economic progress in developing countries will be lost. For this reason, international development cooperation is indispensable for improvement in developing countries lacking capital and technology. One must thus consider what kinds of international cooperation are necessary to advance mitigation and adaptation in developing countries.

5-4-3-1 Mitigation and international development cooperation

Regarding international development cooperation for mitigation in a developing country, we assume that cooperation of funds, technology transfer, tropical forest protection and encouragement of lower carbon in the energy field are important (UNDP, 2007: 147; IPCC, 2007c, 2007d).

One important reason for the underdevelopment of the energy field in developing countries is that the average thermal efficiency for coal plants in these countries is around 30 per cent, compared with 36 per cent in OECD countries. This means that one unit of electricity produced in a developing country emits 20 per cent more CO_2 than an average unit in developed countries (UNDP, 2007: 150). Furthermore, forest conservation and rehabilitation are important not only to preserve CO_2 sinks for mitigation, but also to supply basic goods to poor people in terms of adaptation.

Since negotiations of the UNFCCC began in 1992, there has been much argument on the importance of international development cooperation in fields such as energy and forests. Under the terms of the UNFCCC, international cooperation was identified as a key element in

climate change mitigation. Developed countries pledged to take all practicable steps to promote, facilitate and finance mitigation. The importance of technology transfer was confirmed in the Marrakesh Accords in 2001; however, there was no positive behaviour on the part of developed countries. The role of developed countries in promoting a shift to a low-carbon energy structure in developing countries was discussed in the Kyoto Protocol in 1997, and it was argued that developed countries should invest in climate change as a duty, not as charity.

Under the UNFCCC, the Global Environment Facility (GEF) became a financial instrument to mobilize resources for mitigation and adaptation. Since its inception in 1991 the GEF has allocated US$3 billion, with co-financing of US$14 billion (UNDP, 2007: 154). However, current resource mobilization by the GEF is insufficient to finance low-carbon transformation at the required pace. One estimate of the investment costs to facilitate access to low-carbon technology broadly consistent with a sustainable emissions pathway in developing countries suggests that an additional US$25–50 billion per annum would be required (ibid.: 153–154).

The clean development mechanism (CDM) is another flexible financing instrument and has linked the mitigation agenda to financing for sustainable development in developing countries. This is accomplished through GHG-reducing projects; these generate emission credits in developing countries, which can in turn be used by developed countries to offset their domestic GHG emissions. In 2006 CDM financing amounted to US$5.2 billion (World Bank, 2007).

These mechanisms and other multilateral/bilateral institutions still have limited roles. There are several alternatives proposed by many institutions (UNDP, 2007: 156–157). The UNDP proposed creating an integrated climate change mitigation facility (CCMF) with a wide-ranging role. Its overarching objective would be to facilitate the development of low-carbon energy systems in developing countries. To that end, the aim would be to provide support in key areas through multilateral channels, including financing, technology transfer and capacity development. Operations would be geared towards the attainment of emission reduction targets agreed under the post-Kyoto framework, with dialogue based on nationally owned energy strategies. Rules and governance mechanisms would have to be developed to ensure that all parties deliver on commitments, with CCMF support geared towards well-defined quantitative goals and delivered in a predictable fashion (ibid.: 157).

5-4-3-2 Adaptation and international development cooperation

The creation of national adaptation policies under their ownership is the basis for developing countries' adaptation strategy. Individual countries face

different types and degrees of risk, start from different levels of social development and vary widely in their social capacities (ibid.; IPCC, 2007b).

At present, adaptation planning has been a fringe activity in most developing countries. To the extent that strategies for adaptation are emerging, the focus is on "climate-proofing" infrastructure. This is a critical area. However, adaptation is about far more than infrastructure. The starting point is to implement climate change risk assessment and capacity assessment into all aspects of the policy-making process (Matsuoka, 2007). In turn, risk management requires that strategies for building resilience are embedded in national policies. For countries with limited government and social capacities, this is an immense task.

Adaptation is partly about investment in the "climate-proofing" of basic infrastructure; however, it is also about enabling people to control climate change risk without suffering reversals in human development.

Most developed countries are eagerly working on creating a national adaptation strategy, but they are not so proactive when it comes to supporting developing countries which are trying to achieve the same goal. International development cooperation on adaptation should be thought of as a social insurance mechanism for the world's poor.

The starting point is that donors have to deliver on past commitments. Recent years have witnessed a remarkable change in the provision of aid. During the 1990s development assistance flows went into steep decline, holding back global poverty reduction efforts. The 2000 UN Millennium Summit in New York marked a turning point. It resulted in an unprecedented commitment to achieving shared goals – the MDGs – through a partnership between rich and poor countries. Commitments made at Monterrey in 2002 backed that partnership with commitments on aid. The Monterrey Consensus reaffirmed a long-standing development assistance target of 0.7 per cent of gross national income for rich countries. Commitments made by the European Union and G8 in 2005 included a pledge to double aid flows by 2010 – a US$50 billion increase, with around half earmarked for Africa (UNDP, 2007: 187). These resources could help developing countries meet the challenge of scaling up adaptation efforts.

Multilateral mechanisms for adaptation have been developed under several initiatives. Two UNFCCC funds – the Least Developed Country Fund and the Special Climate Change Fund – have been established under the auspices of the GEF. Both are financed through voluntary pledges by donors (ibid.: 188–190). In 2004 another mechanism, the Strategic Priority on Adaptation, was created to fund pilot projects from the GEF's own resources over a three-year period (ibid.: 188). The stated objective of the GEF funds is to reduce countries' vulnerability by supporting projects which enhance adaptive capacity. With the implementation of the Kyoto Protocol in 2005, another potential source of financing was created in the form of the Adaptation Fund – a facility to be funded through the CDM.

By mid-2007 actual multilateral financing delivered under the broad umbrella of initiatives set up under the UNFCCC had reached a total of US$26 million (ibid.: 190–191). This is equivalent to just one week's worth of spending on flood defence in the United Kingdom. Looking to the future, total committed financing for adaptation through dedicated multilateral funds amounts to US$279 million (ibid.: 190).

Bilateral and multilateral donors are gradually increasing support for adaptation. One review of 10 bilateral agencies accounting for almost two-thirds of international development assistance attempted to identify projects in which climate change adaptation was an explicit consideration. It documented total commitments of US$94 million over a five-year period from 2001 to 2005, less than 0.2 per cent of average development assistance flows (ibid.).

Using the OECD Development Assistance Committee's reporting system, the UNDP has developed an "aid-sensitivity" analysis for donor portfolios averaged across the period 2001–2005 (ibid.: 190–191). The results suggest that 17 per cent of all development assistance falls into the narrow band of intensive risk, rising to 33 per cent for the wider band. Expressed in financial terms, US$16–32 billion are at immediate risk. These figures suggest that "climate-proofing" aid should be viewed as an important part of the adaptation challenge. Approximate costs for such aid are around US$4.5 billion, or 4 per cent of 2005 aid flows.

Key lessons emerging from the adaptation experience of developing countries are reforming dedicated multilateral funds, revising PRSPs (poverty reduction strategy papers) and putting adaptation at the centre of aid partnerships.

5-4-4 Concluding remarks

The state of international development cooperation and measures focusing on mitigation and adaptation, and the cost of the impact of climate change on developing countries, are serious issues.

Average temperature increases higher than 2°C since the Industrial Revolution pose a risk, which has a remarkable negative influence on both advanced and developing countries. However, developing countries are especially vulnerable to climate change risk because of various factors: natural geography, as many of these countries are located in tropical areas; industry, with an emphasis on farming; and socio-economics, which includes low income and a large income disparity.

The future generations in developing countries and the social cost at stake due to climate change were indicated in the Stern Review, which emphasized a firm climate policy and early action, as well as cost-benefit analysis.

Mitigation and adaptation are important measures for developing countries to handle climate change; most importantly, these countries first need to adopt a national policy. But it is impossible for developing counties with low social capacity to make and to implement an effective climate policy without support by effective international development co-operation (Matsuoka, 2007).

Support for developing countries has been accelerated by the UNFCCC regarding mitigation and adaptation by developed countries through negotiation of the Kyoto Protocol in 1997, but the situation is insufficient. It is time seriously to consider forming a new international system to support mitigation and adaptation in developing countries.

REFERENCES

Matsuoka, Shunji (ed.) (2007) *Effective Environmental Management in Developing Countries: Assessing Social Capacity Development*. London: Palgrave Macmillan.
Ministry of Foreign Affairs, Japan (2009) "Responsible Leadership for a Sustainable Future", available at www.mofa.go.jp/mofaj/gaiko/summit/italy09/index.html.
Nordhaus, William (2007) "The Stern Review of the Economics of Climate Change", *Journal of Economic Literature* 45(3), pp. 686–702.
Stern, Nicholas (2006) "The Economics of Climate Change: Executive Summary", available at www-iam.nies.go.jp/aim/stern/SternReviewES(JP).pdf.
——— (2007) *The Economics of Climate Change: The Stern Review*. Cambridge: Cambridge University Press.
IPCC (2007a) *Climate Change 2007: The Physical Science Basis*. Cambridge: Cambridge University Press.
——— (2007b) *Climate Change 2007: Impacts, Adaptation and Vulnerability*. Cambridge: Cambridge University Press.
——— (2007c) *Climate Change 2007: Mitigation of Climate Change*. Cambridge: Cambridge University Press.
——— (2007d) "Climate Change 2007: Synthesis Report", available at www.ipcc.ch/publications_and_data/publications_ipcc_fourth_assessment_report_synthesis_report.htm.
Roberts, Timmons and Bradley C. Parks (2007) *A Climate of Injustice: Global Inequality, North-South Politics and Climate Policy*. Cambridge, MA: MIT Press.
Tol, Richard (2006) "The Stern Review of the Economics of Climate Change: A Comment", available at www.mi.uni-hamburg.de/fileadmin/fnu-files/reports/sternreview.pdf.
UNDP (2007) *Human Development Report 2007/2008: Fighting Climate Change*. New York: Palgrave Macmillan.
World Bank (2007) *The State and Trends of the Carbon Market 2007*. Washington, DC: World Bank.

6

Transformation of social systems and lifestyles

6-1

Induction to a low-carbon city – Innovation of urban form and human activities

Keisuke Hanaki

6-1-1 Introduction

Human activity in cities impacts the surrounding environment on a local as well as a global scale. This means that cities offer great opportunities for reduction of CO_2 emissions in a future low-carbon society.

Fundamental countermeasures to reduce greenhouse gas emissions in urban areas include reducing energy consumption and lowering the carbon intensity of the supplied energy. Many energy-saving devices and systems belong in the former category, and conversion from coal to gas and renewable energy sources is an example of the latter. Together, many technologies have been developed to reduce CO_2 emissions.

However, a low-carbon city needs more than well-integrated implementation of these countermeasures. A change in human behaviour is also needed to decrease the overall environmental burden. Energy and material consumption causes greenhouse gas emissions. In the future, humans will need to lower consumption of energy and materials, while at the same time maintaining or raising the current level of quality of life.

6-1-2 The city as a CO_2 emitter

Large amounts of CO_2 are emitted by cities in both developed and developing countries. Total CO_2 emissions are the summation of the emissions from a variety of sources in various sectors, which are usually categorized

Climate change and global sustainability: A holistic approach, Sumi, Mimura and Masui (eds), United Nations University Press, 2011, ISBN 978-92-808-1181-0

as industry, household, business and commercial, and transportation. Industrial CO_2 emissions depend on the type of industry and process efficiency. Energy consumption in households depends on appliance use, type of heating and cooling systems, size and type of the house and local climate conditions. Except for climate, all of these can be viewed as lifestyle issues in a broad sense. A typical energy-wasting lifestyle includes the use of many appliances, with lots of lighting and a low-efficiency heating and cooling system in a large house with poor insulation. Generation of power by photovoltaic cells can reduce the amount of electricity purchased from the grid and result in reduced CO_2 emissions. CO_2 emissions from the business and commercial sector are also derived from buildings, and the level of emissions again depends on climate conditions, building performance, type of heating and cooling system and business style. A large portion of energy used in transportation is for passenger cars. Public transport systems, especially railways, can decrease CO_2 emissions markedly.

CO_2 emissions can be reduced in all these sectors by the appropriate implementation of energy-saving technologies, but social aspects, such as lifestyle and business style, house size and length of commute, are also important factors. To convert our current society to a low-carbon society will require these types of social aspects to change. The form of urban areas, including factors such as population density and distribution of buildings, influences many aspects of daily life, including transportation modes and demand and energy consumption from buildings.

Figure 6.1.1 shows per capita CO_2 emissions for large cities in the United Kingdom, Japan and China as well as the national averages. Per capita emissions in London and Tokyo are lower than the respective national averages, suggesting that urban areas may be more energy efficient than rural areas. However, per capita emissions in Kawasaki City, which is in the Greater Tokyo region and has a large industrial area, are much larger than those of either Tokyo or the national average. Hanaki (2008) showed that industrial activity is an important factor in determining per capita CO_2 emissions in Japanese cities. The share of industrial CO_2 emissions in London and Tokyo is only about 7 per cent and 9 per cent, respectively, whereas it is 77 per cent in Kawasaki. But although cities like London and Tokyo apparently have better than average performance in terms of CO_2 emissions, they actually consume huge amounts of goods produced in other areas, which in turn causes increased emissions in those areas.

According to Dhakal (2009), the share of industrial CO_2 emissions in Beijing and Shanghai is 43 per cent and 64 per cent, respectively. These fractions are higher than those of London and Tokyo, but these high shares of industrial emissions do not alone explain why per capita CO_2

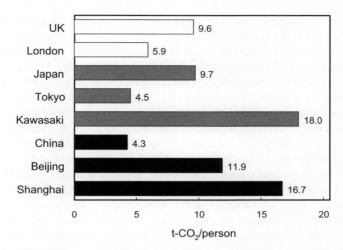

Figure 6.1.1 Per capita CO_2 emissions in large cities in the UK, Japan and China
Sources: National average data – Energy Conservation Center, Japan (2006); London – London Mayor's Office (2009); Japanese cities – local government websites; Chinese cities – Dhakal (2009).

emissions in these cities are so much higher than the Chinese national average. One possible reason is that urban and rural lifestyles are different in terms of energy consumption in developing countries. The International Energy Agency (2008) compared per capita primary energy demand between urban areas and regional averages in 2006. There were slight differences in the demands in the United States, European Union and Australasia, but energy demand in urban areas was 1.82 times that of the regional average in China. This report concludes that this difference is a result of higher average incomes in urban areas than in rural areas. In other words, the urban lifestyle in China is different from the rural lifestyle.

6-1-3 Urban form

6-1-3-1 Compact cities

The compact city has been proposed to reduce energy consumption and CO_2 emissions. Buildings in a compact city are constructed in a limited area in which population density as well as building density is high. Brown, Southworth and Sarzynski (2008) analysed the carbon footprint from transportation and building energy use in the 100 largest US metropolitan areas and found a negative correlation between carbon footprint

(per person CO_2 emissions) and population density. The footprint of a city with very low population density is almost double that of a city with high density. Although a more densely populated city appears to have advantages over a sparsely populated city from the context of energy consumption, further study is needed to learn how best to apply this concept in urban design.

The effect of compactness on transportation is easier to understand. Higher density generally means shorter trip lengths and, in some cases, enables the use of public transport. The most significant reductions in energy consumption occur if a shift can be made from cars to trains.

A series of well-known statistical analyses of transportation in numerous large cities around the world have been conducted by Newman and Kenworthy (1989), Kenworthy (2007) and others. The research clearly shows that low population density is correlated with longer car passenger trip lengths and higher energy consumption. Although other factors influence trip length, population density is the most significant factor. Kenworthy (ibid.) also demonstrated that the relationship can be observed within a city. Similar results were reported by van de Coevering and Schwanen (2006) for 11 European, seven Canadian and 13 US cities and by Stone et al. (2007) for the US Mid-Western metropolitan statistical area.

Unlike transportation, the effect of population density on energy consumption in buildings is not obvious. Theoretically, there is no effect of population density on the floor area and type of house, but apartment buildings usually consume less energy per capita than detached houses. In a study of Quebec, Canada, Larivière and Lafrance (1999) demonstrated that per person building electricity use decreases with population density.

It should be noted that a high population density does not necessarily cause people to live in apartments, and there is no guarantee of low energy consumption in buildings even if a city is compact. More importantly, there are also ways to lower energy consumption in buildings without changing the structure of a city. Changing the urban form will take a very long time and a good deal of planning. Shifting from detached houses to apartments, however, can be realized in a shorter time period.

6-1-3-2 Strategies for cities of various sizes

In many of the megacities, such as Tokyo and New York, population density is already high and train systems are effective. Forming a compact city in such megacities will not, therefore, bring about additional benefits from public transportation. Conversely, many small cities cannot support a rail transport system even if their urban form becomes compact because

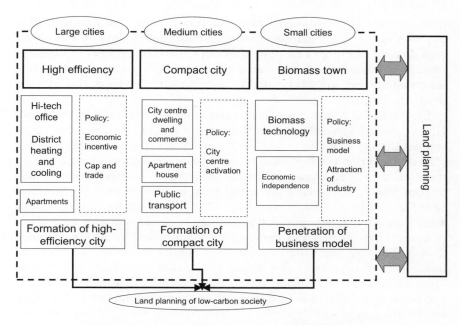

Figure 6.1.2 Strategies for low-carbon cities of various sizes

of their small size and population. The compact city concept is most suitable for mid-sized cities.

Different appropriate strategies for forming low-carbon cities at various scales are shown in Figure 6.1.2. Increasing the efficiency of building performance in large cities is the highest priority. District heating and cooling is one possible way to reduce energy consumption in these areas. Economic incentives for reduction of CO_2 emissions may also work in these areas. In small cities, however, utilization of biomass resources should be promoted, especially in towns near agricultural or forested areas. Mid-size cities should be redesigned to become more compact.

6-1-4 Standard of living, energy consumption and societal change

6-1-4-1 Per capita GDP as a controlling factor

It has long been accepted that per capita energy consumption increases as per capita income increases. However, we now also know that significant reductions in CO_2 emissions are required to mitigate severe climate change. The magnitude of the reduction has been estimated to be as high as 70–80 per cent for the developed countries.

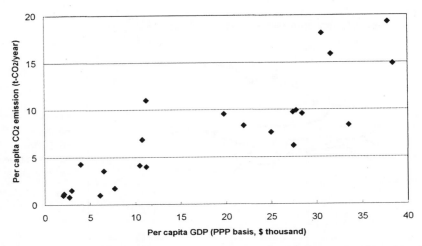

Figure 6.1.3 Per capita CO_2 emissions versus per capita GDP for various countries in 2006

In the traditional pollution case, such as air pollution caused by sulphur oxide in flue gases, the environmental Kuznets theory can be applied. As per capita income increases, the environment will first deteriorate and then improve. When pollution levels are plotted in relation to gross domestic product (GDP) across time for a country, a typical inverted U-shaped Kuznets curve is the result. In addition, for a given year a plot of different countries with different levels of GDP shows a similar tendency.

This theory is valid when technology for controlling pollution is available. It has questionable validity in the case of climate change because, unlike the case of air pollution, no end-of-pipe technology currently exists to solve this problem completely.

Figure 6.1.3 shows the relationship between per capita GDP on a purchasing power parity (PPP) basis and per capita CO_2 emissions for various countries in 2006 (based on data from Energy Data and Modelling Center, 2009). Per capita CO_2 emissions increase as per capita GDP (the standard of living) increases, and there is no tendency of a decrease in CO_2 emissions even at high levels of per capita GDP. These results do not lead to an optimistic outlook for the formation of a low-carbon society in the future.

A more detailed analysis for each country shows, however, that it may be possible to reduce CO_2 emissions while improving the standard of living. The United Kingdom and France have shown gradual decreases in per capita CO_2 emissions in relation to GDP since the 1970s (Figure 6.1.4). Japan reached an emissions peak in 2000, but emissions in Australia continue to increase. There seems to be no clear value of per capita GDP at which CO_2 emissions decrease, and the situation varies markedly

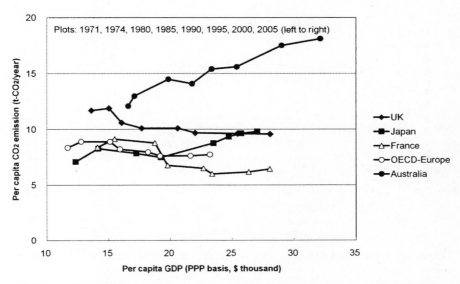

Figure 6.1.4 Trends of per capita CO_2 emissions in relation to per capita GDP for some developed countries
Note: Plots from 1971 to 2005 are shown mostly from the left to the right.

between countries. However, it does seem at least to be possible to re-duce CO_2 emissions at high levels of per capita GDP.

Even if per capita CO_2 emissions do decrease at a very high level of per capita GDP, the world cannot wait until developing countries in-crease their CO_2 emissions to the current level of developed countries before they begin to reduce emissions. The Kuznets curve describes a process of development and adaptation, but the world needs more than this type of incremental process to decrease CO_2 emissions.

Dhakal (2009) compared per capita energy consumption with per cap-ita gross regional product for 34 large Chinese cities (Figure 6.1.5). He categorized these cities into three groups: low energy consumption and high economic output, high energy consumption and low economic out-put, and a middle group between the two. These comparisons show that income level is an important factor, but there seem to be other factors that determine urban energy consumption.

6-1-4-2 Societal change

Because of the difficulties in reducing CO_2 emissions and the seriousness and urgency of the problem, an integrated technological, social and eco-nomic approach towards sustainability is needed. The current incremental approach will not work quickly enough to realize the goal of low-carbon

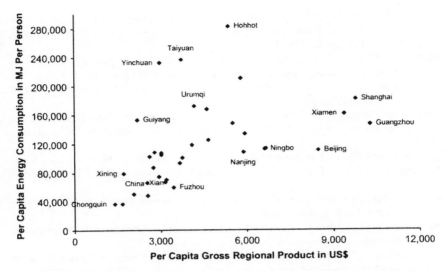

Figure 6.1.5 Energy consumption and standard of living in 34 large Chinese cities in 2006
Source: Dhakal (2009).

cities. Society must devise ways to consume less energy and use fewer materials.

To reduce energy and material consumption while maintaining functions and services, the industrial sector should move towards the concept of "product servicing". Instead of merely producing and selling new products to customers, companies should provide services. Examples are a copying service instead of selling copying machines, and rental, repairing and car-sharing services. In the household sector there are many ways to change the size and type of housing and to live a less energy-intensive lifestyle while maintaining a high quality of life. The business and commercial sector can also shift to systems that consume less energy and materials, and new types of business opportunities will be created in future low-carbon cities. Improved urban design to create more compact cities will reduce trip lengths and increase the use of public transportation.

REFERENCES

Brown, M. A., F. Southworth and A. Sarzynski (2008) *Shrinking the Carbon Footprint of Metropolitan America.* Washington, DC: Brookings Institution.

Dhakal, S. (2009) "Urban Energy Use and Carbon Emissions from Cities in China and Policy Implications", *Energy Policy* 37(11), pp. 4208–4219.

Energy Data and Modelling Center (2009) *EDMC Handbook of Energy & Economic Statistics in Japan (2009 Version)*. Tokyo: Energy Conservation Center, Institute of Energy Economics.

Hanaki, K. (2008) "Global Climate Change and Cities", in K. Hanaki (ed.) *Urban Environmental Management and Technology*. Tokyo: Springer, pp. 175–194.

International Energy Agency (2008) *World Energy Outlook 2008*. Paris: International Energy Agency.

Kenworthy, Jeffrey (2007) "Urban Planning and Transport Paradigm Shifts for Cities of the Post-petroleum Age", *Journal of Urban Technology* 14(2), pp. 47–70.

Larivière, Isabelle and Gaëtan Lafrance (1999) "Modelling the Electricity Consumption of Cities: Effect of Urban Density", *Energy Economics* 21(1), pp. 53–66.

London Mayor's Office (2009) "Climate Change Action Plan", pp. 15–16, available at www.london.gov.uk/mayor/.

Newman, Peter and Jeffrey Kenworthy (1989) *Cities and Automobile Dependence: An International Sourcebook*. Aldershot: Gower.

Stone, Brian Jr, Adam C. Mednick, Tracey Holloway and Scott N. Spak (2007) "Is Compact Growth Good for Air Quality?", *Journal of the American Planning Association* 73(4), pp. 404–418.

van de Coevering, P. and T. Schwanen (2006) "Re-evaluating the Impact of Urban Form on Travel Patterns in Europe and North America", *Transport Policy* 13(3), pp. 229–239.

6-2

The process of political decision-making on climate change and journalism in Japan

Tokuhisa Yoshida

6-2-1 Introduction

More than a decade has passed since the Kyoto Protocol stipulated that greenhouse gas (GHG) emissions of Japan should be reduced by 6 per cent compared to the 1990 level. During this time, political decision-making on climate change in Japan has gone astray amid a three-way conflict among the Ministry of the Environment (MOE), which supervises environmental policy, the Ministry of Economy, Trade and Industry (METI), which oversees energy policy, and industry, which centres on Nippon Keidanren (Japan Business Federation).

Climate change policy began in earnest around 1997, when the Kyoto Protocol was adopted. From the very beginning, the government participated in negotiations for the Kyoto Protocol while making a distinction between environmental and energy policies, and industry quickly announced its own initiatives in an effort to discourage the government from using regulatory tools. As a result, the government succeeded in introducing several new measures that would contribute to the development of industry, such as the proliferation and promotion of energy-saving products, but skirted around environmental taxes and emissions trading, which both met with particularly strong resistance from industry. In addition, the government emphasized the importance of changing people's lifestyles, and this, combined with reports by the mass media, raised the nation's awareness of global environmental issues to such a high level that an eco-boom was created in the country.

Climate change and global sustainability: A holistic approach, Sumi, Mimura and Masui (eds), United Nations University Press, 2011, ISBN 978-92-808-1181-0

However, industrial production grew, consumer spending rose and unexpected troubles occurred at nuclear power stations – more than offsetting the effects of environmental measures. All these things often frustrated the government's scenario for achieving the goal set by the Kyoto Protocol. The government took additional measures each time its plans were upset, but finally entered the first commitment period without a firm prospect of achieving the goal. It is now becoming clear that the government is obliged to rely on credits based on the Kyoto mechanisms in order to make up for a failure to reduce GHG emissions by the level that it had committed to.

On the other hand, driven by industry's strong dissatisfaction with the inequality of target reduction rates allocated to countries under the Kyoto Protocol, the government has striven to construct logic and develop a strategy to recover the ground lost in 1997 in negotiations for international frameworks for the period after 2013.

This chapter traces the twists and turns of climate change policy being formed in Japan, and analyses the influence of journalism on public opinion and political decision-making during the period from the adoption of the Kyoto Protocol to June 2009.

6-2-2 Three-way conflict in political decision-making

Immediately after the Kyoto Protocol was adopted, the government began to paint a scenario for achieving the goal of reducing GHG emissions by 6 per cent, the target set for the first commitment period; however, conflict among the three parties was obvious from the very beginning. According to reports of those days, the scenario of METI (the former Ministry of International Trade and Industry) was to keep emissions of energy-derived carbon dioxide (CO_2) at the 1990 level or lower (*Weekly Energy & the Environment*, 1998). This constituted the core argument that METI had launched prior to the negotiations for the Kyoto Protocol (Takeuchi, 1998), and the ministry did not change its stance even after the Kyoto Protocol was adopted. In synchronization with this, Nippon Keidanren has upheld a slogan of "striving to reduce CO_2 emissions to the 1990 level or lower" as its industry-wide goal for member companies.

There has been a sharp confrontation among Nippon Keidanren, which is strongly dissatisfied with the reduction goal set in the Kyoto Protocol, METI, which focuses on promoting energy conservation efforts and ensuring a stable energy supply in its energy policy, and the MOE, whose environmental policy calls for it to fulfil international commitments under the Kyoto Protocol without fail (Figure 6.2.1).

Japan's policy related to climate change has been implemented through the enactment of related laws and ordinances, administrative plans

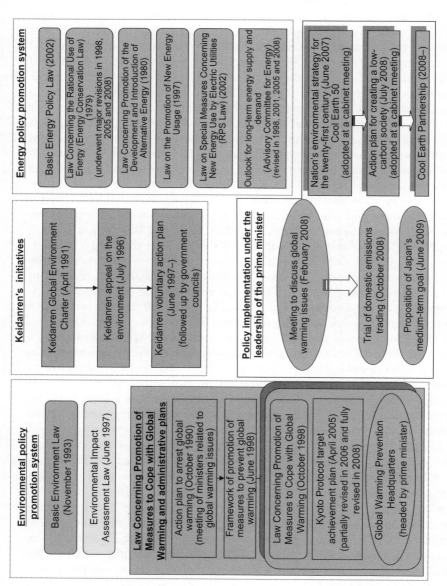

Figure 6.2.1 Three-way conflict in climate change policy and the recent policy implementation under the leadership of the prime minister

worked out by the government and tax breaks and fiscal measures. The response of the three parties mentioned above to climate change issues can generally be summarized as follows.

A harbinger of climate change policy under the government's environmental policy was the action plan to arrest global warming, which was adopted by a meeting of ministers related to the protection of the global environment in October 1990. This action plan covered the period until 2010, and goals set under the plan included keeping CO_2 emissions per capita for the period after 2000 at the 1990 level and endeavouring to stabilize total CO_2 emissions in 2000 and thereafter. In 1998, the year after the Kyoto Protocol was adopted, the Law Concerning Promotion of Measures to Cope with Global Warming was established, with the aim of promoting measures to prevent climate change. The framework of promotion of measures to prevent global warming, developed in accordance with this law, was renamed the Kyoto Protocol target achievement plan two months after the effectuation of the Kyoto Protocol in February 2005. This marked the creation of a statutory plan linked with international commitments, and this plan has remained unchanged since it underwent major revisions in March 2008 as the start of the first commitment period drew near (since the fiscal year in Japan begins in April, the first commitment period for Japan started in April 2008). In addition to prescribing the establishment of the Global Warming Prevention Headquarters as the highest decision-making body for the government's climate change policy, with the prime minister as its head, the Law Concerning Promotion of Measures to Cope with Global Warming provides a basis for the national government to collect data on GHG emissions submitted by business operators nationwide each year, and for local governments to formulate plans to implement measures to cope with climate change at the local level. Furthermore, the law provides a legal basis for implementing educational programmes to promote energy conservation efforts around the nation.

METI's Agency for Natural Resources and Energy, which supervises energy policy, has taken actions steadfastly in this area, which is intimately connected to measures to cope with climate change. The energy policy of Japan, a country that experienced two oil crises in the 1970s, consists of two pillars: advancing energy conservation and promoting introduction of energy sources other than petroleum, with the aim of breaking away from the dependence on oil. The ultimate objective of the policy is to ensure a stable supply of energy while carefully watching the international energy situation. Upholding its unswerving energy policy, METI has revised the Law Concerning the Rational Use of Energy (Energy Conservation Law), enacted in 1979, three times to reinforce it: in 1998, immediately after the Kyoto Protocol was adopted; in 2005, when

the Kyoto Protocol took effect; and in 2008, when the first commitment period began. METI has also pushed forward measures to cope with climate change by establishing the Law on the Promotion of New Energy Usage (New Energy Law) in 1997 and the Law on Special Measures Concerning New Energy Use by Electric Utilities (RPS Law) in 2002 to require electric power companies to use a certain amount of new energy. In addition, in 2002 politicians took the initiative to establish the Basic Energy Policy Law. METI, however, draws a distinction between legislation related to energy policy and legislation related to climate change issues. In defining its purposes, the Basic Energy Policy Law stipulates that Japan's energy policy shall help to protect the global environment and promote sustainable development of the world economy and society, while the Energy Conservation Law, New Energy Law and other individual energy-related laws include only energy policy that meets the energy-related economic and social environment in Japan and abroad in their provisions. The latter do not refer to the direct relationships with climate change issues, nor is their jurisdiction shared with the MOE. In its energy policy, METI has obtained a key list of measures to cope with climate change by enforcing these laws.

Forecasts of future energy supply and demand in Japan, which provide a framework for measures to cope with climate change, have been presented in the outlook for long-term energy supply and demand, which is a report formulated roughly every three to five years by the Energy Supply and Demand Subcommittee under the Advisory Committee for Energy, a consultative organ to METI. These documents, without a solid legal basis, have led the formation of a policy-making framework while painting an integrated scenario for energy security and climate change measures since global warming became an important policy issue in Japan. These forecasts contain the intentions of policy-makers. The May 2008 revised version of the outlook came to have an important meaning. It presented prospects of emissions of energy-derived CO_2 for the period until 2030. The results of a trial calculation of total GHG emissions in 2020 were also presented, expecting them to be 14 per cent lower than the 2005 level if the most advanced technology was introduced to the fullest. This figure anticipated the policy the government adopted when it set the medium-term goal in June 2009.

Another major force that has continued to affect Japan's climate change policy is industry, which centres on Nippon Keidanren. Keidanren announced its Global Environment Charter in April 1991, six months after the government formulated its action plan to arrest global warming. In describing its basic philosophy, the charter states that "business activities must strive to realize a future society in which the environment is protected on a global scale". With respect to global warming, it urges

member companies actively to take effective and reasonable energy-saving measures, and take part in international initiatives to cope with the issue. Later, in the appeal on the environment it published in 1996, Keidanren stated that it would carry out responsible environmental initiatives voluntarily and actively; with respect to climate change issues, it pledged to formulate a voluntary action plan for each industry, including specific goals and means for achieving them, and conduct periodic reviews of the action plans. Voluntary action plans were formulated in 1997, and since 1998 the Industrial Structure Council, an advisory body to METI, has reviewed annually the progress of their implementation in a transparent manner. As described earlier, the goal for all industries participating in the voluntary action plans is to reduce emissions of CO_2 to the 1990 level or lower. Industries joining the voluntary action plans include major manufacturing, energy conversion and other sectors. In the base year (1990), CO_2 emissions from these sectors accounted for 45 per cent of total CO_2 emissions in Japan and 84 per cent of CO_2 emissions from all industries. Each industry set a reduction goal for the 2008–2012 period. For example, the Federation of Electric Power Companies of Japan aims to reduce the emission factor of CO_2 for electricity generation by 20 per cent compared to the 1990 level, and the Japan Iron and Steel Federation aims to reduce energy consumption by 10 per cent compared to the 1990 level.

By developing and carrying out these firm voluntary action plans, Keidanren has successfully prevented the government from introducing regulatory measures under its climate change policy. As advocated in its Global Environment Charter, Keidanren has consistently taken a stance of attaching importance to technological breakthroughs and cooperating with the government in "effective and reasonable measures". The content of the voluntary action plans was incorporated into the Kyoto Protocol target achievement plan in 2005, which was drawn up with the international effectuation of the Kyoto Protocol; Keidanren, however, demanding that its plans be strictly voluntary goals, did not allow them to be considered as its agreement with the government.

In addition, Keidanren has approached the nation by publishing its opinions about climate change policy in the extensive issue-advocacy advertisements it placed in major national newspapers. For example, in November 2005, when the nation was gradually becoming interested in the introduction of environmental taxes, Keidanren swiftly inserted an issue-advocacy advertisement in national newspapers arguing that it was doubtful whether environmental taxes were effective and that such taxes ran counter to measures to cope with global warming. More recently, in March 2009, Keidanren published a similar advertisement warning that efforts to reduce CO_2 emissions would place a major economic burden

on the lives of people; this came under fire from leading environmental NGOs in Japan (WWF Japan, 2009). Moreover, in late May 2009, in response to the government on the issue of how its medium-term goal for reducing GHG emissions for the period after 2013 should attract public attention, Keidanren, together with the department store and hotel industries as well as trade unions such as the Japan Federation of Basic Industry Workers' Unions, ran an issue-advocacy advertisement in national newspapers arguing that from the viewpoint of international equality, heavy burdens placed on Japanese citizens and practicality, it was appropriate to set the goal of a 4 per cent reduction in CO_2 emissions compared to the 2005 level (Alternative 1 in Table 6.2.1).

There was a new development after Yasuo Fukuda assumed office as prime minister in autumn 2007. It was decided that policy discussions for an international framework for the period after 2013 would be held while coordinating the three parties concerned under the leadership of the prime minister. In February 2008 a meeting to discuss global warming, presided over by the prime minister, was organized. The objective of this forum, which comprises a dozen or so experts, is to decide a framework for climate change policy for the period after 2013, and its members include Hiroshi Okuda, former chairman of Nippon Keidanren, as well as two leaders from the steel and electric power industries. The meeting has formed three subcommittees under its control: the "medium-term goal", "model city planning for a low-carbon society" and "policy methods" for discussions about emissions trading.

In June 2008, as the G8 Hokkaido Toyako Summit drew near, then Prime Minister Fukuda unveiled the vision for a low-carbon society (the so-called Fukuda Vision), suggesting a medium-term numerical goal to reduce GHG emissions during the period after 2013. At the Hokkaido Toyako Summit, G8 nations reached a basic agreement on the long-term goal of halving the world's GHG emissions by 2050 as advocated in the Fukuda Vision, and the Japanese government expressed its intention to reduce GHG emissions by 60–80 per cent by the same year. The Fukuda Vision was documented as the action plan for creating a low-carbon society, and was adopted at a cabinet meeting in July 2008. Although this plan was criticized as lacking novelty and not being drawn up based on opinions from the public, it determined the direction of Japan's climate change policy for the period after 2013. It proposed a sectoral approach (working out a national goal by adding up each industry's GHG emissions) as a methodology; it sought participation by all countries worldwide and fairly set a total GHG emission goal for each country. In the Cool Earth Partnership Program under the action plan, Japan expressed its intention of providing a fund of $10 billion over five years to encourage many developing countries to join the plan. Among the economic

Table 6.2.1 Six alternatives of the medium-term goal proposed by the government

	Reduction rate: compared to the 2005/1990 levels	Decrease in household income/increase in fuel and lighting expenses (per month)	GDP/ unemployment rate	Basis for alternatives and international comparison
Alternative 1	−4 / +4%	Standard case	Standard case	Same marginal abatement costs as those for the United States and European Union
Alternative 2	−6 to −12 / 1 to −5%			The reduction goal for advanced countries as a whole is set at 25% with marginal abatement costs equally borne by each of the countries
Alternative 3	−14 / −7%	−3,000 yen/+2,000 yen	Down 0.5–0.6% / Up 0.2–0.3%	Introducing most efficient equipment to the fullest (making the maximum efforts as urged in long-term prospects of energy supply and demand)
Alternative 4	−13 to −23 / −8 to −17%			The reduction goal for advanced countries as a whole is set at 25% with costs per GDP equally borne by each of the countries
Alternative 5	−21 / −15%	−8,000 yen/+5,000 yen	Down 0.8–2.1% / Up 0.5–0.8%	Newly introduced equipment should have the highest level of efficiency, and people are required to replace a certain volume of existing equipment with new
Alternative 6	−30 / −25%	−18,000 yen/+11,000 yen	Down 3.2–6.0% / Up 1.3–1.9%	Both newly introduced and existing equipment should have the highest level of efficiency, and carbon taxes and emissions trading will be introduced

Note: The European Union proposed to reduce emissions by 20 per cent compared to the 2005 level; the United States proposed 14 per cent compared to the 2005 level (±0 per cent compared to the 1990 level).
Source: Cabinet Office of Japan (2009).

methods which the MOE, METI and industry had intensely argued for or against over the past decade, the action plan stated that emissions trading would begin in autumn 2008 on a trial basis by integrating the domestic markets. The plan avoided making a clear reference to environmental taxes (carbon taxes), and only mentioned that it would promote the greening of the whole tax system.

After this action plan was worked out, the meeting was commissioned to discuss important matters that would help form Japan's climate change policy, such as the trial implementation of emissions trading and consideration of a medium-term goal. Reflected in this political decision-making system led by the prime minister is the extraordinary determination of the Japanese government and industry, which have both been preparing for over 10 years for a fight to make up the ground lost since the Kyoto Conference (COP-3).

6-2-3 The 6 per cent GHG emission reduction scenario has gone astray

Japan's total GHG emission volume in the base year was 1,261 million tonnes (in CO_2 equivalent), and its target set by the Kyoto Protocol is 1,186 million tonnes. However, its GHG emissions have continued to grow, although they fluctuate, and in 2007 reached 1,374 million tonnes, a record high and over 9 per cent more compared to the base year. Since 2000 CO_2 has accounted for 94–95 per cent of total GHG emissions, with emissions of energy-derived CO_2 representing about 90 per cent. Therefore the top priority in climate change policy should be how to change the fossil energy consumption structure. But since it was fully recognized that it is difficult to reduce emissions of energy-derived CO_2, from the very onset the basic scenario was to ensure that these emissions remained almost at the same level (±0 per cent) and achieve the 6 per cent reduction goal by other means. This scenario has so far undergone little change. In fact, the breakdown of reduction rates expected in the Kyoto Protocol target achievement plan, which was revised in March 2008, indicates about 1.5 per cent for CO_2 (from the non-energy sector), methane (CH_4) and nitrous oxide (N_2O) combined; about 3.8 per cent for forest absorption; about 1.6 per cent for the utilization of the Kyoto mechanisms; and about 1.6 per cent for chlorofluorocarbon (CFC) substitutes. Emissions of energy-derived CO_2 are expected to grow 1.3–2.3 per cent, taking into account the greater reduction in CFC substitutes than initially projected.

In other words, this means that Japan's climate change policy, aiming to check the rise in emissions of energy-derived CO_2, has focused on spreading energy conservation technology that could be used for the immediate

future, promoting wider use of some renewable energy and increasing nuclear power generation. In its periodical policy evaluations, the government was never confident that it could achieve the 6 per cent reduction goal, but at each policy evaluation it announced additional measures in part to resolve the shortfall in the reduction of GHG emissions, calculated their effects in quantitative terms and explained to the nation that the goal could be achieved but with some difficulty.

The following is a brief history of the important measures that have been taken in Japan. Prior to the adoption of the Kyoto Protocol, Keidanren began its initiatives for voluntary action plans in January 1997. In April the Law on the Promotion of New Energy Usage was enacted, and in October Toyota Motors launched the Prius, which has become a synonym for hybrid cars. In spring 1998 the Energy Conservation Law was revised, and energy conservation standards were introduced for consumer electronics and automobiles under the "top-runner system", which makes the highest energy efficiency attained in a given product category a standard efficiency level for that category. The Energy Conservation Law covers a wide range of areas, including energy conservation at factories through improved energy management, and the improvement of energy conservation performance for automobiles, consumer electronics, other product categories and for buildings, through higher heat-insulating performance and other measures. Later, the law was revised several times to tighten regulations, and has continued to be a sure-fire measure for achieving the goal set by the Kyoto Protocol.

Based on the Law on Special Measures Concerning New Energy Use by Electric Utilities, the target of utilization of electricity from new energy by electric retailers for the year 2010 has been set at 12.2 billion kilowatt hours. Moreover, the government aims to introduce in 2010 a total of 19.1 million kilolitres of new energy in crude oil equivalent, including 3,000 MW of wind power and 4,820 MW of solar power, as well as use of biomass and other types of new energy; this is estimated to account for around 3 per cent of the total primary energy supply. However, both wind and solar power generation facilities operating in March 2006 were less than half the goal. In 1994 the government began granting subsidies to households when they introduced photovoltaic power generators, and increased the subsidy budget thereafter. The subsidy system was abolished in 2005, according to a decision by the Ministry of Finance that the role of the government in terms of using subsidies to boost demand for solar panels had come to an end. However, in January 2009 it restored the subsidy system for photovoltaic power generation. As shown by these events, the government's policy was inconsistent. In February 2009 METI finally announced its policy of introducing the feed-in tariff system for power generated by solar panels, but whether this system will

produce satisfactory effects within the first commitment period is doubt-ful. The government advocates massive proliferation of photovoltaic power generation in housing as one of the principal measures to achieve its medium-term goal for 2020.

The government placed its greatest hope on the spread of nuclear power generation as a measure that was expected to bring results by around 2010 without fail. In 1998 METI launched an aggressive plan to build 20 addi-tional nuclear reactors by the first commitment period; but thus far only four new reactors (4,450 MW) have begun operation, with three (about 3,670 MW) under construction. At present (as of April 2009), 53 nuclear reactors capable of generating about 48,000 MW are in operation, supply-ing approximately 30 per cent of the total electric power. Their average operation rate, however, which peaked in 1998 at 84.2 per cent, has dropped to 60–73 per cent since 2002 due to several shutdowns of reactors caused by human error or earthquakes. Seven reactors (8,200 MW) at the Kashiwazaki-Kariwa nuclear power station, the largest in Japan, which caught fire after the Niigata Chuetsu-oki earthquake in July 2007, com-pletely discontinued operation for the two subsequent years.

Due to the decline in the operating rate for nuclear power plants and the increase in coal consumption exceeding the growth in natural gas consumption, CO_2 emission factors of electricity generation, which had fallen in 1998 to 0.354 kg-CO_2/kWh, a record low, grew 28 per cent in 2007 to 0.453 kg-CO_2/kWh, an 8 per cent increase compared to the 1990 level. Furthermore, the proportion of the electric power sector's CO_2 emissions in total CO_2 emissions, which had been only 25 per cent in 1998, rose to nearly one-third in 2007, when the electric power sector emitted 417 million tonnes of CO_2, a remarkable 51.6 per cent increase compared to the 1990 level (Ministry of the Environment, 2009; Nippon Keidanren, 2008).

Another problem is the liberalization of the electric power sector, which has been advanced in phases since 1995. Many of the new opera-tors that entered the electric power business use low-cost coal, residue oil and other substances for fuel, and this has boosted total CO_2 emissions. In the process of environmental impact assessment for newly planned coal-fired thermal power plant, the MOE has often demanded that elec-tric power companies do their utmost to reduce CO_2 emissions. However, that is inevitably limited to partial policy discussions about the national energy supply plans. Japan has not yet established a strategic environ-mental assessment system, and is urged to build a legal system for evalu-ating energy supply plans in a comprehensive manner from the viewpoint of climate change policy.

Figure 6.2.2 indicates changes in total GHG emissions in Japan and CO_2 emissions by sector. CO_2 emissions resulting from energy conversion

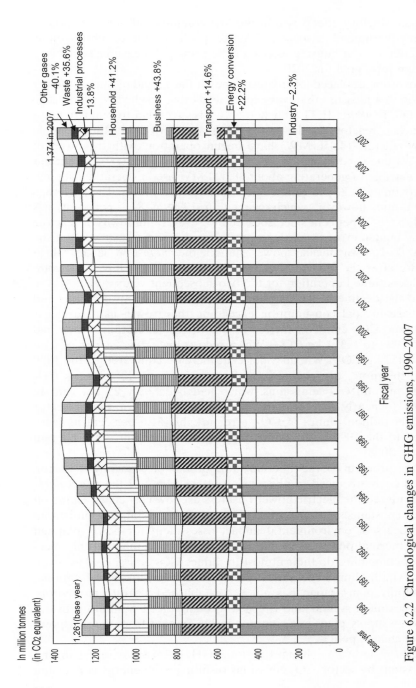

Figure 6.2.2 Chronological changes in GHG emissions, 1990–2007
Source: Based on Ministry of the Environment (2009).
Notes: The figure indicates the sum of carbon dioxide emissions by sector and other gas emissions. Data were collected in each Japanese fiscal year. The percentage for each sector shows the rate of increase or decrease in the sector's emissions in 2007 compared to the base year. Other gases include only CH_4 and N_2O for 1990–1994, because the base year for HFCs, PFCs and SF_6 is 1995 in Japan.

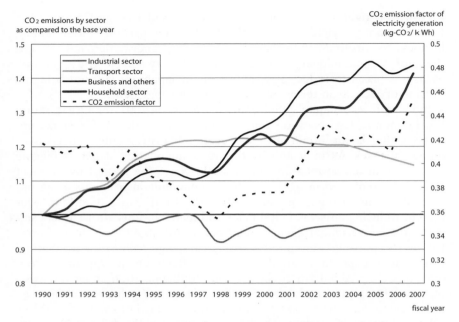

Figure 6.2.3 Increase or decrease in CO_2 emissions by sector and CO_2 emission factors of electricity generation, 1990–2007
Source: Based on Ministry of the Environment (2009).

(electricity generation, oil refining, etc.) are allocated to the final energy consumption sector. Large volumes of CO_2 are emitted by the iron and steel, chemicals, petroleum, paper and pulp and cement industries. Total CO_2 emissions for this sector are lower than the 1990 level, but the iron and steel industry, which emits the largest volume of CO_2, has not yet achieved the goals in its voluntary action plan (Nippon Keidanren, 2008).

The business, private household and transport sectors emit large volumes of CO_2 and have seen their CO_2 emissions grow at a high rate. (It is necessary to note that increases or decreases in CO_2 emissions from businesses and private households are easily affected by the fluctuation of the CO_2 emission factor for electricity generation.) The transport sector, however, has seen its CO_2 emissions fall after they peaked in 2001 (see Figure 6.2.3). This is due to the improvement in fuel efficiency and the reduction of traffic volume of passenger cars. Moreover, the automotive green tax system was introduced in 2001, under which lighter taxes are levied on fuel-efficient, low-emission cars and heavier taxes are imposed on fuel-inefficient cars, and this contributed to the fall in CO_2 emissions from the transport sector.

However, tighter regulations under the revised Energy Conservation Law have not yet yielded noticeable effects in the private household and business sectors, indicating that growth in total energy demand exceeds the improvement in energy efficiency of machinery and electric apparatus. Measures taken to reduce CO_2 emissions in Japan are still not bringing satisfactory results in terms of demand-side management.

In its reviews of Japan's environmental policy in 2001, the Organisation for Economic Co-operation and Development (OECD, 2002) recommended that Japan should introduce economic instruments such as environmental taxes. As indicated by this recommendation, Japan is lagging far behind in taking measures in this field. Since the Basic Environment Law was established in 1993, stipulating economic instruments as an important means of environmental policy, the MOE has patiently considered introducing environmental taxes and made various efforts to consult with other government agencies and politicians about such taxes. Industrial circles, however, mounted a strong campaign against environmental taxes out of concern about their adverse effects on the Japanese economy; this, coupled with discussions about double taxation under the existing energy tax systems and raising consumption tax rates, makes the issue complicated. For this reason, the Tax System Council of the former ruling Liberal Democratic Party, which was practically the highest decision-making body in tax system reforms, put off arriving at a conclusion each year, stating that "it would continue to consider this issue in a comprehensive manner".

As the carbon market grew rapidly on a global scale, on the other hand, the Subcommittee on Policy Methods of the meeting to discuss global warming issues made progress in considering emissions trading in Japan. In October 2008 emissions trading started on a trial basis to integrate carbon markets in Japan. Over 500 companies from the key manufacturing, electric power and other industries participate in the integrated carbon market. Based on CO_2 emissions for the period until 2012, allocating emissions to market players using the benchmarking system is being considered.

The governor of Tokyo, Shintaro Ishihara, who has exerted a great influence over the national government's policy by implementing advanced environmental policies such as automotive exhaust gas regulations, has created a sensation in addressing climate change issues. Before the national government, the Tokyo metropolitan government has decided to introduce a system in April 2010 under which, in a tie-in with emissions trading, it imposes a duty of reducing total GHG emissions upon some 1,300 business sites in Tokyo. Attention is being focused on the effects of the regulatory measures taken by the Tokyo metropolitan government, because local governments have so far concentrated on the intangible aspects of measures to cope with global warming.

The national government has also been enthusiastic in taking soft measures to reduce GHG emissions by inspiring national movements. These measures helped to arouse people's interest in climate change issues and were responsible for causing an eco-boom. In particular, since the Kyoto Protocol took effect in 2005, the MOE has attached importance to the development of national movements. Especially well known in Japan are the "Cool Biz" and "Warm Biz" campaigns proposed by then Minister of the Environment Yuriko Koike in the summer of 2005. These campaigns aim to reduce energy consumption for air-conditioning systems in homes and offices by encouraging people to dress lightly in summer and wrap up well in winter. Team Minus 6% is a virtual national movement operated on the internet. By June 2009 more than 30,000 companies and associations and over 3 million individuals had joined the organization, making it a centre for a national campaign that aims at lifestyles and societies with less CO_2 emissions. However, the effects of intangible measures overlap those of other measures, making them difficult to grasp; moreover, the quantities of the effects are limited. In addition, since 1998 politicians have on several occasions announced a plan to introduce a summer-time system in Japan, but this has not materialized because definite positive effects cannot be expected and it may lead to overwork and other undesirable results.

The volume of primary energy supplied in Japan during the 2004–2007 period on a calorie basis increased 15–16 per cent compared to the 1990 level. During this interval, the country's dependence on petroleum declined from 56 per cent to around 45 per cent. The natural gas supply nearly doubled, with its share up from 11 per cent to 17 per cent, and the coal supply rose from 17 per cent to around 21 per cent. But nuclear power supply has remained sluggish since 2001, with its share hovering at around 10 per cent, and the natural energy supply is negligibly small. During the same period, emissions of energy-derived CO_2 grew 12–15 per cent compared to the 1990 level. This means that the degree of carbon intensity was slightly lowered, due chiefly to a growth in natural gas consumption.

Despite the many measures taken by the government, GHG emissions have continued to grow since the Kyoto Protocol was adopted, and at each evaluation of the policy's effects, the government has seen the gap between its goal and the results become clearer. The list of effective additional measures that can be taken during the remaining period is becoming scanty. Based on the results for 2005, the Kyoto Protocol target achievement plan, which was revised in March 2008, offered additional measures – equivalent to a reduction of 37 million tonnes of CO_2 – to achieve the goals. It became clear at the end of April 2009, however, one year after the revision of the plan, that GHG emissions for fiscal year 2007 were 1,374 million tonnes, a record high and 16 million tonnes more

than in fiscal year 2005. On the face of it, the Kyoto Protocol target achievement plan has failed.

It is believed that the only realistic way left to ensure the attainment of the target is for the electric power and steel industries to make up the shortfall in the reduction of CO_2 emissions by acquiring credits from overseas in order to achieve the goals of their voluntary action plans, in addition to the government's utilization of the Kyoto mechanisms (about 100 million tonnes of CO_2). Currently, the total Kyoto mechanism credits that these two industries will utilize over the five-year first commitment period are estimated to be about 250 million tonnes of CO_2 (Agency for Natural Resources and Energy of Japan, 2009).

6-2-4 Climate change policy and journalism

Reports by the Japanese mass media on climate change issues have taken on a look of being event-driven, concentrating on major events in Japan and abroad such as the Earth Summit in 1992, the adoption of the Kyoto Protocol in 1997, the withdrawal by the United States from the Kyoto Protocol in 2001, the publication by the IPCC of its series of Fourth Assessment Reports starting in February 2007 and the G8 Hokkaido Toyako Summit in 2008. In particular, the coverage of IPCC reports, which asserted that the causal relationships between human activities and climate change had become clear, and the winning of the Nobel Peace Prize by the IPCC and former US Vice-President Al Gore, aroused Japanese interest in the environment, to the extent that it was reported that an eco-boom had been created in Japan. In their TV commercials, many businesses emphasize products that emit less CO_2, joining the mass media in calling for viewers to "think about the future of the Earth" and "prevent global warming". Citing the results of his studies in the United States, Mikami (2001) points out that the number of reports by the mass media on climate change increases during periods when discourses on its threats and adverse effects are extensively taken up for discussion, and decreases during periods when scientific arguments over the authenticity of climate change theories and the economic aspects of climate changes are extensively discussed. This applies to the reports by the Japanese mass media on IPCC-related events in 2007.

Many researchers in journalism have indicated that reporting on climate change is particularly difficult (Ikunaga, 2001; Okajima, 2001). Climate change issues involve a complex mixture of many different elements, such as wavering scientific knowledge, the practicability of technology, economic effects, complicated international politics and people's ethical views. How to analyse these huge issues and what opinions to express

vary depending on the guiding principles of the mass media, as well as the characteristic traits of departments (politics, economy, city, science, etc.) and reporters responsible for news gathering. Segawa (2009) analysed some 1,000 editorials published in three national newspapers (*Asahi*, *Mainichi* and *Nikkei*) during the period from 1987 to 2007 whose titles included the term "global warming". Subjects often taken up in the editorials include environmental taxes, domestic emissions trading, renewable energy, nuclear power and bureaucratic sectionalism. Based on the results of these analyses, Segawa points out that not only does opinion vary from one newspaper to another, but even editorials on the same subject – environmental taxes, for example – in the same newspaper have made comments that have changed over time. He also says that these newspapers have not gone as far as to affect governmental policy-making by raising questions at their own initiative and presenting a roadmap for solving the problems.

If the foregoing is taken into consideration, it can be said that as far as climate change issues are concerned, storms of reporting have buffeted the nation without complete "agenda setting", as journalism experts call it. "Agenda setting" is explained as a particular agenda being such a serious problem that it is taken up as a policy agenda, with its existence as a threat generally recognized through specific data and objective facts, and socially defined through arguments and conflicts among various sectors of society (Mikami, 2001).

As the position of reporting by the mass media remained unfixed, people were asked to express their opinions about the government's proposals concerning the setting of a medium-term goal as international post-Kyoto negotiations approached. It is extremely interesting to find out their opinions in this opportunity to express their views about the government's proposals.

From April to May 2009 the government collected public comments while showing six alternatives of Japan's medium-term goal, as listed in Table 6.2.1. In addition, in May it conducted an opinion poll by interviewing, on an individual basis, 4,000 people nationwide aged 20 or older chosen by random sampling. In this opinion poll respondents were asked to choose from among four alternatives, with the second and fourth alternatives excluded from the six.

When it collected public comments and conducted the opinion poll, the government explained the intentions of the six alternatives of the medium-term goal. Explanations included the equivalency of Japan's target reduction rate with those of the United States and European Union in terms of marginal costs and GDP, as well as the effects that each alternative had on decreasing GDP and individual income, increasing the unemployment rate and fuel and lighting expenses for households during

Relative frequency (%)

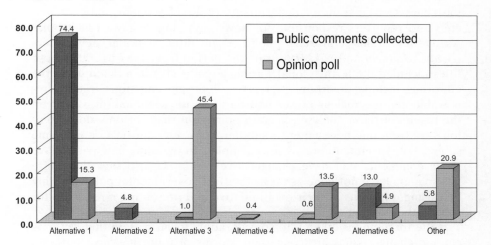

Figure 6.2.4 Results of public comments and the opinion poll on the medium-term goal
Source: Based on materials submitted to the meeting to discuss global warming, Cabinet Secretariat of Japan, May 2009.

the period until 2020 as calculated on a trial basis. This indicates the government's strong intention to urge people to choose a practicable version of the medium-term goal that is fair from an international point of view. Over 10,000 opinions were submitted when public comments were collected, and the number of valid replies to the opinion poll exceeded 1,200. Figure 6.2.4 shows the results of these two surveys as relative values for each of the six alternatives.

As seen in this figure, the collected public comments are polarized, with opinions that support Alternative 1 commanding a majority, at 74 per cent, and those supporting Alternative 6 representing 13 per cent. This is probably because organized votes of trade associations under Keidanren and labour unions of the key industries concentrated on Alternative 1, while those of environmental NGOs concentrated on Alternative 6. The results of the opinion poll, on the other hand, indicate that respondents who support Alternative 3 stand out, accounting for more than 45 per cent of the total. The results of previous opinion polls on climate change policy show there is no doubt that people are highly interested in climate change issues (Cabinet Office of Japan, 2005, 2007). While many of the questions in these opinion polls concerned respondents' moral and idealistic views of environmental issues, however, questions about the medium-term goal in the recent opinion poll urged respondents to make a more realistic decision by presenting its negative effects on their lives and the economy as a whole.

On the evening of 10 June 2009, based on these public views, Prime Minister Taro Aso announced the government's policy after discussions at the meeting to discuss global warming issues, over which he presided. The policy involved adding 1 per cent to Alternative 3 politically and aiming to reduce GHG emissions in Japan alone by 15 per cent compared to the 2005 level (8 per cent compared to the 1990 level) without using forest sink measures or the Kyoto mechanisms.

On the day after this political decision was made, the morning editions of various newspapers carried an editorial on the medium-term goal set by the government. The contents of these editorials are summarized in Table 6.2.2.

While *Yomiuri* supported the government's policy in its editorial, the tone of argument in the *Mainichi* and *Nikkei* editorials was negative. *Yomiuri* endorsed the government's arguments for practicability and international fairness, and reminded the government that in international negotiations it should not accept the unrealistic demands of developing countries without studying them. *Mainichi* criticized the government for its failure to present, in the process of setting the medium-term goal, a vision of how the Earth and Japan should be in the future. *Nikkei* was also critical of the government, arguing that it lacked a strong will for economic and social reforms. The newspaper expressed its concern about the low target reduction rate, saying that strategically it would prevent the government from taking leadership in international negotiations. *Asahi* proposed that rather than focusing on the medium-term goal alone, the government should take daring measures to advance structural reforms for industry and society with the aim of early achievement of a long-term goal. All these newspapers agree, however, that moving towards the realization of a low-carbon society with high technological capabilities will bring economic benefits to Japan some time in the future. But there are no original or specific proposals in these editorials; all cited measures and means for achieving the medium-term goal that are ordinary today, like further promotion of energy conservation and introduction of new energy (*Asahi* and *Yomiuri*) and carbon taxes and emissions trading (*Asahi*).

Domestic discussions over the medium-term goal have not yet settled down. With both industry and environmental NGOs left dissatisfied with the government's policy decision, the stage for policy-making on climate change will shift to international negotiations. Many doubts remain as to whether the way the government sought people's opinions on its medium-term goal adequately took into account a quarter of a century of discussions about climate change issues, and whether it was neutral. Analyses of the medium-term goal-setting process reveal, however, that the news media in Japan have not been able to form solid opinions about the

Table 6.2.2 Comparison of editorials on setting the medium-term goal in four leading newspapers

Comparison item	Asahi Shimbun	Mainichi Shimbun	Yomiuri Shimbun	Nihon Keizai Shimbun
Evaluation of target figure	It is courageous to set the target domestic effective reduction rate at 15%, but this is just the first step towards international negotiations	The target figure shows the government's lack of strong intention and philosophy to realize a low-carbon society It is a half-hearted figure that takes industry's interests into account	The government set a goal that exceeds that of the EU and US, but it poses a high hurdle for Japan, which is advanced in energy conservation efforts	Affected by discussions in Japan, this target reduction rate lacks power to drive international negotiations
Basis for goal setting	Based on the six alternatives of the reduction rate, the medium-term goal was set by taking a figure somewhere between the opinions of economic circles and those of environmental NGOs	The medium-term goal attaches importance to future heavy burdens on people and the intentions of economic circles The government made it look high by comparing it with the 2005 level	The medium-term goal remains within the range of being considered fair and practicable even by international standards The government has determined that the idealism of boasting a high target reduction rate is irresponsible	The government calls it a target domestic effective reduction rate, but made it look like being on the same level as the proposals of the EU and US by shifting the base year to 2005

Measures and visions	The government should change industrial and social structures by taking bold measures such as emissions trading and carbon taxes, and thereby prevent global warming, its ultimate goal, without sticking to the medium-term goal alone	In setting its medium-term goal, the government does not paint a vision of how the Earth and Japan should be in the future Although there is little hope that even the goal for the first commitment period will be achieved, there is no mention of it	It is necessary to promote wider use of the most advanced energy conservation technology and new energy in homes and workplaces It is also necessary to increase photovoltaic power generation by 20 times	The government's strong will for economic and social reforms is not found in its vision and the measures it is going to take The government does not ask industry to bear a big burden or intend to introduce economic control methods This means that the government will place a big burden on consumers
Creation of a low-carbon society	The path that Japan should follow for survival is to maintain top-level international competitiveness through innovative low-carbon technology	Depending on policy, people consider it as investment for the future to pay costs for low-carbon technology Technological innovations can lead to positive economic effects	It is necessary for more people to understand that goal achievement will lead to realization of a low-carbon society	It is necessary to spread Japan's environmental technology throughout the world, thus establishing a system to accelerate a low-carbon revolution

Table 6.2.2 (cont.)

Comparison item	Asahi Shimbun	Mainichi Shimbun	Yomiuri Shimbun	Nihon Keizai Shimbun
Participation by developing countries	The government should facilitate participation by developing countries and emerging economies while using technical assistance and financing as a bargaining chip	Additional strategy is needed to take leadership in encouraging participation by emerging economies	The government should lead emerging economies into a fair framework It should avoid accepting unrealistic demands without studying them	If the EU and US act in concert through policy coordination, making emerging economies accept one goal or another, Japan will be unable to make its presence felt in international negotiations
International negotiation strategy	The 15% reduction goal is low The focus of international negotiations is how far the goal is raised by taking into consideration forest sinks and emissions trading	Politicians should further display their leadership in negotiations to decide the next international framework	It is necessary to allocate a fair target reduction rate to each of the advanced countries according to the progress made by them in energy conservation Otherwise, negotiators will go the same way as with the Kyoto Protocol	The strategy of starting from small reduction rates and discussions about fairness does not allow Japan to take leadership in international negotiations

government's climate change policy. And it is likely that people's recognition of the importance of climate change as an environmental issue is separated from realistic policy decisions and pushed to the back of their minds.

6-2-5 Conclusion

Japan's industry and energy policy-makers, who regard the Kyoto Protocol as an unequal treaty, have continued to demand that a fair total GHG emission reduction goal be allocated to each country from a global perspective. According to their arguments, it is more important to aim at recovering lost territory in post-Kyoto negotiations than to make strenuous efforts to achieve the target set by the Kyoto Protocol.

Japan's strategy for bargaining in post-Kyoto international negotiations, which went into full swing in 2008, was revealed to the nation in the administrative process of medium-term goal setting. But with the government focusing on pursuing this strategy, drastic economic and social reforms to create a low-carbon society have been left completely untouched by debate. There has been no discussion as to who should bear the huge economic burdens that will weigh heavily on Japan in the future as climate change progresses, and how. Nor has any government policy been worked out with respect to what measures should be taken to adapt to the adverse effects of climate change.

There is no doubt that global trends in efforts to grapple with climate change have determined the direction of industrial and technological development in Japan. It cannot be denied that climate change has accelerated the improvement of energy conservation performance for automobiles and consumer electronics, as well as that of new energy technology such as photovoltaic power generation, and these improvements are the result of policies that have supported such industrial and technological development. Many experts expect that Japan's industrial technology, which is unrivalled in the world, will continue to lead a low-carbon society and drive the economy in the future, and these expectations cannot be denied, either. What the government's policy has achieved during the past dozen years or so, however, was no more than just a ripple on the surface of a deep lake, and it is still uncertain whether the government can make sure that total emissions of energy-derived CO_2 will peak by 2020.

Just as Japan struggled to cope with the recent serious economic slump, the government drew up a large supplementary budget for fiscal year 2009 worth ¥15 trillion to revitalize the economy, and appropriated 10 per cent of it to the cause of facilitating a low-carbon revolution. In

particular, the "green new deal policy" aimed at protecting the environment and increasing consumer spending attracted people's attention; ¥290 billion in subsidies was allotted to popularize energy-saving home appliances, and ¥370 billion in subsidies and major tax cuts to encourage the replacement of existing cars with fuel-efficient ones. We cannot help but feel baffled by a government's temporary fiscal measures to encourage people to replace products with a lifespan of about 10 years with new ones on an extensive scale being presented as environmental protection measures. The environmental policy, which accepted the necessity of making the environment compatible with the economy after the Earth Summit, now seems to be forced to make a difficult decision while being buffeted by energy and economic policies.

REFERENCES

Agency for Natural Resources and Energy of Japan (2009) *Energy White Paper 2009*. Tokyo: Government of Japan.
Cabinet Office of Japan (2005) "Report on an Opinion Poll on Measures to Cope with Global Warming", Government of Japan, Tokyo.
────── (2007) "Report on an Opinion Poll on Measures to Cope with Global Warming", Government of Japan, Tokyo.
────── (2009) "Alternatives of the Medium-term Goal to Cope with Global Warming", April, Government of Japan, Tokyo.
Ikunaga, Meguri (2001) *Global Environment*, Studies of Environmental Media. Tokyo: Chuohoki Publishing.
Mikami, Shunji (2001) *The Present Condition of Studies of Environmental Media and Their Tasks*, Studies of Environmental Media. Tokyo: Chuohoki Publishing.
Ministry of the Environment (2009) "Emission Volumes of GHG in 2007", April, Government of Japan, Tokyo.
Nippon Keidanren (2008) "Voluntary Environmental Action Plan 'Measures to Cope with Global Warming': Results of 2008 Follow-up", Nippon Keidanren, Tokyo.
OECD (2002) *Environmental Performance Review: Japan*. Paris: OECD.
Okajima, Shigeyuki (2001) *The Present Condition of Newspapers and Their Tasks*, Studies of Environmental Media. Tokyo: Chuohoki Publishing.
Segawa, Shiro (2009) "Climate Change Issues and Environmental Journalism", report of Waseda Initiative on Sustainability Science for Political Decision Making and Journalism, Waseda University, Tokyo.
Takeuchi, Keiji (1998) "Politics of Global Warming", *Asahi Sensho* 604.
Weekly Energy & the Environment (1998) No. 1501, 11 June, pp. 2–5.
WWF Japan (2009) "Comments on Advocacy Advertisement of Keidanren etc.", available at www.wwf.or.jp/activity/climate/news/2009/20090317opt.htm.

6-3

The conceptions of "environment" and eco-philosophy

Hideo Kawamoto

"Environment" is an ambiguous, suggestive concept. In essence, an environment is something that encompasses systems (of people, things, organizations, lives, etc.) while existing alongside those systems. The environment is not the natural world in general. This notion of environment emerges clearly as a concept in European thought with the use of "environment" in Darwin's evolutionary theory to mean the "set of conditions governing survival". Living creatures do not inhabit the world as such. The "world as such" and "nature as such" are, as it were, conceptual constructs that come into being as objects of perception. And these constructs obviously only come into being when they have been isolated and separated from human life.

Living systems exist within an environment, though not in the sense that a rock occupies a certain position in space. An environment is not uniform, nor does it exist independently of the systems. Moreover, environments are peculiar to individual life forms of the system, or at least to each species. However, as life forms thus have their own environment-world, how can the peculiarities of such environments be defined? The environment in which systems exist is itself, neither a world that can be apprehended by an observer objectively nor a thing with an objective subsistence. Still, should one attempt to control the environment, one must apprehend its basic mechanism through some technique. When we try to define something as explicitly as possible that cannot reveal itself in its entirety, we confront a difficult problem that is also an issue in philosophy. One research technique is phenomenology, and there are similar

Climate change and global sustainability: A holistic approach, Sumi, Mimura and Masui (eds), United Nations University Press, 2011, ISBN 978-92-808-1181-0

mechanisms of experience belonging to various kinds of Eastern thought. As instances of Eastern thought, this chapter will consider Taoism and the Sohto-Zen Buddhism of Dohgen. These sought to develop and express clearly a way of experience so as to identify "the workings of things that, naturally, are as they are". Zinen (nature) is the word used to talk about such workings.

The chapter will also consider another form of peculiar human experience, namely the act of making, or production. There are deeply rooted issues related to environmental problems here. After all, production has a way of always surpassing human stature. Production, moreover, is characteristic of an ever-advancing civilization, be it Eastern or Western. Production involves situations that carry with them choices that have yet to be explored. Finding the paths by which to realize this potential and its development is one important concern of eco-philosophy. From that vantage point, one can examine the possibilities that develop as a result of these ideas once it is realized that the environment itself and human civilization form a kind of system. This will reflect on arguments about self-organization since the 1960s as they apply to the environment. The basic arguments in this chapter will be on the cutting-edge of dynamic equilibrium, or "double-stability", and on "hypercycles", a higher order of self-organization.

6-3-1 Things that are what they are naturally

In Chinese Taoism, practical action centres on *mui shizen* (doing nothing and being natural). The foundation of this practical philosophy is in compliance with, and does not deviate from, *ten no michi* (the way of heaven). "The king obeys the earth, the earth obeys the heavens, the heavens obey the way, and the way obeys nature." In this context, nature means that "things are, naturally, the way they are", and does not mean the great outdoors. Still, in several descriptions "the natural world" is used repeatedly as a literary metaphor. In effect, nature is the essence, force or mechanism that makes the great outdoors what it is naturally; thus, in the context of Taoism, there is little difference whether one calls nature the great outdoors or the essence of mind. Both people and the great outdoors are said to exist in conformity to the fundamental principle of the cosmos. All things, that is, exist as part of the cosmos in conformity with the cosmic principle that "things are, naturally, the way they are". People exist as people, mountains as mountains. The force by which people exist as people, or mountains as mountains, comes from the way of the cosmos.

Some philosophers found the idea for conceptual models of physics in Taoist nature studies, known generally as the New Science (Capra, 1975;

Bohm, 1976). Capra (1975) stressed the fact that Eastern thought, including Taoism, contained within it many of the logical categories that leading physicists had found and revealed. Under Taoism's fundamental conception of unity, all things are one and mutually connected. Being mutually connected within the cosmos, and thus inseparable, all things, it was held, were nothing more than the various manifestations of one ultimate reality. Such a conception was even said to have offered a way of thinking similar to quantum mechanics. At the very least, under Taoism the world is not something made up of mere individual entities.

Moreover, in this respect, things are no longer to be grasped objectively from the perspective of an observer. Rather it is the very organization of one's relationship to things that constitutes observation. This organization of relationships, or the idea that interactions inhere in observation, is one found in Taoism. It is the critical fact that became clear with the measurement problem in quantum mechanics. An object exists under such special conditions that the act of observation falls within the limits of measurement error; when such special conditions are eliminated, there is nothing that does not interact. In other words, observation itself is one kind of interaction. At the extreme, experience is able to come into being to the point that the very difference between observers and observed things vanishes. This is one of Taoism's distinctive features.

The complementarity of opposed entities is also apparent. In Taoism there is no such notion that evil might be defeated and a pure good attained. Absolute good, pure good and so forth cannot be regarded as human ideals to achieve. Good and evil are mutually opposed and, in fact, complementary. They are phenomena that manifest themselves at either extreme; indeed, intimately related, they form a dynamic pair. Such complementarity signifies the limitations of each independent concept, and this fact is similarly evident, it is claimed, in the complementarity of position and momentum in quantum mechanics.

There is no doubt that various concepts that have been overlooked by classical physics – intimate connections between a part and its whole, interactions between individual elements, the indivisibility of subject and object, the mutual complementarity of seeming opposites – were, albeit latently, a part of the Taoist world. In general, we are compelled to feel through the statements of Taoism that these concepts are in some measure only simple analogies, or even forced rationalizations. It is, however, a distinguishing feature of Capra (ibid.) and the New Science that they identify these levels of analogy between physics and narrative arguments by Taoism.

Among Zhuangzi's anecdotes are many pieces that are distinct from his systematized concepts, yet rich in implication. Taking the form of allegories and parables, they give us many insights in a way that differs

from a systemized understanding of his writings. In fact, we have many issues that we can understand simply by relating them in parable form. A parable, in effect, is a microcosm that exists of itself and suggests something that cannot be related in any other form. For this reason, the parable may appear anecdotal; however, it is in fact more than a mere anecdote.

For example, there is the story about Hundun (Chaos), whose body had no openings (Legge, 1962: 266–267). In appreciation of the courtesy shown them by Hundun, two guests offer to create openings in his body like any normal person's. Guessing that the guests probably made their offer in good faith, he accepts. Each day the guests create one opening in Hundun's body until he has seven openings by the seventh day, like a normal person, whereupon he dies. While the parable seems to suggest that his death occurred because the guests' actions were not in keeping with *mui shizen*, "doing nothing and being natural", it is too rich in implication to interpret in such a way.

We can consider how intentional artifice is at work in this scene. People have seven openings innate in their bodies. This situation is a natural state. There should be nothing intentionally artificial about making a person resemble this. Common sense would suggest that creating openings in Hundun's opening-less body should bring him closer to a natural state. Yet Hundun dies. Does this mean that there is a problem concerning creating openings from outside one's own body? People naturally have openings that serve as innate sensory systems. Is there a problem with creating such openings from the outside, in a way that differs from the process by which they are formed naturally? If so, then normal plastic surgery seems to be completely invalid and there should be no choice between simply creating an opening from outside and an opening forming naturally from the inside. In the case that an opening is created from inside as an opening to the world, the inside and the outside have been already distinguished by an outside observer. The observer on the outside seems to conclude that the lack of an opening is an obstruction that prevents any connection with the world. Yet anyone without openings ought to feel neither that his own body is inside nor that he cognizes he is connected to the world by the process of creating openings. After all, Hundun had no knowledge of the outside. He ought not to have felt that creating an opening would connect him to the outside from the inside. Intentional artifice, one might conclude, lies in the fact that the gap between outside and inside is never covered by the creation of an opening.

This fact conveys more deeply the essential truth of what "doing nothing and being natural" means. While the outward appearance of two identical states – one formed of its own accord, the other created by outside intervention – may be the same, their actual conditions will differ. At

the same time, this is not a mere problem of perspective – that is, of whether to apprehend conditions from the outside or from the inside. After all, Hundun had presumably not understood what it meant to apprehend his circumstances from the inside. The implication of doing nothing and being natural has nothing to do with the question of which perspective is to be adopted. The fundamentals of doing nothing and being natural subsist in three points. First, it is necessary to elicit functioning that conforms to a thing's own peculiarity. Second, any external operations will, in that context, only provide an impetus to the functioning of this peculiarity, intervening in a way that supports it. All interventions that do not encourage such functioning are, in all cases, extrinsic. Third, in this context it is not a matter of transferring the outside perspective to the inside, but rather one of initiating a process by which perspective as such can emerge.

How might one go about identifying such natural functioning? To take notice of natural functioning in everyday life alone is probably difficult. After all, many people live, as they must, amid the vicissitudes of the mundane world and are swayed by their emotions in their perception of things. This natural functioning thus represents itself through conditions that cannot be perceived without some kind of disciplinary practices. Zen meditation is one such practice.

The Sohto sect of Zen Buddhism, founded by Dohgen, is Japan's most widespread Zen sect, and its Zen riddles ("problems" upon which to meditate) are well known. Roughly speaking, practitioners use breathing techniques to slow their thinking, decreasing their breaths to two or three per minute. They can thus move from a state of active thoughts to one of half-sleep, or perhaps reach a place where the boundaries of consciousness are thrown into relief by neutralizing its workings. At this stage they begin to see phenomena appearing of themselves naturally and vividly, instead of using consciousness to grasp matters in a controlled fashion. Perception at this stage is thought to grasp the natural way of things, a kind of process that Dohgen called *shinshin datsuraku* (shedding mind and body). Once consciousness is neutralized, normal human perception becomes but one interpretation of reality. From that position they seek to grasp the reality of things.

Similar ideas are seen in both Aristotle and phenomenology. The father of all learning and thinking, as he is called, Aristotle stressed *theoria* (contemplation) as a method that involved keeping one's mind neutral while in a state of mental quiet. From this vantage point one could grasp nature's relations. What he called contemplation was the emotionally peaceful observation of nature in a state free from relations of interest. Hence, for Aristotle, though it carried no meaning akin to environment, nature was a topic of study in which all things had their own natural

essence, or peculiarity, that could be identified. Therefore, for instance, the essence of things subsists in the purposes or goals towards which they move. The essence of physical objects lies in the earth; hence things fall downward in conformity with their essence. This was his way of thinking and manner of grasping nature. Concluding that a thing's essence subsists in the aim towards which it tends, he looked to its end to grasp the natural way of a thing's being. It was a way for the observer to reach neutrality independent of his emotions and values in order to grasp the natural course of the way things are.

Phenomenology (Husserl, 1931) attempts a thorough elucidation of conditions that are already occurring within the workings of consciousness. The fact that they have occurred at the level of experience in life means that the essence of consciousness has played a role in the already experienced life, and has already experienced the world. To the extent that the world of experience is continuous with being alive, there is no distance between being alive and the world; before it can ever be perceived for what it is, the world is already as it is. There is no distance between consciousness and the world *vis-à-vis* a world that has come into being before it is ever perceived. The classic example of experiences with no such distances is phenomena that appear directly before one's eyes. The operation that creates distance, in this experience without distance, is what is called "phenomenological reduction". Phenomenology is the method of describing the world at the level of experience as mediated by this operation. It does not only neutralize consciousness, but also research at the point of neutralization of the already-in-effect workings of consciousness as an action itself.

For example, were one to attempt to know the kind of essence that is an apple, one would normally gather as many apples from around the world as possible, analyse them and seek to know their shared qualities. Such shared qualities are extracted by a method of induction. In the course of gathering apples of various colours, shape and taste, one would presumably exclude pears, mandarins and so on. That is, before one ever examines the apples by scientific and analytical methods, one already knows well what an apple is. At work at this stage is the "substantive intuition", that is the intuition upon which survival depends. Such intuition has no way of answering how one knows an apple is distinct from a pear, yet nonetheless the distinction has already been put into effect in life.

In Dohgen's case, similar to phenomenological reduction, the effort to grasp matters with a neutralized consciousness involves a distinctive method by which the things one can actually see are cognized as if set in brackets. This method is his frequent use of negation, by which he tries to perceive reality's true form. "Life and death are not one, but neither are they different. They are no different, yet they are not equivalent. They

are not equivalent, but neither are they varied. For this reason, when life manifests its workings in their entirety, many different phenomena exist; likewise, when death manifests its workings in their entirety, many different phenomena exist." This chain of negations attempts to grasp workings as a whole, as the appearances of *zenki* (all processes). Negation is the performable method in order to grasp this "appearance of all processes" in which the workings of consciousness are neutralized (Dohgen, 2008: 355–357). As suggested by expressions like "the mountains run, the rivers stay", he also sought to distance himself from reality by negating it in peculiar ways.

It was the pre-war physiologist and wartime Minister of Education Kunihiko Hashida who thought it possible to apply these methods to the science of physiology, by applying Dohgen's insights on life to a physiological theory of life as well. Given that the substance of life lay in *zenki*, he believed it necessary to grasp activity, through an act of intuition, as the manifestation of activity of life (Hashida, 1935, 1977: 25–39). What he expected to grasp in this way was nature the way it exists naturally. The distinguishing quality of that which we call an environment subsists in the fact that we already live alongside it before we ever apprehend it rationally or analytically. For that reason, in terms of phenomena at the level of experience of life, nature in this sense was precisely akin to what today we call "the environment".

6-3-2 Transcending oneself

Scientific technology, according to common belief, has transformed nature, creating a man-made nature while destroying nature as such. In the background, the Christian view of the hierarchy of nature and Bacon's empiricist control can both be cited. In the Christian view of nature's hierarchies, God is at the zenith, spirits in physical form and rational humanity next, followed by plants and animals and other natural creatures. In this context, nature falls below humanity, which controls and exploits it. This view differs completely from the Eastern view of nature. In the Christian view, however, control over nature is accompanied by responsibility towards nature. Both interest in and awareness of nature preservation are thought for this reason to be stronger than in the East.

In fact, during its high-growth period after the war, Japan was one of the planet's great polluters. The fruits of scientific technology that were imported from the West during this time were fully accepted by people and companies, while wastewater and other toxic waste were entrusted to the purifying power of nature as mother, in what was truly a convenient distinction. In this context, responsibility towards nature may have

been both clearer and stronger in Christian cultural spheres than in Japan.

That being the case, one expects that the question is not at the root of whether to choose a Western or Eastern view of nature. Replacing a Western view of nature with an Eastern one will not perhaps resolve the problem. With his Christian view of nature, Bacon is said to have replaced the Aristotelian conception by stressing empiricist control over nature. Explaining that "knowledge is power", he announced that knowledge was not simply to know something about nature, but rather to wield power over it and actually affect it. In this case as well one must know what nature is. The scientific method Bacon advocated then was "induction". As Bacon himself explains, however, to subjugate nature one must conform to nature; without obedience to nature, nature can never be subjugated (Sakamoto, 1981). One would locate a path for conforming to nature, and conceive how one might go about controlling nature along that path. For that reason, what Bacon calls "control over nature" in fact locates nature's rules and adjusts to them; it draws one into nature in order to control it. That being the case, the rational control of nature as such is not necessarily irrational as a view of nature. The root of today's environmental problems is then not, one might conclude, on this level of one's view of nature.

Rather, production – the making of things – in general has major problems as regards environmental problems. According to philosophical anthropologist Gehlen (1971), there are two human situations that emerged in tandem with the making of things. The first is release from burden (functional substitution). For instance, replacing one's hands with a shovel means a lighter physical burden. A portion of physical work is transferred to and substituted with tools (things for making). In the event, both the workings of a person's body and the workings of perception change themselves. With tools, because they are instruments akin to one's body but outside it, one's bodily movements normalize one's bodily posture within their limits. When a person tests the ground with a stick as he walks, his hand senses not the movement of the stick but the rise and fall of the ground surface. A person uses the stick to gain direct knowledge of the ground such that the tool itself, as a medium of perception at the site of perception, becomes transparent, its tip a means of directly perceiving the environment. As this implies, our means of perception are at once vastly expanded. The second situation is excess substitution. For instance, the work of a shovel far exceeds that which a human hand can accomplish, just as calculations performed by a computer far exceed any human ability to calculate. In such a case, a person must stretch the abilities of his body to adjust the functionality of the tools that have been

made; and the tool is not only, for this reason, an extension of a person's body, but also a transformation of the person's body advancing naturally in response to the tool's functionality. With the manufacture of tools, then, humanity is no longer able to keep to human proportions. A body equipped with tools is a body that has taken specialized form under the tool's functionality, and one that is compelled to adapt itself to the tool's standards of functioning.

Beyond Gehlen, there is additionally a process by which reality is idealized, or ideals realized, as production advances. No matter how many attempts a person makes at levelling an uneven surface to make it flat, it will not easily flatten. If the flattening task includes tiny bumps the surface will be almost hopelessly difficult to flatten physically. At the same time, however, this work enables us to grasp what "flat" is. Once we extract in isolation this thing we have grasped, it gives meaning to "flat", a thing which, although it cannot be actualized, has through the act of making now come into being as something known. This is what Husserl (1970) so vividly depicts. And indeed geometry, that which schematizes in isolation a world of mere meanings and extracts from it a network of symbols, is brought forth in the matrix of making and measuring, just as Husserl explains.

The prehistory of geometry is one that rests on the effort to grasp the extremes of reality that lie one step beyond sensory facts. Though never actualized in reality, we know very well what it is, and in a form that engenders a world of meanings that are, as it were, incorporated in action. These meanings function, in the act of making, as an anticipation of directed action. With the emergence of meanings this side of geometry, meaning is achieved along with bodily action through our daily lives in reality. For instance, prior to acquiring the linguistic meaning of what "flat" is, we comprehend it through experience and our bodies. When sleeping on a bumpy floor, the question of what is "flatter" or "smoother" is something that we comprehend through experience and our bodies, not something we do not learn until we see it with our eyes. A discrete reality thus exists in the level of making. The content that emerges with this making is not an extension of our experiences; rather, for experience, it assumes a kind of transcendental quality.

In both East and West, making as such begins and advances ahead of, as it were, the making of language. Thus, independently of self-consciousness and reflection, the human body and its gestures undergo transformation, while civilization can no longer keep to human proportions. And because human civilization incorporates this situation in which it "always surpasses human proportions", it always includes situations that are impossible to control. It is not just that civilization changes the

environment, but that it is structured such that the environment always contains something that surpasses human proportions. It is a situation that cannot be resolved by suppressing human desire or the like. At a glance, it also seems to be a situation that cannot be overcome by an Eastern view of nature.

Hence we consider where the real problem lies. The speed of civilization, or of changes in natural conditions that accompany civilization, surpasses the speed with which humanity can respond. For instance, imagine the polar ice-caps were to melt, raising water levels and with them coastlines. Even so, if the rate were, say, 10 centimetres in 100 years, there would still be plenty of opportunity to respond. Occurring situations that surpass human proportions constitute a discrete system. It is the system of production. Regulating this system is problematic for both consciousness and the body, and merely changing the rules and conventions of society makes us no more able to respond. Rather, the solution must be conceived on the level of the discrete system. That is, production requires a solution at the production level. Situations that surpass human proportions are not part of a pathway capable of reproduction. To be capable of reproduction, certain distinctive techniques are necessary, techniques that must also fit with the structure of the system.

6-3-3 System

The word *system* is one that German Idealism invoked frequently. It appears at the start of the 1800s in works by Schelling. Prior to that, system was used in French Enlightenment encyclopaedias to mean a comprehensive collection of elements. The meaning of system is completely transformed under German Idealism. Regardless of how any given system is conceived, there are three features they commonly share: relations and integrity of the parts, the creation of a whole and organizational stratification. The idea of a system, then, is always near the heart of philosophy, the question of how to conceptualize it having been posed over and again. During this period, the basic idea of self-organization appeared often. Today, however, system theory no longer stresses knowledge of the whole. Rather, at present it stresses localized emergence, multiple parallel distribution and multidimensional interconnectedness. In that sense, the conception of system design has always been a central philosophical concern, and is today a practical concern.

In connection with environmental problems, one can draw attention to two new system structures. The environment is itself a kind of self-organizing, self-sustaining system in which lies a new structure yet to

be recognized. Considering environment-related problems, a model that conceptualizes multidimensional interconnectedness is required.

6-3-3-1 Double stability

For complex modes in the formative process, "double stability" has taken on clear form (Amamiya, 2006). That is, even within a system of similar elements there are transformational modes that assume different processes, and there are complex operating modes for which peripheral conditions must be in place at the time when an element among complex elements is activated.

Such an example was actually observed with eutrophication in a famous lake in the Netherlands, in which an increase in the concentration of phosphorus generally corresponded to a decrease in surface plant life. When the concentration of phosphorus increased rapidly, plant life diminished precipitously at a certain stage; yet at the same time, if the concentration of phosphorus was gradually lowered, the volume of plant life would gradually decrease along a different path. However, this is not a reversible process, but rather an indication that water pollution and environmental restoration must take different paths (Figure 6.3.1). Similarly, the transparency of pond water involves a phase transition in the changing context of *aoko* (algal bloom). When the amount (per cubic unit concentration) of *aoko* passes a certain critical point, the water gets clouded immediately. In addition, self-restoration is difficult. The level of *aoko* decreases with the release of carp and by other means, and the

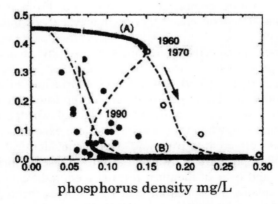

Figure 6.3.1 The process of eutrophication with historicity in a lake

process of clarifying the water will only commence once this level falls well below the critical point. An increase in chemical nutrients is met with a gradual increase in phytoplankton; however, given a certain level of plankton, the latter will continue to increase for some time even after chemical nutrients have been decreased. The biomass, then, has two states of stability.

Similarly, grasses diminish with the release of cattle, and decreasing the number of cattle does not restore the grasses every time. Grasses are known to regrow when "crescent tilling" with water and fertilizer is used to change the agricultural state of the land. "Double stability" is the term used to refer to the condition evident in these examples.

A system with double stability has what may seem its normal state, yet within it there is a repair mechanism with a certain built-in width. This repair mechanism has variables that define the various states of the system – that is, states that are selected according to the varying paths set by these variables. In this context, it is important to establish a process and procedure for restoration, rather than restoration to a defined state. The restoration of an ecological environment is not a matter of simply putting it back as it was. Rather, the question is which variables can be most effectively varied. Stability is supported by at least two or more variables, and how subsequent variables will change depends on which variable is altered first.

It is difficult to determine the critical point at which self-restoration in general, phase transition, becomes problematic. This is something that makes environmental problems challenging. That is, both extreme pessimism and extreme optimism exist side by side. Then there is the appearance of a special chaos-like state at the limits of double stability where mathematically some phase transition occurs. It is here that waveforms appear, substituting complexity for confusion. From mathematical approximations based on chaos theory, it may be possible to predict the critical points.

In historical perspective, Schelling's philosophy of nature had a mechanics of processes akin to double stability. For instance, in explaining the dynamics of rigid bodies, Kant uses a principle of equilibrium between the opposing forces of attraction and repulsion. However, the thing Schelling was seeking to grasp was a kind of whirlpool, a whirlwind. For Schelling, even when they are stable, these exist in a state of disequilibrium that gets created over and over in an identical form. For him, even a stable rigid body is always in a state of disequilibrium that is produced over and over in identical form (Eigen and Schuster, 1978). Thus Schelling explains the appearance of rigid bodies through two differing principles, one a state of dynamic disequilibrium, the other its repetitious

production. Two different but not contradictory principles working in close tandem is what distinguishes double stability.

6-3-3-2   The structure of hypercycles as the advanced model of self-organization

Emergence is a part of self-organization. However, it is not enough for self-organization that new properties, inherent in no individual elements, should appear. For example, when water forms from oxygen and hydrogen, it contains new properties that neither oxygen nor hydrogen possesses. To the extent that water is all but certain to appear, however, it is logically consistent to say that water's properties are latent in oxygen and hydrogen. In such a case, there is no emergence. Chemical compounding, a classic example of dialectics, is not an example of an emergent system today. Rather, the necessary condition for any self-organizing process is the appearance of new variables. Moreover, the range of variability of such a variable is not pre-determined.

As a formula, self-organization is "the entirety of the process by which individual processes are linked to subsequent processes for which they provide the initial conditions". This formulates the definition of a system built from the maintenance of processes. When some process returns to the start and closes the circle, we have a self-propagating system. By definition, when the chain of formative processes has returned to the start, a system has appeared that proceeds automatically and is autonomous. In such a process, it is normal for multiple processes to contribute simultaneously in parallel. As the formative process is repeated and a certain structure is maintained, we have a "dissipative structure" like a whirlpool or whirlwind.

The classic example of multiple systems interacting is the "hypercycle" as proposed by Eigen and Schuster (ibid.). At the root of their conception is the self-catalysing system. As the formative process proceeds, the products of the process produce themselves, becoming regulating factors in their formation. At this point the system's self is functionally divided in two. Materially speaking, the self is the body of the system brought into being through the formative process, as well as the latter's catalysing function. In terms of the formative process, this self is the production of products, as well as the regulation of the speed at which these products are produced.

A more complexly structured self-catalysing loop results when products of the formative process catalyse the next formative process, the products of which in turn catalyse the next formative process, and so on, in a continuous chain that forms a single large loop. Such a system has a

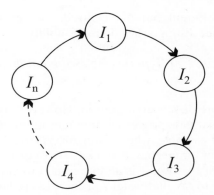

Figure 6.3.2 The hypercycle

higher order of organization and a new level of stratification. As the products of one formative process catalyse the next, and so on, the products of a formative process may at some stage catalyse the initial formative process, thereby forming a complex cycle. This is a hypercycle. A classic example is the coupling between the proteins and DNA that are believed to function in life forms (Figure 6.3.2).

With hypercycles, a system is possible in which individual cycles are regularly capable of substituting for others, while multiple cycles can also work in parallel. In terms of energy sources, various energy sources – wind, water, solar, geothermal – that can substitute for fossil fuels create a functionally diverse cycle. At the same time, however, any energy source that cannot connect forward with a subsequent cycle will naturally vanish. Also, it is possible to increase the cycle types that interact. For instance, were the chemical fixation of carbon dioxide possible, then chemical fixation technology could be installed at the end of systems used by companies producing carbon dioxide so that it could be used effectively. In a reciprocally catalysing system, the operation of the system as a whole can be regulated by endowing the catalytic segment with a regulatory function. In systems without catalytic interactions, the priority would be to introduce a catalytic cycle. One example would be environment-related taxation. An economic/taxation system should always be considered when doubling the system's operation. Hypercycles offer the best example of a model case for multiple systems in a state of symbiosis. Moreover, because these symbiotic relations are sustained by the system's operation, various decision points can be incorporated. This is symbiosis, then, that includes choice.

The model of hypercycles is not a Hegelian synthesis of elements, nor is it something that requires the a priori appearance of new properties, as

with dialectics. Rather, each element exists independently as such, its activities entailing both its individual functioning and functioning as a substitutable portion of the system as a whole. When new properties arise, they do so naturally within the workings of the system and, as such, are properly labelled emergent.

A system, then, through such workings as it proceeds of its own accord without the imposition of deliberate restrictions, is an apparatus by which intended results can be indirectly achieved. Speed and direction of operations can both be adjusted as part of the system activity. A hypercycle is a system built with many selective and alternative points.

In Japan today, the government and people alike are engaged in "sustainable" projects. To clarify research topics, our project sets in place three systems to be sustained: a global system, a social system and a human system. Numerous scholars have now joined in re-examining several strategies regarding global warming, social environment education and human values. However, these three systems are areas of research, not a cycle in which the system itself is interconnected. For instance, demands made in the name of sustaining the global system take form only as extrinsic restraints on social and human systems. Consumer behaviour that is easy on the planet or conserves electrical power requires deliberate effort by people. There is no mutually catalytic relationship between the individual systems. For this reason, the goals set for the system from the outside and towards which it moves are half-coerced constraints on the system's operation. Such external goals are fundamentally repressive towards the human system and, to the extent they remain so, they are not sustainable environmental countermeasures. For companies, global warming countermeasures, while a business opportunity, do no more than replace the substitution cycle.

By contrast, we will try to consider the introduction of different values into everyday human life. Consider the introduction of values other than convenience or comfort and the implementation of new choices. For instance, following the second period of growth, everyone has need of rehabilitation to sustain his or her individual skills, health and life. Consider an environmental design that meets that requirement. If an environment incorporating these new values were meaningfully implemented, on the one hand the emergence of an environment with such values would itself become a business opportunity, while on the other hand the natural reduction of carbon dioxide gases would become one element in a new hypercycle. To put it in extreme terms, it would be good were we to build a kind of staircase that was an alternative to elevators and escalators because it was more interesting, linked to the development of individual abilities and better for one's health. In this context, individual cycles have a dual function. One is an environment that promotes and develops

Photo by Luis Perez-Griffo Viqueira

Figure 6.3.3 Bioscleave house, 2008

human abilities, the other a choice to live a life with a small carbon footprint. Were it possible to introduce anew such dual-function cycles, they
would not only create business opportunities on the side of emergent
values, but also make it possible to conceive of a mechanism for contributing naturally to the reduction of carbon dioxide.

Consider, for instance, the reversible destiny house conceived by Shu-
saku Arakawa, an architect living in New York (Figure 6.3.3). Its design
creates an environment intended to exhume the latent abilities lying dor-
mant in humanity. Through the introduction of new choices such as this, a
contribution is made at the same time to the reduction of carbon dioxide,
forming interconnections between multiple systems. Moreover, the introduction of these new values is not repressive, and creates various
small-scale business opportunities. What hypercycles present is how such
secondary effects of interconnecting cycles are creative, as well as what
use these ideas can be.

REFERENCES

Amamiya, Takeshi (2006) "Ecological Environmental Problems as Complex Sys-
tems", *Kagaku* (Iwanami Shoten) 76(10), pp. 1047–1052.
Bohm, D. J. (1976) *Fragmentation and Wholeness*. Jerusalem: Van Leer Jerusalem
Foundation.
Capra, F. (1975) *The Tao of Physics*. Berkeley, CA: Shambhala.

Dohgen (2008) *Shobogenzo*. Berkeley, CA: Numata Center for Buddhist Translation and Research.

Eigen, M. and Schuster, P. (1978) "The Hypercycle", *Die Naturwissenschaften* 64, pp. 341–369.

Gehlen, A. (1971) *Der Mensch: Seine Natur und seine Stellung in der Welt*. Frankfurt: Athenäum Verlag.

Hashida, K. (1935) *Sciences as Action*. Tokyo: Iwanami Shoten.

——— (1977) *The Life as All Functions*. Tokyo: Kyodoisho Shuppan.

Husserl, E. (1931) *Ideas: General Introduction to a Pure Phenomenology*. London: Allen & Unwin.

——— (1970) *The Crisis of European Sciences and Transcendental Phenomenology*. Evanston, IL: Northwestern University Press.

Legge, J. (trans.) (1962) *The Texts of Taoism*. New York: Dover Publications.

May, R. M. (1977) "Thresholds and Breakpoints in Ecosystems with a Multiplicity of Stable States", *Nature* 269, pp. 471–477.

Sakamoto, K. (1981) *Bacon*. Tokyo: Kodansha.

7

Integration of a low-carbon society with a resource-circulating and nature-harmonious society

Toshihiko Masui

7-1 Environmental problems in achieving a sustainable society

7-1-1 Overview of sustainable development

There has been much discussion about sustainable development. It is said that "sustainable development" was firstly proposed in the World Conservation Strategy in 1980. The World Commission on Environment and Development (1987) introduced the concept of sustainable development in its final report, *Our Common Future*, as "development that meets the needs of the present without compromising the ability of future generations to meet their own needs. It contains within it two key concepts: the concept of 'needs', in particular the essential needs of the world's poor, to which overriding priority should be given; and the idea of limitations imposed by the state of technology and social organization on the environment's ability to meet present and future needs."

The eight Millennium Development Goals (MDGs) are to be achieved by 2015 to respond to the world's main development challenges. The MDGs are drawn from the actions and targets contained in the Millennium Declaration, which was adopted by 189 nations and signed by 147 heads of state and governments during the UN Millennium Summit in September 2000 (United Nations, 2009). As shown in Table 7.1, ensuring environmental sustainability is one goal. The definition of sustainability under the MDGs and in other references indicates that the

Climate change and global sustainability: A holistic approach, Sumi, Mimura and Masui (eds), *United Nations University Press, 2011, ISBN 978-92-808-1181-0*

Table 7.1   Goals of MDGs and indicators for Goal 7

Goal 1: Eradicate extreme poverty and hunger
Goal 2: Achieve universal primary education
Goal 3: Promote gender equality and empower women
Goal 4: Reduce child mortality
Goal 5: Improve maternal health
Goal 6: Combat HIV/AIDS, malaria and other diseases
Goal 7: Ensure environmental sustainability
  Target 7.A: Integrate the principles of sustainable development into country
  policies and programmes and reverse the loss of environmental resources
  Target 7.B: Reduce biodiversity loss, achieving, by 2010, a significant reduction
  in the rate of loss
    7.1 Proportion of land area covered by forest
    7.2 CO_2 emissions, total, per capita and per \$1 GDP (PPP)
    7.3 Consumption of ozone-depleting substances
    7.4 Proportion of fish stocks within safe biological limits
    7.5 Proportion of total water resources used
    7.6 Proportion of terrestrial and marine areas protected
    7.7 Proportion of species threatened with extinction
  Target 7.C: Halve, by 2015, the proportion of people without sustainable
  access to safe drinking water and basic sanitation
    7.8 Proportion of population using an improved drinking water source
    7.9 Proportion of population using an improved sanitation facility
  Target 7.D: By 2020, to have achieved a significant improvement in the lives of
  at least 100 million slum dwellers
    7.10 Proportion of urban population living in slums
Goal 8: Develop a global partnership for development

economic and social aspects of environmental sustainability cannot be separated.

In Japan, the Ministry of the Environment (2007) has published a very long-term vision in which the socio-economic activities and the environment in Japan in 2050 were discussed and quantified from the viewpoints of not only the social and economic situation, which includes population, economy, lifestyles, national land and social infrastructure, self-sufficiency and international society, but also risks to sustainability, which include global warming, material circulation, ecosystems and quality of the environment for living. Figure 7.1 shows the results of the quantification.

The Central Environment Council (2007) formulated a strategy for becoming a leading environmental nation. The strategy proposes that we aim to build a sustainable society through comprehensive measures integrating three aspects of society: a low-carbon society, a sound material-cycle society and a society in harmony with nature. We can apply our wisdom and tradition of living in harmony with nature to the present-day situation and utilize our world-renowned environmental and energy

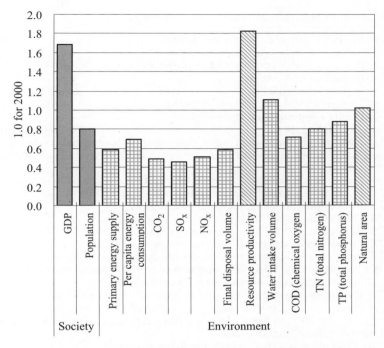

Figure 7.1 2050 changes in indicators from 2000 in the "Very Long-term Vision"

technologies, our experience and knowledge of having overcome serious pollution, and our abundant earnest and capable human resources to create a driving force that can bring forth environment-oriented economic growth and invigorate local communities. Under this strategy, the following eight points are to be implemented as priorities in the next one to two years.

- 1: International leadership to overcome the climate change problem.
- 2: Conservation of biodiversity for the sustainable use of nature's blessings for the current generation and generations to come.
- 3: Creation of sustainable material cycles through the 3Rs (reduce, reuse and recycle).
- 4: International cooperation utilizing the experience and knowledge derived from having overcome pollution.
- 5: Economic growth centred on environmental and energy technologies.
- 6: Creation of vibrant local communities that utilize the blessings of nature.
- 7: Educating people to feel for the environment, think for the environment and act for the environment.
- 8: Creating a system to support a "leading environmental nation".

In this chapter, the three aspects of environmental sustainability at the global level in 2050 – a low-carbon society, a resource-circulating society

and a nature-harmonious society – are discussed and quantified in relation to future socio-economic activity.

7-2 Scenarios and the environment

7-2-1 Why are scenarios used for environmental assessment?

Global environmental problems, including climate change, are regarded as one of the most important issues in international policy discussion. However, as shown in the international negotiations for greenhouse gas emission reduction, it is not easy to decide effective reduction targets because of the involvement of various stakeholders. This kind of issue is called an "ill-structured" problem in political science (Miyagawa, 1994). In the process of resolving this type of problem, structuralizing rather than solving the problem is the focus.

In order to treat climate change as an ill-structured problem, both policy and science have important roles that intertwine. Policy is implemented based on scientific knowledge, while science evaluates the countermeasures examined in policy. After repeating these processes, the most effective countermeasures to combat climate change are implemented.

Alcamo (2001) pointed out that scenarios can be useful tools for assessing either the future implications of current environmental problems or the future emergence of new problems, since scenarios are helpful for thinking about the future. He also stated that scenarios can be used to:

- provide a picture of future alternative states of the environment in the absence of additional environmental policies ("baseline scenarios"); in this way scenarios are a device to illustrate the impacts of society on the natural environment, and to point out the need for environmental policies to avoid these impacts
- raise awareness about the future connection between different environmental problems
- illustrate how alternative policy pathways can achieve an environmental target
- combine qualitative and quantitative information about the future evolution of an environmental problem
- identify the robustness of environmental policies under different future conditions
- help stakeholders, policy-makers and experts to "think big" about an environmental issue, i.e. to take into account the large time and space scales of a problem
- help raise awareness about the emergence of new or intensifying environmental problems in Europe over the next few decades.

7-2-2 Environmental scenarios

Many types of environmental scenario, combining qualitative storyline and quantitative simulation, have already been developed. With regard to the climate change problem, Nakicenovic and Swart (2000) edited an IPCC special report on future greenhouse gas emission scenarios as business as usual, and Morita and Robinson (2001) summarized the GHG stabilization scenario based on this IPCC report. All of these scenarios examined greenhouse gas emissions up to 2100. The Millennium Ecosystem Assessment (2005) quantified ecosystem services and human well-being; its definitions of ecosystem services are shown in Table 7.2.

With regard to more comprehensive environmental scenarios, UNEP (2007) published the "Global Environment Outlook (GEO) 4" and the OECD (2008) published the *OECD Environmental Outlook to 2030*. In the GEO4, based on the four different types of future scenarios up to 2050 – market first, policy first, security first and sustainability first – the changes to the atmosphere, land, water, biodiversity and human well-being and vulnerability are indicated. The OECD outlook categorizes the three levels of environmental change as shown in Table 7.3.

7-2-3 Achieving a low-carbon society in Japan by 2050

At the national level, many scenarios have been developed. The National Institute for Environmental Studies and other research communities proposed two types of future scenarios which will achieve a 70 per cent reduction of CO_2 emissions in Japan by 2050 under the Japan Low-carbon Society Scenarios towards 2050 (LCS) project (Japan LCS 2050 Scenario Team, 2008). Table 7.4 presents a summary of the socio-economic scenarios; Figure 7.2 shows the countermeasures for achieving the 70 per cent reduction target.

In 2009, at the G8 summit held in L'Aquila, it was declared a goal of developed countries to reduce aggregate greenhouse gas emissions by at least 80 per cent by 2050 compared to 1990 or more recent years. Based on this long-term target, revised scenarios which will reduce CO_2 emissions by 80 per cent by 2050 were presented (Minister of the Environment, 2009). In the new vision, total energy demand will be reduced to achieve a 40 per cent cut in CO_2 emissions and low-carbon energy will be introduced to achieve a 70 per cent cut in CO_2 emissions.

Development of national scenarios for a low-carbon society has already been started by developed countries, and also developing countries such as China.

Table 7.2 Ecosystem services examined by the Millennium Ecosystem Assessment

Provisioning services: products obtained from ecosystems

Food	This includes the vast range of food products derived from plants, animals, and microbes
Fibre	Materials such as wood, jute, cotton, hemp, silk and wool
Fuel	Wood, dung and other biological materials serve as sources of energy
Genetic resources	This includes genes and genetic information used for animal and plant breeding and biotechnology
Biochemicals, natural medicines and pharmaceuticals	Many medicines, biocides, food additives such as alginates, and biological materials are derived from ecosystems
Ornamental resources	Animal and plant products, such as skins, shells and flowers, are used as ornaments, and whole plants are used for landscaping and ornaments
Fresh water	People obtain fresh water from ecosystems and thus the supply of fresh water can be considered a provisioning service
	Fresh water in rivers is also a source of energy
	Because water is required for other life to exist, however, it could also be considered a supporting service

Regulating services: benefits obtained from regulation of ecosystem processes

Air quality regulation	Ecosystems both contribute chemicals to and extract chemicals from the atmosphere, influencing many aspects of air quality
Climate regulation	Ecosystems influence climate both locally and globally
	On a local scale, for example, changes in land cover can affect both temperature and precipitation
	On a global scale, ecosystems play an important role in climate by either sequestering or emitting greenhouse gases
Water regulation	Timing and magnitude of runoff, flooding and aquifer recharge can be strongly influenced by changes in land cover, including in particular alterations that change water storage potential of the system, such as the conversion of wetlands or the replacement of forests with croplands or croplands with urban areas
Erosion regulation	Vegetative cover plays an important role in soil retention and prevention of landslides

Table 7.2 (cont.)

Water purification and waste treatment	Ecosystems can be a source of impurities (for instance in fresh water) but also can help filter out and decompose organic wastes introduced into inland waters and coastal and marine ecosystems, and can assimilate and detoxify compounds through soil and subsoil processes
Disease regulation	Changes in ecosystems can directly change abundance of human pathogens, such as cholera, and can alter abundance of disease vectors, such as mosquitoes
Pest regulation	Ecosystem changes affect prevalence of crop and livestock pests and diseases
Pollination	Ecosystem changes affect distribution, abundance and effectiveness of pollinators
Natural hazard regulation	Presence of coastal ecosystems such as mangroves and coral reefs can reduce damage caused by hurricanes and large waves

Cultural services: non-material benefits people obtain from ecosystems through spiritual enrichment, cognitive development, reflection, recreation and aesthetic experiences

Cultural diversity	Diversity of ecosystems is one factor influencing diversity of cultures
Spiritual and religious values	Many religions attach spiritual and religious values to ecosystems or their components
Knowledge systems (traditional and formal)	Ecosystems influence the types of knowledge systems developed by different cultures
Educational values	Ecosystems and their components and processes provide the basis for both formal and informal education in many societies
Inspiration	Ecosystems provide a rich source of inspiration for art, folklore, national symbols, architecture and advertising
Aesthetic values	Many people find beauty or aesthetic value in various aspects of ecosystems, as reflected in the support for parks, scenic drives and the selection of housing locations
Social relations	Ecosystems influence the types of social relations that are established in particular cultures; fishing societies, for example, differ in many respects in their social relations from nomadic herding or agricultural societies
Sense of place	Many people value the "sense of place" that is associated with recognized features of their environment, including aspects of the ecosystem

Table 7.2 (cont.)

Cultural heritage values	Many societies place high value on the maintenance of either historically important landscapes ("cultural landscapes") or culturally significant species
Recreation and eco-tourism	People often choose where to spend their leisure time based in part on the characteristics of the natural or cultivated landscapes in a particular area

Supporting services: necessary for the production of all other ecosystem services; they differ from provisioning, regulating and cultural services in that their impacts on people are often indirect or occur over a very long time, whereas changes in the other categories have relatively direct and short-term impacts on people

Soil formation	Because many provisioning services depend on soil fertility, the rate of soil formation influences human well-being in many ways
Photosynthesis	Photosynthesis produces oxygen necessary for most living organisms
Primary production	Assimilation or accumulation of energy and nutrients by organisms
Nutrient cycling	Approximately 20 nutrients essential for life, including nitrogen and phosphorus, cycle through ecosystems and are maintained at different concentrations in different parts of ecosystems
Water cycling	Water cycles through ecosystems and is essential for living organisms

7-3 Development of a low-carbon society integrated with a resource-circulating society and a nature-harmonious society

7-3-1 Forecasting and backcasting

As shown in the previous section, many types of environmental scenarios have been proposed. Many of these are "forecasting"-type scenarios, which show the present day as a starting point and are not constrained by a predetermined end vision. That is to say, they are forward-looking scenarios. In "forecasting"-type scenarios, realization of a sustainable society in the future is not promised. However, in order to develop a sustainable society there are many environmental and social targets to achieve. In this case, the "backcasting"-type scenario approach is more useful. Backcasting scenarios indicate how to achieve a desired target or avoid an undesired target.

Table 7.3 Future environmental changes identified in the OECD outlook

	Green light	Yellow light	Red light
Climate change		Declining GHG emissions per unit of GDP	Global GHG emissions Increasing evidence of an already changing climate
Biodiversity and renewable natural resources	Forested areas in OECD countries	Forest management Protected areas	Ecosystem quality Species loss Invasive alien species Tropical forests Illegal logging Ecosystem fragmentation
Water	Point-source water pollution in OECD countries (industry, municipalities)	Surface water quality and wastewater treatment	Water scarcity Groundwater quality Agricultural water use and pollution
Air quality	OECD country SO_2 and NO_x emissions	Particulate matter and ground-level ozone Road transport emissions	Urban air quality
Waste and hazardous chemicals	Waste management in OECD countries OECD country CFC emissions	Municipal waste generation Developing country CFC emissions	Hazardous waste management and transportation Waste management in developing countries Chemicals in environment and products

Notes:
Green light = environmental issues which are being well managed, or for which there have been significant improvements in management in recent years but on which countries should remain vigilant.
Yellow light = environmental issues which remain a challenge but for which management is improving, or for which current status is uncertain or which have been well managed in the past but are less so now.
Red light = environmental issues which are not well managed, are in a bad or worsening state and require urgent attention.
All trends are global, unless otherwise specified.

Table 7.4 Scenarios in Japan for 2050 under the LCS project

Scenario A	Scenario B
Vivid, technology-driven	Slow, nature-oriented
Urban/personal	Decentralized/community
Technology breakthroughs	Self-sufficient
Centralized production/recycling	Produce locally, consume locally
Comfortable and convenient	Social and cultural values
2%/yr GDP per capita growth	1%/yr GDP per capita growth
High import dependency for primary industry	Low import dependency for primary industry
Globalization of production bases	Limited production of diversified products with local brands
Reducing market regulation	Penetration of market rules with moderate regulations

7-3-2 Targets for achieving a sustainable society

A sustainable scenario for Japan has already been developed, as shown above. This section will extend the scenario on a global scale. In this study, as conditions for a sustainable world, the following three aspects have been taken into account: a low-carbon society, a resource-circulating society and a nature-harmonious society.

The final target of the low-carbon society (LCS) is substantial reduction of global greenhouse gas (GHG) emissions. GHG concentrations will be stabilized at levels that will not affect humans or human-survival foundations for the future. The IPCC (2007) shows that the global GHG emissions in 2050 will be half the 1990 level. As noted, the L'Aquila G8 Summit agreed to reduce GHG emissions in developed countries 80 per cent by 2050. At the following MEF (major economic forum), no agreement was reached on a proposal to reduce global GHG emissions 50 per cent by 2050 because the proposal was rejected by the newly emerging nations. In this study, a 50 per cent reduction by 2050 is set as the target for achieving an LCS.

The resource-circulating society (RCS) is assessed from the viewpoint of material flow change. At present, no appropriate global targets for an RCS have been proposed. At the national level, for example in Japan, three types of target have been proposed: "resource productivity", defined as GDP divided by input such as natural resources, is an index that comprehensively shows how effectively materials are being used by industries and in people's lives; "cyclical use rate", defined as the cyclical use amount divided by the natural resources input and cyclical use amount, is an index that shows the percentage of cyclical use within the total input amount injected into an economic society; and "final disposal

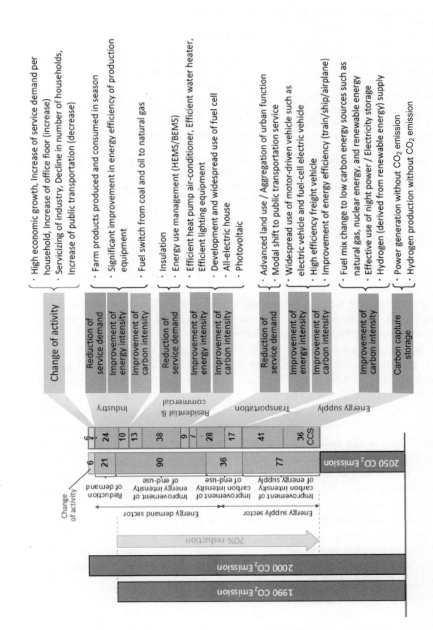

Scenario A

Note: Please see page 315 for a colour version of this figure.

268

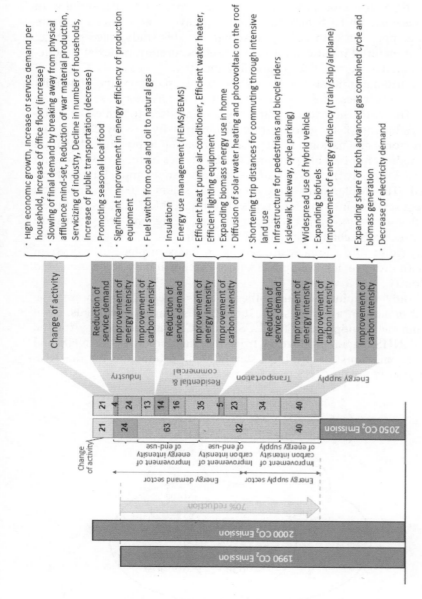

Scenario B

Figure 7.2 List of countermeasures for achieving a 70 per cent reduction in CO$_2$ emissions
Note: Please see page 316 for a colour version of this figure.

269

amount" is an index that directly concerns the urgent issue of addressing the shortage of landfill capacity at final disposal sites.

In an RCS, resource productivity will be improved substantially. In order to achieve an RCS, material input will have to be reduced substantially in comparison with economic activity. In this study, since the total volume of material input cannot be assessed accurately, material production is treated as an index for examining the RCS.

The nature-harmonious society (NHS) is assessed from the viewpoint of ecosystem services, because assessment of biodiversity itself is quite difficult. The 2010 Biodiversity Target was committed to achieving a significant reduction of the current rate of biodiversity loss by 2010 at the global, regional and national levels as a contribution to poverty alleviation and to the benefit of all life on Earth by the parties of the Convention on Biological Diversity. In this target, seven focal areas and 11 targets are indicated. The Millennium Ecosystem Assessment (2005) categorized ecosystem services into the four types shown in Table 7.2. Ecosystem services influence various aspects of human well-being, and ecosystems are in turn affected by changes in human well-being.

In this study, forest area is utilized as an index in place of ecosystem services. In order to achieve an NHS, forest area will have to be increased continuously.

This study examines whether these three types of society will be achieved or not on a global scale. It will assess various materials: fossil fuels from the standpoint of the LCS and RCS, biomass energy for the LCS and NHS, paper production from the standpoint of the NHS and RCS, CO_2 emissions for the LCS, steel-making production for the RCS and forest area for the NHS (see Figure 7.3).

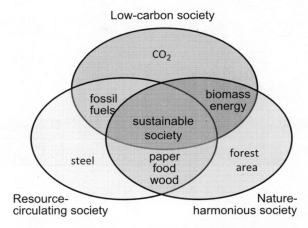

Figure 7.3 Factors for assessing the LCS, RCS and NHS

7-4 Quantification of a low-carbon society with a resource-circulating society and a nature-harmonious society

The National Institute for Environmental Studies and The University of Tokyo have quantified a low-carbon society with a resource-circulating society and a nature-harmonious society at the global level in the Integrated Research System for Sustainability Science. In this section, the method of quantification and the tentative results are introduced.

7-4-1 Model

In order to quantify the low-carbon, resource-circulating and nature-harmonious societies, a global computable general equilibrium model was developed. This model includes 13 regions and 16 sectors, as shown in Tables 7.5 and 7.6, respectively.

As the benchmark for economic data, GTAP 6 is adopted. In addition to this economic dataset, GHG emissions data provided by EDGAR, land-use data provided by the FAO and energy demand and supply data provided by the IEA have been included. Material production and consumption, such as for paper and steel, have also been estimated and included in the model, the basic structure of which is shown in Figure 7.4.

The final demand sector, including household and government, is endowed with production factors such as land and resources in addition to capital and labour. These factors are provided to the production sectors, and the household sector receives income such as wages and rent. The

Table 7.5 Regional definitions for the global model

North America (NAM)	Indonesia (IDN)
Japan (JPN)	Rest of Asia (RAS)
Oceania (ANZ)	Middle East/Asia (MEA)
Western Europe (WEU)	Africa (AFR)
Eastern Europe and Russia (EEU)	Brazil (BRA)
China (CHN)	Rest of Latin America (LAM)
India (IND)	

Table 7.6 Sectoral classifications for the global model

Oil (OIL)	Mining (MIN)
Coal (COA)	Steel (STL)
Gas (GAS)	Food (FOD)
Electricity (ELY)	Pulp and paper (PPL)
Agriculture (AGR)	Other manufactures (OTM)
Livestock (LVK)	Construction (CNS)
Forestry and wood (FRS)	Transportation (TRS)
Fishery (FSH)	Service (SER)

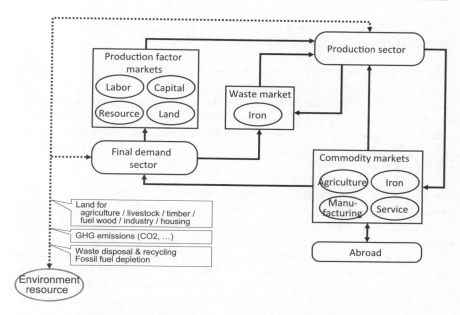

Figure 7.4 The economic activity and commodity flow in the model

household sector selects final consumption goods to maximize utility subject to income. The production sectors produce specific commodities by
inputting production factors and materials as intermediate goods. The
produced goods are provided to the domestic market or the foreign
market as exported goods. The domestic market handles both domestic
goods and imported goods. In the processes of production and consumption, various wastes are generated, and the valuable wastes are input into
the appropriate production sectors.

Final disposal wastes and CO_2 are released into the environment. In
this model, this activity is treated as utilization of environmental services.
Resource extraction and land use are treated as utilization of environmental resources.

7-4-2 Future scenarios

In this analysis, future economic activity and the related environmental
burdens are calculated sequentially from 2001. Driving forces are assumed to be as follows.

Regarding population change, we used the medium projections by the
United Nations (2007). For economic growth we assumed the SRES B2
scenario presented by the IPCC (2000). Energy efficiency improvement

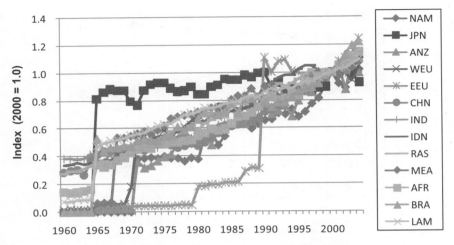

Figure 7.5 Changes in land productivity in regions in the model
Note: Land productivity is calculated by dividing the GDP of the primary sector by agricultural land.

was assumed to reproduce the SRES B2 scenario for four regions (OECD90 region, countries undergoing economic reform, Asia and Middle East, Africa and Latin America). Future land productivity change was defined based on past trends (see Figure 7.5) and the potential of land productivity by region was set to be the maximum productivity. Past land productivity was calculated from the agricultural area estimated by the FAO and the GDP in the primary sector estimated by the United Nations (2008). It is assumed land productivity will improve by half the past improvement rate, and that total factor productivity is 0.5 per cent/year for developed regions and 1 per cent/year for developing countries.

To quantify the countermeasures for achieving integration of the three societies, the following scenarios are presented.

- *Scen_0: Reference case.* In this scenario, no additional countermeasures will be introduced.
- *Scen_1: Energy efficiency improvement scenario.* In order to reduce CO_2 emissions by half by 2050, energy efficiency improvement is assumed to be 2.5 times that of the reference case.
- *Scen_2: Long-lived capital stock scenario.* This scenario indicates the lifespans of building materials will become 50 per cent longer than those of the reference case in addition to the assumption of Scen_1.
- *Scen_3: Less paper in household sector scenario.* This scenario indicates that paper demand by households will be reduced by the introduction of information technology in addition to the assumption of Scen_1.

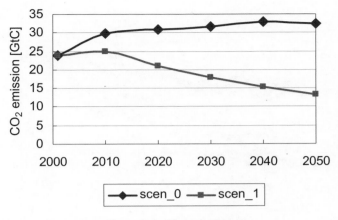

Figure 7.6 CO_2 emissions

- *Scen_4: Land productivity improvement scenario.* This scenario includes the assumption that land productivity will improve at the same rate as during 1960–2000 in addition to the assumption of Scen_1.

Scen_1 is a scenario for achieving a low-carbon society, Scen_2 and Scen_3 are scenarios for achieving a resource-circulating society and Scen_4 is a scenario for achieving a nature-harmonious society.

7-4-3 Simulation results

Figure 7.6 presents the CO_2 emission trajectories for Scen_0 and Scen_1. In Scen_0, CO_2 emissions will increase. In contrast, in Scen_1 emissions will decrease after 2010, and the CO_2 emissions in 2050 will be half the present emissions level.

In the previous section, resource productivity is a more suitable index for assessing the resource-circulating society. However, because of the lack of information, material production is an index representing the achievement of a resource-circulating society. Figure 7.7 presents trends in steel production. It shows that production will decrease compared to Scen_0 through the introduction of twice the capital stock lifetime. In contrast, steel production will increase continuously because of economic growth, especially in developing countries. Steel is used not only as building material but also in vehicles and machinery. In order to achieve a resource-circulating society, other countermeasures such as utilization of waste scrap are required when we maintain economic growth.

Figure 7.8 presents trends for paper products. In this scenario, the speed of paper production will decrease, but the volume of production

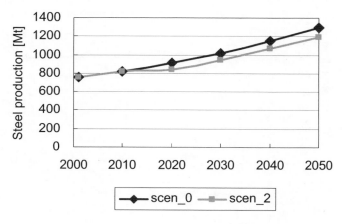

Figure 7.7 Steel production

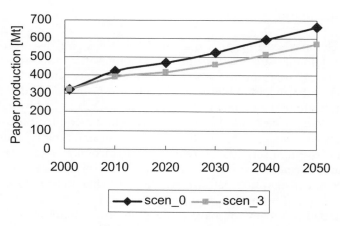

Figure 7.8 Paper production

will continue to increase. Since not only the household sector but also production sectors consume paper, countermeasures for production sectors will have to be considered. Waste-paper recycling will also be a countermeasure for decreasing natural material input.

Forest areas are used to assess the nature-harmonious society. As shown in Figure 7.9, the forest area in Scen_0 will be flat up to 2050. In contrast, in Scen_4 the area increases because improvement in agricultural land productivity will help to recover forest area.

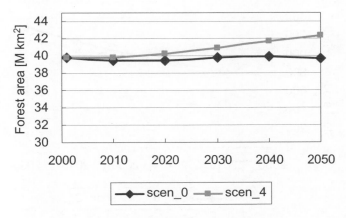

Figure 7.9 Changes in forest area

7-5 Conclusion

In this chapter, existing environmental scenarios are discussed, and a global sustainable society from the standpoints of a low-carbon society, material-circulating society and nature-harmonious society is assessed using the global computable general equilibrium model. The simulation results indicate that a sustainable society will not be created by extensions of past trends. If past trends continue, we will experience unsustainable conditions such as increased CO_2 emissions, increased material input and reduced ecosystem services. To realize a low-carbon, resource-circulating and nature-harmonious society, efficiency must be improved drastically. In addition, consumption patterns will have to change to reduce demand for materials and promote long-term use.

Developed countries will have to develop new technologies to achieve the goals of a sustainable society. However, developing countries will not follow the conventional development paths but will use new development paths to achieve a sustainable society more efficiently. Cooperation among all countries is an essential condition for achieving a sustainable world.

REFERENCES

Alcamo, Joseph (2001) "Scenarios as Tools for International Environmental Assessments", Environmental Issue Report No. 24, available at www.eea.europa.eu/publications/environmental_issue_report_2001_24.

Central Environment Council (2007) "Becoming a Leading Environmental Nation Strategy in the 21st Century: Japan's Strategy for a Sustainable Society", available at www.env.go.jp/en/focus/070606.html.

IPCC (2000) *Emissions Scenarios.* Cambridge: Cambridge University Press.

IPCC (2007) *Climate Change 2007.* Cambridge: Cambridge University Press.

Japan LCS 2050 Scenario Team (2008) "Japan Scenarios and Actions towards Low-carbon Societies (LCSs)", available at http://2050.nies.go.jp/material/2050_LCS_Scenarios_Actions_English_080715.pdf.

Millennium Ecosystem Assessment (2005) *Ecosystems and Human Well-being: Scenarios.* Washington, DC: Island Press.

Minister of the Environment (2009) "Vision for 80% Reduction of Greenhouse Gas Emissions in 2050", available at www.env.go.jp/earth/info/80vision/vision.pdf.

Ministry of the Environment (2007) "Very Long-term Vision", available at www.env.go.jp/policy/info/ult_vision/ (in Japanese).

Miyagawa, Tadao (1994) *Foundations of Policy Sciences.* Tokyo: Toyo Keizai, pp. 216–224.

Morita, Tsuneyuki and John Robinson (2001) "Greenhouse Gas Emission Mitigation Scenarios and Implications", in IPCC Working Group III *Climate Change 2001: Mitigation.* Cambridge: Cambridge University Press, pp. 115–166.

Nakicenovic, Nebojsa and Rob Swart (eds) (2000) *Emissions Scenarios.* Cambridge: Cambridge University Press.

OECD (2008) *OECD Environmental Outlook to 2030.* Paris: OECD.

United Nations (2007) *World Population Prospects: The 2006 Revision.* New York: United Nations Department of Economic and Social Affairs, Population Division.

United Nations (2008) *Statistical Yearbook 2006: Fifty-first Issue.* New York: United Nations Department of Economic and Social Affairs.

United Nations (2009) "Millennium Development Goals", available at www.un.org/millenniumgoals/.

UNEP (2007) "Global Environment Outlook 4", available at www.unep.org/geo/geo4/media/.

World Commission on Environment and Development (1987) *Our Common Future.* Oxford: Oxford University Press, available at www.un-documents.net/wced-ocf.htm, pp. 43–66.

8

Future vision towards a sustainable society

Akimasa Sumi

8-1 Historical background

We do not live alone. We exist in a stream of life from the past to the future. The human race was born and has evolved on Earth, and Earth, in turn, has evolved from the universe (Nakano, 1994: 107). Therefore, we have to regard ourselves as historical entities and remember that we are responsible for the future. It is always important to study the past when we learn new things.

When we survey the environment in its entirety, numerous issues surround us and the solutions seem few and far between. In such difficult situations, it is easy to be captured in a "trap of pessimism". Pessimism itself is not entirely bad because when we look upon the future as a challenge, we pay more attention to the risks involved. However, the drawback of pessimism is losing motivation to overcome these issues. We should remember that we have suffered many troubles through the entire history of the human race. In other words, there has been no easy time for human beings, and we have learnt to fight for survival. We have strengthened our knowledge during this fight. Science and technology are examples of this accumulated knowledge. Using information accrued from scientific experimentation and thought and applying technology, we have solved many problems; as a result, many people in developed countries are now leading comfortable lives. However, it should be remembered that difficulties are co-evolving with the development of our society. Our present situation is different from that in the past. Although

Climate change and global sustainability: A holistic approach, Sumi, Mimura and Masui (eds), United Nations University Press, 2011, ISBN 978-92-808-1181-0

new technologies have solved many existing issues, some have also created new problems. For example, mobile phones have improved our lifestyle but brought with them a new type of crime. Therefore, we are constantly confronted with new issues.

Since the Industrial Revolution, mankind has been seeking wealth and prosperity by making maximum use of energy and natural resources. Nature was believed to have an infinite capacity to process waste energy and resources. It was thought that whatever the burden, nature would renew and repair all our actions; and while the human activity domain remained small, this was indeed true. However, we have learned that proper disposal of waste matter is a necessity. As the activity domain of mankind has expanded, the limits of nature and possible growth have surfaced (Meadows, et al., 1972: 212).

Today, we are trying to achieve well-being under various constraints imposed by current situations. Since it is obvious that energy and natural resources are limited and the capacity of our environment is finite, the main constraint at present is to limit the use of energy, materials and the environment.

8-2 Restructuring the system of our society

There is no doubt that we have to reduce GHG emissions in order to stabilize the behaviour of the Earth's climate system. To achieve this task and realize a low-carbon society, mitigation and adaptation options should be well mixed. Mitigation potential to reduce CO_2 emissions, which represents amounts of reduction of CO_2 emissions, was summarized by the IPCC (2007) and is shown in Figure 8.1.

It has been clearly demonstrated that the potential to mitigate greenhouse gas emission remains in many sectors. In particular, construction, transport and energy supply have large potential, especially at lower carbon prices, which means that many options are possible at a relatively low cost. In buildings, for example, high thermal insulation and longer lifetime contribute to reduction of CO_2 emission, which may contribute to improvement of our quality of life. In the transport sector, various new technologies are proposed, including solar and fuel-cell vehicles. However, advancement in automobile engineering itself is not sufficient for reduction of CO_2. If numbers of vehicles increase dramatically, total amounts of CO_2 emission will increase. Therefore, it is also necessary to address the design of transport systems and ensure that the social system and people's lifestyles are consistent with this design.

In this book we insist that a low-carbon society is not enough for a sustainable society, and three societies should be integrated (see Chapter

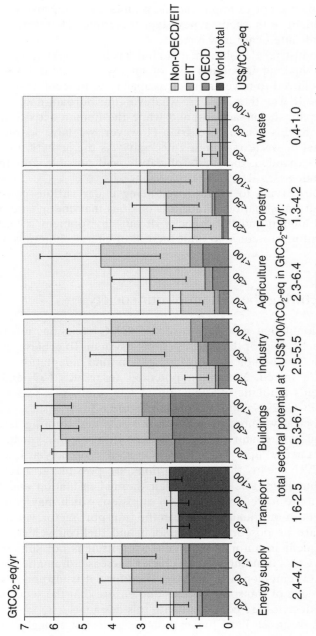

Figure 8.1 Estimated economic mitigation potential by sector in 2030 from bottom-up studies, compared to the respective baselines assumed in sector assessments

Note: The potentials do not include non-technical options such as lifestyle changes.

7). Mitigation potential as described above should be reviewed from this viewpoint. If action for mitigation in each sector is taken in an unorganized way, in other words if each action is conducted independently, it does not work very well. Action should be conducted under a clearly defined concept in a systematic way.

When we look at the high mitigation potential sectors, such as construction, transport and energy, we find these are strongly related to regional development. Regional development is still a key issue in developing countries, and it is necessary to find a pathway for how these countries can reach a developed state in a sustainable way. Within issues relating to regional development, "sustainable cities" and "megacities" are among the most urgent and important. It has been predicted that in 2030 60 per cent of the world population will live in cities (United Nations, 2005). Many people will migrate to cities from rural areas, partly because of rural poverty. Cities are growing. You can easily imagine the future status of a city when it expands in an unorganized way. Hence it is critical to design the growing city from the sustainability point of view.

When we discuss issues relating to cities, we tend to focus only on city regions. However, a city is not independent from other regions. For example, a city needs energy, food and fresh water, and discharges waste. Regarding mitigation potential, we should note that the agricultural and forestry sectors also have a considerable amount of potential for CO_2 reduction, and should not be neglected. These sectors are strongly related to primary industry and rural areas. There is an urgent need to develop an equitable rural economy; to achieve this goal, we can reconstruct rural regions by adopting mitigation methods in these sectors through political and economic institutions. It is important to remember that urban and rural areas are closely linked, and issues should be handled in an interdisciplinary and integrated way. Cities require many natural resources, such as food, fresh air and water as well as a healthy ecosystem, most of which are produced in rural areas. So both city and rural regions should be restructured in a consistent way.

In conclusion, city and rural issues cannot be separated and should be considered within the same framework. Under the concept of "integration of three societies", harmonization between cities and villages should be pursued. This will entail restructuring our existing society.

8-3 Evaluation criteria

When the IPCC AR4 was presented to the public, one could sense a view that more attention should be paid to the adaptation strategy in addition to mitigation. In the past, adaptation has been less discussed because it

hinders us from developing a mitigation option. Although we expect the global community to continue to make efforts to reduce CO_2 emissions, it is inevitable that a warmer climate will come in the future. Consequently, we have to prepare for future climate change. Needless to say, this does not mean that mitigation is useless, but we have to use the best mix of mitigation and adaptation options.

Although it is often stressed that mitigation and adaptation strategies should be optimized, there are no general criteria concerning evaluation of optimality. Optimality and efficiency are terms used frequently in discussions of the merits of each method. Optimality should, however, be judged with respect to certain criteria or evaluation functions, which are often based on assumptions. There is no guarantee that such criteria are correct, and the process should be approached with caution. Money is not the sole criterion, although the monetary aspect cannot be neglected. New criteria with emphasis on sustainability should be used. For example, natural capital, social capital and human capital are emphasized in the recent economics. A global system, a social system and a human system are emphasized in this book. All are similar concepts. Criteria including these three aspects should be developed.

8-4 Sharing the concept of a future society

When we think about designing a sustainable society, we need to make decisions about resource allocation. As explained previously, we are surrounded by issues requiring resources, and it is impossible to satisfy all these requests. We need to select and prioritize cases and agree on resource allocation. It would be desirable for this process to be conducted with the agreement of the wider population; however, our society consists of a variety of stakeholders with differing interests and concerns. It is crucial to achieve agreement between different stakeholders and share future perspectives. If we can reach a common view about our future situation, it will be easier to agree on the best course of action. There are many ways to present the future view. Computer simulations of future climate change and its impacts to the society are one way to contribute to sharing future views, and the IPCC is an example of such an activity.

Rational methods will contribute well to an agreement in society (Sumi, 2007). In Chapter 7 of this book we proposed a new concept for future societies, described as "integration of a low-carbon society with a resource-circulating society and a nature-harmonious society". Model results are also presented. Although it is at an early stage, this research is very promising and a clear pathway to a future sustainable society will be presented by accelerating research in this track. We believe that this con-

cept will be accepted by readers and societies and contribute to realization of a sustainable society.

It is true that the pathway towards a new society is not yet clearly presented, and we have to exert all possible efforts to reach this goal. It should be remembered that the pathway is not unique: there are many pathways in the world. In this respect, evaluation criteria are very important, as explained above. In the past, much emphasis has been placed on quantitative properties such as money and material, while damage to the environment and ecosystems has been neglected. However, in the twenty-first century our evaluation criteria should be changed in favour of the happiness and well-being of people. We should remember that mankind has evolved not only in physical and socio-economic environments but also in historical and cultural environments.

REFERENCES

IPCC (2007) "Summary for Policy Makers", Climate Change 2007 Synthesis Report, available at www.ipcc.ch.

Meadows, D. H., D. L. Meadows, J. Randers and W. W. Behrens III (1972) *The Limits to Growth*. New York: Universe Books.

Nakano, Y. (1994) *Miraculous Life Chain: The Essence of Evolution from the Universe to Mankind*. Deddington: Helix Editions.

Sumi, A. (2007) "On Several Issues Regarding Efforts Toward a Sustainable Society", *Sustainability Science* 2, pp. 67–76.

United Nations (2005) *World Urbanization Prospects. The 2005 Revision*. New York: UN Population Division, Department of Economic and Social Affairs.

Index

acidification of oceans, 49, 95–96
adaptation
  adaptive capacity of each country and
    local community, depends on, 56
  biological, to changes in marine
    environments, 108
  capacity development and, 144–46
  to climate change, 78, 143, 148, 161–62,
    192, 201
  climate change, proactive, 141
  climate change, to adjust human and
    natural systems to, 133
  "climate-proofing" aid, 205
  in "climate-proofing" of basic
    infrastructure, 204
  CO_2 emissions, to decrease, 214
  coastal defences, new, 113
  to coastal disasters, 124
  to coastal flooding, 51
  coastal revetment and agricultural, 21
  coasts of developing countries, 111
  development objectives, to accomplish,
    146
  disaster, investment cost for, 73
  disaster prevention plans, 56
  effectiveness and costs are not yet clear,
    21
  efforts will not be realized for several
    decades, 55

  financing for, 204–5
  to flooding, 72–75
  for GHG emissions, 56
  to global environmental changes, 125
  global warming, measures against, 55
  global warming, of human activities to
    future, 95
  impacts of, 8
  insurance schemes and risk management,
    16
  international development cooperation
    and, 203–5
  international framework addressing, 137
  key question, 15
  for low-carbon society, 279
  measures, climate change, 4, 55, 135,
    141–42
  measures, long-term, 52, 68, 70
  measures for developing countries, 206
  mechanisms at the local scale, 73
  meteorological extreme events,
    countermeasures against current, 56
  mitigation and, 6, 9, 125, 133, 135, 137,
    142–44, 147, 282
  to mobilize resources for, 203
  multilateral mechanisms for, 204
  in natural and human systems, 137
  planning, 142, 204
  policies, creating national, 203–4

policies to mitigate certain impacts, 32
policy-making, 30, 32–36
political intentions, based on clear, 137
poor people, to supply basic goods to, 202
to population growth, 124
to prevent additional vulnerabilities and
    negative impacts, 125
process, 142
to reduce damage and countermeasure
    costs, 141
research resources, few, 26–27
risk communication for public opinion
    formation and motivation, 36–41
river water quality, 82
to sea-level rise, 124–25
by sector, 138–40
sedimentation disasters, 75–77
snow-water resources, 77–80
social structure, contributes to
    establishment of new, 8
society must promote policies and
    technologies adapted to warmer world,
    13
Stern Review, 201–2
strategies, 21–22, 137–42, 204, 281–82
sustainability, 146–47
sustainable development, 56–57, 125, 131,
    146–47
targets, short-term and mid- to long-term,
    143
technologies, 11, 15
water quality problems, 80–82
water-treatment plants, 82
"wise adaptation," guidelines for, 147
Adaptation Fund, 204
aerosols, 13, 15, 17, 23
afforestation, 133, 135, 143
Africa
    development assistance, 204
    floods and droughts in, 46
    food shortage in, 200
    food trade and population growth, 50
    malaria, range and transmission potential
        of, 52
    population increase, 113
    social infrastructure, 56
    submergence areas, 117
    submergence population, 118
    water resources, decrease in, 47
AGCM. See Atmospheric General Circular
    Model (AGCM)

agriculture
    in Asia, 92–94
    climate change and acute malnutrition,
        194
    CO_2 fertilizing effect enhances plant
        productivity, 54
    cold stress, less, 38
    farm practices, change in, 141
    global food production potential of, 50
    in Latin America, 86, 91–94
    planting times and crop types, changing,
        33
    productivity, reduced, 194
    rice yields in Japan, 59, 68
    simulations of impact areas, 34–35
    in sub-Saharan Africa, 86, 92–94
    temperature rise, sensitive to low, 54
    in the West, 91, 93–94
    in West Africa, 92, 94
AIM/Impact [Policy], 60–61
Aleutian Low Pressure Index (ALPI), 97
ALPI. See Aleutian Low Pressure Index
    (ALPI)
Amazon, 7, 49, 117, 200
Andean inter-tropical glaciers, 47
Antarctic ice sheet, 39, 51, 55
anthropogenic
    climate change, 34
    CO_2 concentrations, photosynthetic, 95,
        97
    CO_2 emission, 95–96
    GHG emissions, increase in, 15, 21
    socio-economic activities and GHG, 8, 15
aoko (algal bloom), 251
aquifer recharge, 263
AR4. See Fourth Assessment Report (AR4)
    [IPCC]
Arctic, 54
Arctic Ocean sea ice, 7, 46
Asia
    cereal production, 85–86
    cereal yield and nitrogen fertilizer input,
        87
    floods and droughts in, 46
    food supply, 92–94
    food trade and population growth, 50
    meat production, 87–88
    mega-deltas, 51, 54, 113
    population of, 84, 113
    submergence areas, 117–18
    submergence population, 118

Aso, Prime Minister Taro, 235
astronomical tides, 112–14, 117
Atmospheric General Circular Model
(AGCM), 72–73
Australia, 46, 93, 117, 182, 213

Bangladesh, 51, 56, 93–94, 117, 119, 122–24
BaU. *See* business as usual (BaU)
biochemical oxygen demand (BOD), 80–82
biofuels, 179–85
Bioscleave house, 256
Bolivia, 47
boreal forests, 49
Borneo, 117
Buddhism, Sohto-Zen, 242, 245
business as usual (BaU)
climate change cost and reduced
consumption per head, 198
climate change estimated cost *vs.*
reduction in consumption per head,
199
climate change on, cost of, 198
climate change on the business, cost of,
198
conditions, GHG emissions, 61
flood damage cost, maximum, 65
flooded areas, nationwide, 62
forests, impact on, 67–68
GHG emissions, 144, 157
GHG emission scenarios, future, 262
global emissions, deviation from baseline
and climate change stabilization
scenarios, 157
global emissions of developing and
developed countries, 156–57
heat stress (heatstroke) mortality, cost of
damage from, 69–70
heat stress mortality risk, 69
low-carbon technologies and changes in
land use, 198
rice yields, impact on, 68
sandy beach loss from sea level rise, cost
of, 68
sea-level rises by the 2090s, 64–65
sectoral impacts in Japan, 62
slope failure, 65, 67
social costs of carbon, 199–200
storm-surge flooding in Japan, 69
temperature increase of 3.8°C in 2100,
61, 197
world, 180

CAFE. *See* Corporate Average Fuel
Economy [USA] (CAFE)
carbon
circulation model, 23
cycle, 8, 13, 15, 23, 27
emissions, 156–57, 161–62, 187
energy for goods and services, 158
footprint, 210, 256
sink, 23, 198
tax, 23, 170, 173, 175, 182, 224–25, 235,
237
trading, 182, 186, 192
carbon capture and storage (CCS)
carbon emissions trading scheme and, 187
clean-energy technologies, 178, 180
climate change research, keyword, 23
ecosystems, potential adverse impacts
on, 135
emission reduction, 15-20 percent, 189–90
forest management techniques and, 16
new technology, 180
technology by 2050, 189
technology is not a silver bullet, 191
carbon dioxide (CO$_2$)
agricultural and forestry sectors, 281
atmospheric, desirable levels of, 179
atmospheric, rate of growth of, 180
automobile engineering and, 279
buildings with high thermal insulation
and longer lifetime, 279
capture and underground storage after
2020, 189
carbon sinks for mitigation of, preserving,
202
chemical fixation of, 254
clean-energy technologies, 178
climate, causes warmer, 4
compact city reduces energy consumption
and, 210
concentration in warm season and rice
yield, 64
concentrations, photosynthetic, 95, 97
from developing countries, 202
electricity generation, 227, 229
electric power sector, 227
electric vehicles, mass-market, 186
emission, anthropogenic, 95–96
emission allocations and carbon trading
framework, 192
emission allowances, Europe imposes
stricter, 188

emission allowances and fuel-efficient cars, 188
emissions, 40 per cent reduction by reducing energy demand, 262
emissions, 70 per cent reduction with low-carbon energy, 262
emissions, 70 to 80 per cent reduction in future scenarios, 262
emissions, adaptation to decrease, 214
emissions, economic incentives for reduction, 187, 212
emissions, global community to reduce, 282
emissions, technologies to reduce, 208
emissions and CCS technologies, 189
emissions and mitigation strategies, 135, 279
emissions as threat to human well-being, 179
emissions by cities, 208–10
emissions by sector, 227–29
emission scenarios for six alternative stabilization levels, 20
emissions credits and electrical power, 232
emissions credits from overseas, 232
emissions for electricity in developing countries, 202
emissions for large UK cities, per capita, 209–10
emissions from electric power sector, 227
emissions from energy conversion, 227, 229
emissions from fossil fuels, 20
emissions in Beijing and Shanghai, 209
emissions in future low-carbon society, 208
emissions in large cities, 209–10
emissions in UK, per capita and GDP, 213–14
emissions per capita and GDP, 212–14
emissions per capita and Japanese government, 220
emissions reduced by electrification, 190
emissions reduction of 70 per cent by 2050, 262, 269
emissions target at 1990 level, METI, 208
emissions target at 1990 level, Nippon Keidanren, 218
emissions trading in Japan, 230

emissions vs. per capita GDP of various countries, 213–14
emission target for products, lower, 232
energy-derived, 218, 225–26, 231, 239
energy efficiency of machinery and electric apparatus, 230
energy-oriented, 164
Energy Supply and Demand Subcommittee [METI] and emissions until 2030, 221
equivalent concentration for GHG under BaU, 61–62
Federation of Electric Power Companies of Japan, 222
fertilization effect and enhanced plant productivity, 46, 50, 54, 64
fertilization effect and rice yield, 68
fertilizing effect enhances plant productivity, 54
final disposal wastes and, 272
future scenario models, 273–74, 276
G8 summit in L'Aquila, 262, 267
GHG concentration level stabilized and unavoidable damage, 70
GHG concentrations and equilibrium temperature increase, 61–62
GHG emissions increase from 2006 to 2007 and, 164–65
GHG emissions target in terms of, 197
goals of MDGs and indicators for goal 7, 259
Japan Low-carbon Society Scenarios and 70 per cent emissions cut, 262, 269–70
Japan's total GHG emission volume in base year, 223
Keidanren's publication about climate change policy, 222–23
Keidanren Voluntary Action Plan on the Environment, 166
Kyoto mechanisms, government's utilization of, 232
Kyoto Protocol target achievement plan, 231–32
land-use changes and release of stored CO_2 in soil, 183
in low-carbon society, 12
low-carbon society and emissions reduction, 208, 262, 269
low-carbon society and emissions stabilization, 12

carbon dioxide (CO$_2$) (cont.)
  low-carbon society *vs.* high emissions per
    capita, 213
  management, international approach to,
    189
  management practices, market-driven,
    186
  national campaign targeting lifestyles and
    societies with less CO$_2$ emissions, 231
  National Institute for Environmental
    Studies, 262
  natural reduction of, 255–56
  ocean acidification, 49
  ocean surface pH, 49
  power plant, coal-fired thermal, 227
  pricing mechanism for carbon, 187
  pricing stimulates energy efficiency and
    electrification, 191
  reduction policy enforcement on GHGs,
    197
  reduction to mitigate severe climate
    change, 212
  by sector, 165, 225, 228
  social cost of carbon, 200
  Subcommittee on Policy Methods on
    global warming, 230
  transport systems design and people's
    lifestyle, 279
  voluntary action plans by industry, 222
cars, fuel-efficient, 240
catalytic cycle, 254
CBDR. *See* common but differentiated
  responsibilities (CBDR)
CCCC. *See* Climate Change and Carrying
  Capacity Program (CCCC)
CCMF. *See* climate change mitigation
  facility (CCMF)
CCS. *See* carbon capture and storage (CCS)
CCSP. *See* Climate Change Science
  Program [USA] (CCSP)
CDM. *See* clean development mechanism
  (CDM)
Center for Global Trade Analysis, Purdue
  University, 153
cereal production/trade, 84–87, 89–90
CFC. *See* chlorofluorocarbon (CFC)
CGE. *See* computable general equilibrium
  (CGE)
CH$_4$. *See* methane (CH$_4$)
Changchiang delta, 117
Chao Phraya delta, 125–31

China
  carbon-intensive energy for goods and
    services, 158
  cereal imports from the West, 92
  climate change and forest of, 49
  CO$_2$ emissions in large cities, 210
  coal industry, 182
  drought in inland, 94
  economic growth, energy-intensive, 179
  energy efficiency country, least, 158
  environmental degradation, local, 182
  GETS, international transfers under, 159,
    161
  GHG emissions, 152
  global warming and increased food
    production, 94
  Kyoto Protocol and GETS, comparison
    between, 160
  Kyoto Protocol and no quantitative
    emissions targets, 155, 157
  meat production/supply, 88, 91
  mega-deltas and megacities of, 122
  North Pacific Marine Science
    Organization, 98
  population, flooded, 122
  population growth, 119
  soybean import, 89
  storm surges and coastal vulnerability,
    117
chlorofluorocarbon (CFC), 137, 252, 262
CIESIN, 114
clean development mechanism (CDM), 16,
  23, 136, 203
climate
  prediction, 4, 11, 23
  proofing, 144, 204–5
  scenario, 23, 61
  shocks, 178, 196
climate change
  adaptation, 78, 143, 148, 161–62, 192,
    201
  anthropogenic, 34
  coastal zones, 59
  countermeasures against, 55–56
  drought, 49
  ecosystems, 21, 49–50
  European Union (EU), 174–75
  flooding, 53, 62–67, 141
  food production, 91–94
  forests, 59, 67–68
  GHG, 8, 13, 133–34

heat stress mortality, 69–70
human health, 59–60
malnutrition, acute, 194
mass media, 232–39
media coverage of, 232
mega-deltas, 125
mitigation, 32, 185, 192
OECD, 195
policy and journalism, 232–39
policy based on scientific information,
   42
research, keyword for, 23
rice yields, 59, 68
sandy beach loss, 68
social resilience to, 147–48
storm-surge flooding, 69
sub-Saharan Africa, 51, 54
sustainable society, 28, 147
water resources, 13, 46–47, 58, 72
Climate Change and Carrying Capacity
   Program (CCCC), 98
climate change mitigation facility (CCMF),
   203
Climate Change Science Program [USA]
   (CCSP), 26
climate model
   climate change, future estimate of, 141
   climate change research, key word for, 23
   climate change risk projections,
      quantitative, 34
   ensemble mean of the outputs of, 47–48
   future projections by, 17
   global warming on marine
      biogeochemical cycling and ecosystems,
      102
   integrated assessment model and, 6
   projections, treatment of the uncertainty
      in, 35
   simulation in, 4, 8
CO$_2$. See carbon dioxide (CO$_2$)
coal
   about, 180–82, 184–85, 189
   consumption, 227
   electricity, 153
   electric power business, 227
   environmental degradation from, 179
   fired thermal power plant, 153, 165, 189,
      202, 227
   plants, average thermal efficiency for, 202
   prices, decline in, 155
   supply in Japan, 231

coastal
   erosion, 72, 111
   flooding, 51, 195
   protection facilities, 139
   protection programmes, 125
   protection scenario, 123
   zones, 46, 51, 59, 111–13
common but differentiated responsibilities
   (CBDR), 155, 162, 202
computable general equilibrium (CGE),
   153, 271, 276
Conference of Parties (COP), 6, 23, 54, 225
constant-ratio-of-elasticity-of-substitution-
   homothetic (CRESH), 153
consumer behaviour, 255
consumer's fear of change, 187
contingent valuation method (CVM), 63,
   65
"Cool Earth 50" strategy [Japan], 152
COP. See Conference of Parties (COP)
coral reefs, 49, 51, 54, 103–8, 139, 195, 264
Corporate Average Fuel Economy [USA]
   (CAFE), 188
Council for Science and Technology, 11, 24
CRESH. See constant-ratio-of-elasticity-of-
   substitution-homothetic (CRESH)
CVM. See contingent valuation method
   (CVM)

Darwin's evolutionary theory, 241
deforestation
   in the Amazon, 7
   in developing countries, curbing, 201
   GHG emissions and curbing, 201
   in sub-Saharan Africa, 86
degree heating month (DHM), 107
Department of Energy [USA] (DOE), 26
desertification/dryness, 200
DHM. See degree heating month (DHM)
dialectics, 253, 255
disaster(s)
   adaptation by infrastructure construction,
      73
   climate-related, 125, 195
   in coastal zones, 112, 124
   environmental, 31
   flood, 122
   health impacts from, 52
   Indian Ocean tsunami, 112
   landslide, 58
   natural, 46–47, 111, 137, 146

disaster(s) (cont.)
  prevention plans, 56, 58, 125, 133–34, 139,
    146–47
  risk management, 141, 144
  sedimentation, 72, 75–77
  water-related, 72
DOE. *See* Department of Energy [USA]
    (DOE)
Dohgen's case, 246–47
double stability, 242, 251–53
drought
  afforestation and forest conservation to
    stabilize water, 143
  in Asia and Africa, 46
  in Australia, 46, 93
  as barrier for sustainable development,
    49
  BOD change ratio for 10- and 50-year
    return periods of, 81
  climate change and, 49
  climate-related disasters, 195
  in developed countries, 134
  in developing countries, 133–34
  in India, 93
  in inland China, 94
  in Japan, 72
  periods, 80, 82
  risks of natural disasters, 47
  suspended solids load change, 81
  thermal stress and, 134
  water quality, 80
  water transfer during, 138
dual-function cycles, 256. *See also*
    hypercycles
dynamic disequilibrium, 252
dynamic equilibrium, 242

Earth Summit, 232, 240
eco-philosophy, 242
ecosystems
  carbon capture and storage, adverse
    affect of, 135
  climate change, 21, 49–50
  climate change and, 21, 49–50
  collapse, 195
  freshwater for humans and, 49
  GHGs, either sequester or emit, 263
  Global Ocean Ecosystem Dynamics
    (GLOBEC), 98
  global warming and, 102
  human society and, 13, 15

Millennium Ecosystem Assessment,
    262–65, 270, 277
North Pacific Ecosystem Model Used for
    Regional Oceanography, 98–102
  oceanic, 98
  research budget for, 27
  services, 3
  species movement towards poles and
    higher elevations, 46
  sustainability of human beings and, 50
  terrestrial and marine, 46
EDGAR, 271
electricity generation, 153, 222, 227, 229
electric power
  CO_2 emissions credits from overseas,
    232
  companies, 221
  industries, 223
  from nuclear energy, 227
  sector, 227
  sector and integrated carbon market,
    230
  sector and low-cost coal, 227
  sector's CO_2 emissions, 227
electric vehicles, 186, 189
emergence, 253, 255
emissions trading (ET). *See also* global
    emissions trading scheme (GETS)
  capped, 170, 175
  CO_2 pricing mechanism using a carbon,
    187
  by critical mass of nations, 189
  domestic, 173
  duty imposed on business sites by Tokyo
    government, 172, 230
  EU Emissions Trading System cap and
    carbon taxes, 173–74
  industry, strong resistance from, 217
  in Japan, 225, 230
  journalism articles on, 233, 235, 237–38
  Kyoto Protocol, 136, 153
  "policy methods" for discussions about,
    223
  Stern Review and international carbon
    price, 201
  Subcommittee on Policy Methods, 230
  voluntary domestic, 166
Energy Conservation Law. *See* Law
    Concerning the Rational Use of
    Energy (Energy Conservation Law)
energy conservation standards, 226, 235–39

energy consumption
    adaptation measures and, 143–44
    of biomass in Scramble, 184
    of buildings, 209, 211
    carbon intensity of supplied energy,
        reducing, 208
    cars to trains, shift from, 211
    car trips, long, 211
    compact city reduces, 210–11
    "Cool Biz" and "Warm Biz" campaigns,
        230
    densely populated city vs. sparsely
        populated city, 211
    in developing countries, 210
    district heating and cooling, 212
    economic growth means vigorous, 185
    economic output, high, 214
    economic output, low, 214
    electricity generation, oil refining sectors,
        229
    of electricity in Blueprints, 188
    energy conversion, CO_2 emissions from,
        227, 229
    fossil, 225
    gross regional product, per capita, 214
    in households, 209
    income, per capita, 212
    Japan Iron and Steel Federation, 222
    mitigation measures and, 144
    population density in buildings, 211
    production volume and revenue affect,
        166
    by region and primary energy by source
        in Scramble, 183
    by region in Scramble, 182
    in residential and business sectors, 164
    by sector in Blueprints, 190
    shrinking economy contributes to
        reduction in, 4
    standard of living in large Chinese cities,
        215
    urban, 214
    wealthy nations struggle to adapt, 181
energy demand in urban areas, 210
energy efficiency
    alternative energy sources, 185
    climate change encourages, 180, 188
    CO_2 pricing stimulates, meaningful, 191
    electric vehicles, mass-market, 186
    energy conservation standards for, 226
    imported fuels, high dependency on, 159

improvement, 272–73
    measures, 178
    promotion of energy conservation and
        improvement of, 166
    of supply and demand, 135
    of water treatment and distribution
        systems, 144
energy-saving home appliances, 240
Energy Supply and Demand Subcommittee,
    221
Environmental Outlook to 2030 [OECD],
    262, 277
environmental taxes (carbon tax), 217, 222,
    225, 230, 233. See also carbon, tax
ET. See emissions trading (ET)
EU. See European Union (EU)
Europe
    carbon-intensive energy for goods and
        services, 158
    CO_2 emission allowances, imposes
        stricter, 188
    emission reduction strategy changes,
        174–75
    food supply and food export, 84
    heatwave in, 46
    submergence areas, 117
    submergence population, 118
European Union (EU)
    abatement costs, marginal, 224
    biofuel, palm oil and sugar-cane for,
        183
    carbon emissions trading scheme, 187
    climate change policy, 174–75
    climate research in, 27
    development assistance pledge, 204
    emission reduction strategies in, 174–75
    Emissions Trading System cap and
        carbon taxes, 173–74
    energy demand between urban regional
        areas, 210
    energy use in 2055, 192
    GHG reduction by individual countries,
        173
    GHGs reduction by 2020, 152
    low-carbon social economy, transition
        to, 174
eutrophication, 95–97, 138, 251
extinction of wildlife species, 39

FAO. See UN Food and Agriculture
    Organization (FAO)

Federation of Electric Power Companies of
    Japan, 222
financing instrument, flexible, 203
flooded
    areas, 62, 114–19, 124 (*See also*
        submerged areas)
    population, 119–23 (*See also* submerged
        population)
floods (flooding)
    afforestation and forest conservation
        programmes, 143
    in Asia and Africa, 46
    Asian mega-deltas, 54
    in Bangladesh, 93, 123–24
    as barrier for sustainable development,
        49
    climate change, impact of, 53
    climate change adaptation measures
        against, 141
    climate-related disasters, as main driver
        of increased, 195
    coastal, increased exposure to, 195
    coastal, in low-lying areas, 51
    in coastal regions of developing countries,
        124
    countermeasures to, 75
    damage costs, 73
    economic implications of, 75
    flood defence, cost of, 73
    hazards, 47, 73
    impacts of, 62–70
    infectious diseases due to increased, 39
    levee building to prepare for, 33
    main drivers in climate-related disasters,
        195
    meteorological extreme events, 56
    people potentially affected by, 122
    regional countermeasures to protect
        against, 75
    in semi-enclosed sea areas, high risk, 59
    serious damage due to, 134
    simulations of impact areas, 34
    in South Asia, 200
    in Southeast Asia, 200
    storm-surge, in Japan's three major bays,
        59, 64, 69
    storm-surge, in western Japan, 64–65, 69
food production, world
    climate change, forecast with, 93–94
    climate change, forecast without, 91–93
food supply per person, 90–91

forest conservation, 143, 202
forest sinks, 235, 238
Fourth Assessment Report (AR4) [IPCC]
    adaptation strategy and mitigation, 281
    climate change, countermeasures against,
        55–56
    climate change, scientific evidence about,
        193
    climate change and most vulnerable
        regions, 52–54
    climate change awareness by Japanese
        public, 30
    climate change in latter part of twenty-
        first century, 72
    climate change on national, regional and
        global scales, 47
    coastal systems and low-lying areas,
        112–13
    GHG emissions, "developed" countries
        need to reduce, 172
    global warming, restructuring knowledge
        on, 16
    global warming and human activities, 1,
        162, 232
    large scale events and abrupt change,
        54–55
    research findings, measurement of
        certainty, 20
    scientific findings, mapping of, 18–19, 22
    sea level rise from deglaciation and ice
        sheet melting, 55
    social systems, research of, 22, 27
    Working Groups (WG) I–III, 17, 111–12
fuel taxes, 188
Fukuda, Prime Minister, 223

G8
    in Germany (2007), 152
    Gleneagles Summit (2005), 197, 204
    Hokkaido Toyako Summit (2008), 30–31,
        223, 232
    summit in L'Aquila, Italy (2009), 54, 194,
        262, 267
Ganges-Brahmaputra delta, 51, 54, 117
gas-electricity, 153
gas-fired power stations, 153, 189
GASR. *See* Grants-in-Aid for Scientific
    Research (GASR)
GCM. *See* general circulation model
    (GCM)
GDP. *See* gross domestic product (GDP)

GEF. *See* Global Environment Facility (GEF)
general circulation model (GCM), 61, 100, 112–13, 117–19
genetically modified organism (GMO), 16
geographic information system (GIS), 76, 126, 129
geothermal energy, 254
German Idealism, 250
GETS. *See* global emissions trading scheme (GETS)
GHG. *See* greenhouse gas (GHG)
GIS. *See* geographic information system (GIS)
glaciers, 47, 51, 54
global emissions trading scheme (GETS), 153, 157–62
Global Environmental Research Fund Strategic Research and Development Project S-5, 31
Global Environment Charter, 221–22
Global Environment Facility (GEF), 203–4
"Global Environment Outlook (GEO) 4," 262
Global Ocean Ecosystem Dynamics (GLOBEC), 98
Global Trade Analysis Project (GTAP), 153
Global Warming Prevention Headquarters [Japan], 220
GLOBEC. *See* Global Ocean Ecosystem Dynamics (GLOBEC)
GMO. *See* genetically modified organism (GMO)
Gore, US Vice-President Al, 232
GPWv3 model, 114
Grants-in-Aid for Scientific Research (GASR), 23–24
Great Barrier Reef, 49
greenhouse effect, 23
greenhouse gas (GHG)
anthropogenic, 8, 21
carbon, estimates of social cost of, 199
carbon cycle and concentration, 13
clean development mechanism (CDM), 203
climate change and, 8, 13, 133–34
climate change research, keyword for, 23
climate change risk communication, 32
climate shocks, major, 178
CO_2 equivalent concentration, 61–62
concentration constraint scenarios, 62

concentration level not affecting humans or human-survival, 267
concentrations, stabilization of, 61
concentrations and global mean temperature, 60
concentration stabilization target, 61
deforestation in developing countries, curbing, 201
Earth's climate system perturbed by human activity, 3
ecosystems either sequester or emit, 263
emission, target setting for long-term, 200
emission control policies, 61
emission reduction, international negotiations for, 261
emission reduction by 15 per cent without forest sink, 235
emission reduction goal for each country, 239
emission reduction measures in urban areas, 208
emission reduction policy mix in industrial sector, 175–76
emission reduction strategy in Europe and United States, 174–75
emissions, 6 per cent reduction target, 225–32
emissions, 50 per cent reduction by 2050, 223, 267
emissions, anthropogenic, 15
emissions, IPCC special report on future, 262
emissions, medium-term reduction level, 223
emissions, socio-economic activity and, 13
emissions from fossil-fuel-fired power stations, 164
emissions in many sectors, potential to mitigate, 279
emissions submitted by business operators nationwide, 220
emission targets for Japan in Kyoto Protocol, 217
European Union, 20 per cent reduction target, 152
global temperature rise, 33
goal of developed countries to reduce, 262
government policies to reduce, 32
integrated assessment model, 61–70
key questions about, 15

greenhouse gas (GHG) (cont.)
Kyoto Protocol, 6 per cent reduction
target, 217–18
Kyoto Protocol, US failed to ratify, 155
Kyoto-type framework, 155
L'Aquila G8 Summit agreement, 267
management schemes *vs.* potential
damage to economic growth, 182
mitigating policies and technologies to
reduce, 13, 55
mitigation measures, evaluation of, 142
mitigation policy, 32
natural carbon cycle, 8
post–Kyoto Protocol framework, 152
reduction policies, industrial sector,
164–68, 171–74
reduction policies, Japanese corporations,
165–71
reduction target of low-carbon society,
267
reduction timings, 61
regulatory certainty and international
agreements, delays in, 186
SRES scenarios on sea-level rise, 124
stabilization scenario based on IPCC
report, 262
Stern Review, 197–301
United States, Russia, China and India,
need for meaningful action by, 157
US as largest contributor of, 155
Greenland ice sheet, 51, 55
gross domestic product (GDP)
agricultural area, estimated, 273
climate change, economic strength and
vulnerability to, 123
climate change and loss in global, 198
climate change and OECD outlook, 266
CO_2 emissions per capita, as a controlling
factor, 212–14
costs of stabilization, 199
in each country from CIESIN results,
114
emission rights by population, 158
emissions reductions and, expected
annual cost of, 198–99
global emissions trading scheme (GETS),
158–61
goals of MDGs and indicators for Goal
7, 259
land productivity changes and SRES B2
scenario, 273

LCS project, scenarios in Japan for 2050,
267
medium-term goal proposed by
government, six alternatives of, 224,
233
pollution levels plotted in relation to, 213
relative increase in flooded population
and, 123
resource-circulating society (RCS), 267
groundwater, 47, 76–77, 127, 138, 266
GTAP. *See* Global Trade Analysis Project
(GTAP)
GTAP 6, 271
GTOPO30, 114

heatwave warning systems, 33
high tides, 114, 117
Hundun (Chaos), 244–45
Hurricane Katrina, 46, 112
hurricanes, 3, 46, 120, 134, 264
hypercycles, 242, 253–54, 256. *See also*
dual-function cycles

IEA. *See* International Energy Agency
(IEA)
An Inconvenient Truth (film), 30
India, 84, 92–93, 119, 122, 152, 155–61
Indus delta, 117
Industrial Revolution, 205
insect intrusion, 49
insurance
schemes, 16, 137, 139, 141, 196
social, 196, 204
Integrated Research Systems for
Sustainability Science (IR3S), 12, 271
Intergovernmental Panel on Climate
Change (IPCC). *See also* Fourth
Assessment Report (AR4); *Special
Report on Emissions Scenarios* (SRES)
adaptation strategy and mitigation, 281
climate change, assessment reports on, 11
climate change, computer simulations of
future, 282
climate change, magnitude of global, 72
climate change and world food
production, 83, 91–94
climate change on ecosystems, 49–50
CO_2 emissions, mitigation to reduce,
279
coastal regions, vulnerability of world,
124

findings, application of, 16–22
Fourth Assessment Report, 1, 16, 30, 72,
    162, 172, 193, 232
GHG emission scenarios as business as
    usual, 262
GHG emissions in 2050, global, 267
GHG emissions reduction and developed
    countries, 172
GHG stabilization scenario, 136, 262
global society, influence on, 201
global temperature rise in next 20 years,
    33
global temperature rise over 10 years,
    average, 152, 194
global warming, negative effects of, 46
global warming, scepticism and science
    of, 36
global warming, sea-level rise from,
    129
global warming caused by human actions,
    162
keywords for extract research, 23
mapping framework for, 16, 18, 22
mass media on, Japanese reports, 232
mega-deltas and natural disasters, 125
Nobel Peace Prize, 232
policy-relevant stance, 17, 40
population in severely stressed river
    basins, 47
process with structured knowledge, 7
report, executive summary of, 83
runoff, mean change of annual, 48
scientific findings, 19–22
scientific research and relevant policy,
    17, 40
sea level, very large rise in, 55
sea-level rise rate and rate of flooded
    population, 119
surface warming, projected global from,
    53
vulnerable areas, 54
weather events, increased extreme, 195
Working Group II report, 111–13
International Energy Agency (IEA), 210,
    216, 271
inundation, 125–31, 139
IPCC. *See* Intergovernmental Panel on
    Climate Change (IPCC)
IR3S. *See* Integrated Research Systems for
    Sustainability Science (IR3S)
Irrawaddy delta, 117

Japan
    Agency for Natural Resources and
        Energy, 220, 232, 240
    Atmospheric General Circular Model
        (AGCM), 72–73
    carbon-intensive energy for goods and
        services, 158
    climate change and, 217–18
    climate change and coastal zones, 59
    climate change and floods, 62–67
    climate change and forests, 59, 67–68
    climate change and heat stress mortality,
        69–70
    climate change and human health, 59–60
    climate change and rice yields, 59, 68
    climate change and sandy beach loss, 68
    climate change and storm-surge flooding,
        69
    climate change and water resources, 58
    climate change policy and journalism,
        232–39
    climate change policy based on scientific
        information, 42
    CO_2 emissions in large cities, per capita,
        210
    Cool Earth Partnership Program, 223
    destiny house, reversible, 256
    editorials on setting the medium-term
        goal in four leading newspapers,
        236–38
    energy supply and demand, future
        forecasts, 221
    Federation of Electric Power Companies
        of Japan, 222
    Fukuda Vision, 223
    GHG emission reduction of 6 per cent,
        225–32
    GHG emissions, chronological changes
        in, 228
    Global Environment Charter, 221–22
    Global Warming Prevention
        Headquarters, 220
    government, 255
    Industrial Structure Council, 222
    industry, 217–18, 221–23, 225, 229, 235–39
    international negotiations, 42
    Kyoto Protocol, 217–18, 220–22, 225–26,
        231–32, 238–39
    Law Concerning Promotion of Measures
        to Cope with Global Warming, 165–66,
        220

Japan (cont.)
Law Concerning the Rational Use of
Energy (Energy Conservation Law),
168–70, 220–21, 226, 230
Law on Special Measures Concerning
New Energy Use by Electric Utilities
(RPS Law), 221, 226
Law on the Promotion of New Energy
Usage (New Energy Law), 221, 226
Law Regarding the Rationalization of
Energy Use, 166
medium-term goal proposed by the
government, 224
Ministry of Economy, Trade and Industry
(METI), 217–18, 220–22, 225–27
Ministry of the Environment (MOE),
217–18, 221, 225, 227, 230–31
Nippon Keidanren (Japan Business
Federation), 217–18, 221, 223
political decision making, three-way
conflict, 218–25
Project for Comprehensive Projection of
Climate Change Impacts, 60–62
public awareness of climate change, 30
rain and flooding, increased, 72–73
research programmes, governmental,
22–26
sedimentation disasters, 75–77
strategic environmental assessment
system, 227
sustainable projects, 255
Japan Federation of Basic Industry
Workers' Unions, 223
Japan Low-carbon Society Scenarios (LCS),
262
JI. *See* Joint symposium (JI)
Joint symposium (JI), 23

K-1 Model Developers, 101, 104, 109
Keidanren's publication on climate change
policy, 222–23
Keidanren Voluntary Action Plan on the
Environment, 166
Kiribati, 56, 122
Kyoto Protocol
Adaptation Fund, 204
Annex I countries emissions reduced by
40 per cent below the 1990 levels, 157
base year of 1990, 164
cap-and-trade systems as alternative to,
157

carbon trading framework, international,
192
China and India lack emission targets,
155
clean development mechanism (CDM),
136, 187
climate change and Japan, 217–18,
220–22, 225–26, 231–32, 238–39
climate change research, keywords for, 23
costs imposed on countries, 155
developed countries, mitigation and
adaptation by, 206
developed countries and shift to low-
carbon energy, 203
developing countries, no emission
mitigation obligations, 155, 162
emission permits from foreign countries,
Japan's purchase of, 173
emissions trading, 136
European Union, 8 per cent reduction
obligation, 173
expiry in 2012, 187, 192
GETS *vs.*, 160
GHG reduction, international framework
for, 125
global framework after 2013, 152
industrialized countries, emission
mitigation obligations for, 155
Japan's plan to achieve protocol target,
165, 172
joint implementation, 136
mechanisms, 23, 218, 225, 232, 235
mitigation and adaptation, international
framework for, 137
negotiations about future action, 6
reduction obligations on countries, 173
reduction rates expected, 225
reduction target of 6.0 per cent, 165,
217–18
target achievement plan, 231–32
United States has not ratified the
protocol, 155, 174

land subsidence, 125–31, 138
Latin America, 84–87, 91–93
Law Concerning Promotion of Measures
to Cope with Global Warming, 165–66,
220
Law Concerning the Rational Use of
Energy (Energy Conservation Law),
168–70, 220–21, 226, 230

Law on Special Measures Concerning New Energy Use by Electric Utilities (RPS Law), 221, 226
Law on the Promotion of New Energy Usage (New Energy Law), 221, 226
Law Regarding the Rationalization of Energy Use [Japan], 166
LCS. *See* low-carbon society (LCS)
Least Developed Country Fund [UNFCCC], 204
load-quality (L-Q), 80
low-carbon society (LCS)
   CO_2 emissions per capita *vs.,* 213
   CO_2 emissions reduction, 208, 262, 269
   CO_2 stabilized at non-dangerous level, 12
   energy-saving technologies and social changes, 209
   Fukuda Vision, 223
   GHG emissions, reduction of global, 267
   government focus on, 239
   high carbon society *vs.,* 200
   integrated with resource-circulating and nature-harmonious society, 57
   key question, 15
   Mainichi Shimbun newspaper, 236
   mitigation and adaptation options, 279
   mitigation measure, 135
   model city planning for, 223
   national scenarios for, 262
   natural and social systems, balance between, 4
   with resource-circulating society and nature-harmonious society, 259, 261, 267, 271, 276, 282
   scenarios in Japan for 2050 under the LCS project, 267
   sustainable society, 259–61, 267, 270–71, 276, 279, 282
   technological capabilities, high, 235
   Yomiuri Shimbun newspaper, 237
low-carbon technology, 203, 237
L-Q. *See* load-quality (L-Q)

major economic forum (MEF), 267. *See also* G8
Maldives, 51, 122–24
mangroves, 49, 51, 105, 141, 143, 264
marine biogeochemical cycling, 102
marine environments, 95–97, 108

mass media
   exaggerations seen in, 30
   Japanese, 232–39
   national awareness of global environmental issues, 217
MDG. *See* Millennium Development Goal (MDG)
meat
   production, 87–89, 91
   supply, 90–91
   trade, 89
Mediterranean Basin, 47
Meeting of Parties (MOP), 6
MEF. *See* major economic forum (MEF)
mega-delta regions, 125–26
mega-deltas, 51, 54, 113, 122, 125–26
Mekong delta, 51, 117, 125
methane (CH_4), 39, 198, 225
METI. *See* Ministry of Economy, Trade and Industry [Japan] (METI)
Millennium Development Goal (MDG), 202, 204, 258–59, 277
Millennium Development Goals (MDGs), 202, 258, 277
Millennium Ecosystem Assessment, 262–65, 270, 277
Ministry of Economy, Trade and Industry [Japan] (METI), 25, 217–18, 220–22, 225–27
Ministry of Land, Infrastructure, Transport and Tourism [Japan] (MLIT), 25, 63, 73, 75
Ministry of the Environment [Japan] (MOE)
   budget and research on climate change, 25
   climate change and political conflicts, 217
   "Cool Biz" and "Warm Biz" campaigns, 231
   emissions trading, 225
   energy-related laws, 221
   environmental impact assessment for coal-fired thermal power plant, 227
   environmental policy and commitments to Kyoto Protocol, 218
   environmental taxes, 230
   Global Environmental Research Fund Strategic Research and Development Project S-5, 31
   political decision making, three-way conflict, 217

Ministry of the Environment [Japan] (MOE) (cont.)
  "Smart Adaptation to Climate Change," 43
  socio-economic activities and environment, long-term vision of, 259
  "Wise Adaptation to Climate Change" report, 148
MIROC. See Model for Interdisciplinary Research on Climate (MIROC)
MIROC3.2hires, 61
MIROC3.2 model, 101, 104, 109, 113
Mississippi delta, 112, 117
mitigation
  action and, 8
  activities, carbon, 161
  adaptation and, 6, 9, 125, 133, 135, 137, 142–44, 147, 282
  adaptation technologies and, 11, 22
  climate change, 185, 192
  GHG emissions, 197
  of global warming, 125, 133
  global warming, countermeasure to, 55, 70
  global warming, evaluating policies on, 60–61
  human society must reduce GHG emissions, 13
  international cooperation to advance, 202–3
  Japan and, 27
  long-term, 17, 22
  measures, 4, 21, 70, 201, 206
  measures to reduce GHGs, 134–35
  measures with economic incentives, 137
  new technologies and innovative social systems, 135
  obligations, quantitative emission, 155, 162
  options, 8, 19, 27, 160
  policies, 9, 15–16, 30, 32, 36–37, 42, 61, 199
  process, order of priority, 77
  research budget, 23
  resource circulating society and, 146
  strategies, 133, 135–37
  technologies, 16, 21
MLIT. See Ministry of Land, Infrastructure, Transport and Tourism [Japan] (MLIT)
Model for Interdisciplinary Research on Climate (MIROC), 61, 101, 104, 109, 113

MOE. See Ministry of the Environment [Japan] (MOE)
Monterrey Consensus, 204
MOP. See Meeting of Parties (MOP)
MRI-CGCM2 model, 113, 132

N_2O. See nitrous oxide (N_2O)
NAOTIDE model, 114
NASA. See National Aeronautics and Space Administration [USA] (NASA)
National Aeronautics and Space Administration [USA] (NASA), 26, 103, 114
National Institute for Environmental Studies [Japan], 61, 176, 262, 271
National Oceanic and Atmospheric Administration [USA] (NOAA), 26, 100, 114
National Science Foundation [USA] (NSF), 26
natural gas, 227, 231
nature-friendly society, 3
nature-harmonious society (NHS), 57, 259, 261, 267, 270–71, 274–76, 282
NEMURO. See North Pacific Ecosystem Model Used for Regional Oceanography (NEMURO)
NEMURO For Including Saury and Herring (NEMURO.FISH), 98–100
New Science, 242
NGO. See non-governmental organization (NGO)
NHS. See nature-harmonious society (NHS)
Nippon Keidanren (Japan Business Federation), 217–18, 221, 223, 240
nitrous oxide (N_2O), 225
NOAA. See National Oceanic and Atmospheric Administration [USA] (NOAA)
non-governmental organization (NGO), 223, 234–36
North America, 117–18
North Pacific Ecosystem Model Used for Regional Oceanography (NEMURO), 98–102
North Pacific Marine Science Organization (PICES), 98
NSF. See National Science Foundation [USA] (NSF)
Nuclear Non-Proliferation Treaty, 6
nuclear power, 165, 175, 218, 226–27, 231

ocean acidification, 49, 95–96
Oceania, 84, 112, 118–19, 124, 271
oceanic ecosystems, 98
ocean surface pH, 49
ocean tide model, 114
Organisation for Economic Co-operation
    and Development (OECD)
  climate change risk, 195
  coal plants, average thermal efficiency
      for, 202
  countries in temperate regions and
      biofuels, 184
  Development Assistance Committee,
      205
  environmental changes identified, future,
      266
  Japan's environmental policy, reviews of,
      230, 240
  OECD Environmental Outlook to 2030,
      262, 266, 277
  power stations, coal- and gas-fired, 189
Organization of the Petroleum Exporting
    Countries (OPEC), 181, 189

Pacific Decadal Oscillation (PDO),
    100–101
Pathum Thani, 126, 128, 130
PDO. See Pacific Decadal Oscillation
    (PDO)
permafrost, 39, 46
Peru, 47
petroleum dependency, 231
phenomenology, 241, 245–46
photovoltaic cells, 209
photovoltaic power generation, 226–27, 237,
    239
PICES. See North Pacific Marine Science
    Organization (PICES)
PICES/GLOBEC CCCC, 98
population, world, 84
populations affected by, 64–65
population growth and, 125
post-Kyoto Protocol, 137, 152, 174–75
poverty reduction strategy paper (PRSP),
    205
power stations, 164–65, 189, 218, 227
PPP. See purchasing power parity (PPP)
PRSP. See poverty reduction strategy paper
    (PRSP)
public transport systems, 209, 211, 215
purchasing power parity (PPP), 213, 259

RCS. See resource-circulating society (RCS)
Red River delta, 125
Research Programs by Ministries (RPM),
    23–24
resource-circulating society (RCS), 57,
    259–60, 267, 270–71, 276, 282
Rhine-Meuse-Scheldt deltas, 117
risk management, 16, 49, 52, 144–45, 204
river flooding, 54
RPM. See Research Programs by Ministries
    (RPM)
Russia, 93, 98, 155, 157–58, 271

salt marshes, 49, 51
Samut Prakan, 126, 128–31
Samut Sakhon, Bangkok, 129–31
sandy beach loss, 64
sea ice, 7, 46, 50
sea-level rise (SLR)
  Asian mega-deltas, 54
  astronomical tide, 114
  Bangladesh, 124
  beyond 2100, 52
  Chao Phraya delta, 125–26, 128–30
  civilization, effects on today's, 55
  coastal erosion, 111
  coastal flooding, 51, 124
  coastal zones risks, 51
  dual impacts of sea-level rise and land
      subsidence on inundation area, 125–31
  flooded areas, potential, 116
  general circulation model (GCM),
      projected in, 112
  GHG emission scenarios, 124
  glaciers, melting land-based, 51
  global warming, 55, 129
  Greenland and Antarctica ice sheets, 51,
      55
  human development pattern conflicts, 111
  inundation areas in coastal regions, 129
seasonal changes of ground water, 127
Sea-viewing Field-of-view Sensor [NASA],
    103
seawater, caused by thermal expansion of,
    51
seawater volume, 113
self-catalysing loop/system, 253
self-organization, 250, 253
shinshin datsuraku (shedding mind and
    body), 245
SLR. See sea-level rise (SLR)

small islands, 51, 54, 56
snow-water, 58, 72, 77–80
snow-water equivalent (SWE), 77–79
social discount rate (SDR) in the Stern
    Review, 199
social insurance, 196, 204
socio-economic progress, 202
solar power, 168, 189, 226
South America, 47, 89, 117
soybean, 88–89, 92
Special Climate Change Fund [UNFCCC],
    204
Special Report on Emissions Scenarios
    (SRES) [IPCC], 113
  A1B emissions scenario, 48, 53, 114,
      119–21
  A1FI scenarios, 53
  A2 scenario, 47, 51, 53, 114, 119–21, 124
  B1 scenario, 53, 114, 125
  B2 scenario, 53, 62, 272
  scenarios, six, 52–54, 113
  scenarios on sea-level rise, population
      and economic growth, 113, 125
  scenarios provided by CIESIN, 114
  socio-economic development scenarios,
      51
SPM. *See* summary for policy-makers
    (SPM)
SRES. *See Special Report on Emissions
    Scenarios* (SRES) [IPCC]
SRES scenarios of, 113–24
SRTM30 of NASA, 114
SS. *See* suspended solids (SS)
Stern Review, 197–202, 205
storm surges, 15, 54, 114–15, 117
Strategic Priority on Adaptation, 204
submerged areas, 112, 114, 117–18, 120, 124.
    See also flooded, area
submerged population, 118–20. *See also*
    flooded, population
sub-Saharan Africa, 51, 54, 84–87, 92–94,
    194–95
Sumatra, northeastern, 117
summary for policy-makers (SPM), 7, 17,
    19–20, 82
suspended solids (SS), 80
sustainability
  biofuels, first- and second-generation, 184
  city design for, 281
  definition of, 258–59
  environmental, 258–60

environmental countermeasures, 255
evaluation functions, 282
of human beings and ecosystems, 50
Integrated Research Systems for
    Sustainability Science (IR3S), 12, 271
integrated technological, social and
    economic approach to, 214
mapping approaches to, 11
risks to, 259
science, 10–11, 50, 98
sustainable development
  about, 258–61
  adaptation and, 56–57, 125, 131, 146
  barriers for, 49
  Basic Energy Policy Law, 221
  climate change countermeasures, 55–56
  climate change, social resilience to,
      147–48
  developing countries', 193
  drought as serious barrier for, 49
  mitigation agenda linked to, 203
  Our Common Future, 258
  principles of, MDGs, 259
sustainable society
  climate change, 28
  climate change policies and socio-
      economic policies, 147
  conventional disciplines for, linking and
      integrating, 10
  environmental and social targets, 265
  environmental problems, 258–61
  GHG emissions reduction of 50 per cent
      by 2050, 267
  low carbon and resilient society, 147–48
  low-carbon society (LCS), 57, 259–61,
      267, 270–71, 276, 279, 282
  nature-harmonious society (NHS), 57,
      259, 261, 267, 270–71, 276, 282
  resource-circulating society (RCS), 57,
      259–60, 267, 270–71, 276, 282
  scenarios, forward-looking, 265
  systems, global-social-human, 2–3, 9
  targets for achieving, 267–70
SWE. *See* snow-water equivalent (SWE)
symbiosis, 254

Taoism, 242–43
ten no michi (the way of heaven), 242
tides, astronomical, 112–14, 117
TOPEX/POSEIDON, 114, 132
transcending oneself, 247–50

tsunamis, 3, 111–12
tundra forests, Siberian and Canadian, 49
Tuvalu, 51, 56, 122
typhoon, 3, 64–65, 69, 112

UN Food and Agriculture Organization
    (FAO), 271, 273
UN Framework Convention on Climate
    Change (UNFCCC), 6, 23, 155, 203–6
United Kingdom
    CO_2 emissions for large cities, per capita,
        209–10
    CO_2 emissions in relation to GDP, per
        capita, 213–14
    flood defence in, spending on, 205
    Stern Review, 197–201
United States, 155
    abatement costs, marginal, 224
    carbon-intensive energy for goods and
        services, 158
    climate and related environmental
        change research on, 26–27
    climate change, media coverage of, 232
    climate systems and climate projection,
        27
    CO_2 pricing mechanism, 187
    coal plants, 182
    economic growth, fearful of potential
        damage to, 182
    emission reduction strategy, 174–75
    emissions trading system, EU-style, 174
    energy demand in urban areas, 210
    energy use by 2055, projected, 192
    ethanol from maize, 91
    flooded population, projected, 122
    fuel efficiency steps, 187
    GETS, 159
    GHG emission reductions for 2050, 152
    global emissions trading, 157
    global warming and Mid-West grain
        production, 93
    Hurricane Katrina and Mississippi delta,
        112
    Kyoto Protocol, has not ratified, 155,
        232
    marginal abatement costs, 224

North Pacific Marine Science
    Organization (PICES), 98
research programmes, governmental,
    26–27
soybean producer/exporter, 88–89
water resources, decrease in, 47
UN Millennium Summit, 204
US Geological Survey (USGS), 114
US Global Change Research Program
    (USGCRP), 26

value of a statistical life (VSL), 65

water quality, 47, 72, 80–82, 146, 266
water resources
    climate change and, 13, 46–47, 58, 72
    flooding and adaptation, 72–75
    freshwater and water environment, 47–49
    management, 56
    MDG goals, 259
    problems, 72
    sedimentation disasters, 75–77
    snow-water, 77–80
    sustainable development, as barrier to, 49
    temperature increase and distribution of,
        194–95
    water quality problems, 80–82
    water use and, 138
the West, 84–88, 91, 93
West Antarctic ice sheet, 55
West Asia, 84–88, 92, 94
wetlands, 49, 51, 139, 263
WG. See working group (WG)
wildfire, 49
wind power, 189, 226, 254
working group (WG), 1, 17, 111–12
world coastal zone, 113
World Commission on Environment and
    Development, 258, 277
World Conservation Strategy, 258

zenki (all processes), 247
Zen riddles, 245
Zhujiang delta, 54
zinen (nature), 242
zooplankton (ZL), 96–101

Sustainability Science:
A Multidisciplinary Approach

Edited by
Hiroshi Komiyama
Kazuhiko Takeuchi
Hideaki Shiroyama
Takashi Mino

ISBN 978-92-808-1180-3 • paper •
488pp • US$37.00

Sustainability Science
A Multidisciplinary Approach

Edited by Hiroshi Komiyama, Kazuhiko Takeuchi, Hideaki Shiroyama and Takashi Mino

Sustainability Science

Contents overview:

Sustainability science: Building a new academic discipline
Hiroshi Komiyama and Kazuhiko Takeuchi

The connections between existing sciences and sustainability science
Contributors include: Yuya Kajikawa, Hiroshi Komiyama, Riichiro Mizoguchi, Kouji Kozaki, Osamu Saito, Terukazu Kumazawa, Takanori Matsui, Takeru Hirota and Kazuhiko Takeuchi

Concepts of "sustainability" and "sustainability science"
Contributors include: Motoharu Onuki, Takashi Mino, Masaru Yarime, Kensuke Fukushi and Kazuhiko Takeuchi

Tools and methods for sustainability science
Contributors include: Hideaki Shiroyama, Hironori Kato, Mitsutsugu Hamamoto, Masahiro Matsuura, Nobuo Kurata, Hideyuki Hirakawa, Makiko Matsuo and Hirotaka Matsuda

The redefinition of existing sciences in light of sustainability science
Contributors include: Akimasa Sumi, Hiroyuki Yohikawa, Mitsuru Osaki, Gakushi Ishimura, Magan Bailey, Takamitsu Sawa, Jin Sato, Makio Takemura and Kazuhiko Takeuchi

Education
Contributors include: Mitsuhiro Nakagawa, Michinori Uwasu, Noriyuki Tanaka, Makoto Tamura, Takahide Uegaki, Hisashi Otsuji, Harumoto Gunji, Motoharu Onuki, Takashi Mino, Akihisa Mori, Michinori Kimura, Keishiro Hara, Helmut Yabar, Yoshiyuki Shimoda, Nobuyuki Tsuji and Yasuhiko Kudo

Building a global meta-network for sustainability science
Kazuhiko Takeuchi

Designing Our Future
Local Perspectives on
Bioproduction, Ecosystems
and Humanity

*Edited by Mitsuru Osaki, Ademola K.
Braimoh and Ken'ichi Nakagami*

Sustainability Science

Contents overview:

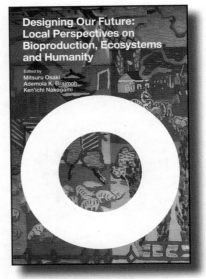

Introduction: From global to regional sustainability
Contributors include: Mitsuru Osaki and
Norihito Tambo

Sustainable land management
Contributors include: Masakazu
Komatsuzaki, Hiroyuki Ohta, Ademola K.
Braimoh, Anthony R. Chittenden, Yutaka
Saito and Makoto Ogawa

ISBN 978-92-808-1183-4 • paper •
504pp • US$39.00

How to make food, biological and water resources sustainable
Contributors include: Fumitaka Shiotsu,
Taiichiro Hattori, Shigenori Morita, Takashi
S. Kohyama, Akihiko Ito, Noriyuki Kobayashi, Masahide Kaeriyama, Michio J. Kishi,
Sei-Ichi Saitoh and Yasunori Sakurai

Regional initiatives for self-sustaining models
Contributors include: Ken'ichi Nakagami, Kazuyuki Doi, Yoshito Yuyama, Hidetsugu
Morimoto, Nobuyuki Tsuji, Toshiki Sato, Juzo Matsuda, Shiho Ishikawa, Marianne
Karpenstein-Machan, Peter Schmuck, Ryoh Nakakubo, Søren Hermansen and
B. Mohan Kumar

Self-sustaining local and regional societies
Contributors include: Yoshiki Yamagata, Florian Kraxner, Kentaro Aoki, Noriyuki
Tanaka, Kazuhiko Takeuchi, Makoto Inoue and Hiroyuki Matsuda

Bridging between sustainability and governance
Contributors include: Nobuo Kurata, Yuka Motoda, Yasuhiko Kudo, Nobuyuki Tsuji,
Hironori Kato, Hideaki Shiroyama and Seiichi Kagaya

How to sustain social, cultural and human well-being
Contributors include: Osamu Saito, Richard Bawden, Tatsuji Sawa, Koji Yamasaki,
Kiyoto Kurokawa, Takumi Kondo, Hong Park, Yoshifumi Miyazaki, Bum-Jin Park,
Juyoung Lee, Tatsuo Omura, Fumikazu Yoshida and Motoyoshi Ikeda

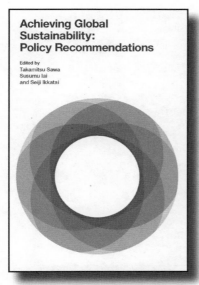

Achieving Global
Sustainability:
Policy Recommendations

Edited by
Takamitsu Sawa
Susumu Iai
and Seiji Ikkatai

Achieving Global Sustainability
Policy Recommendations

Edited by Takamitsu Sawa, Susumu Iai and Seiji Ikkatai

Sustainability Science

Contents overview:

Introduction,
Takamitsu Sawa

Global sustainability
Contributors include: Michinori Uwasu,
Kazuhiro Ueta and Takamitsu Sawa

**Paradigm shift of socio-economic
development**
Contributors include: Kazuhiro Ueta, Takashi
Ohshima and Masayuki Sato

ISBN 978-92-808-1184-1 • paper •
375pp • US$37.00

Strategies for sustainable society
Contributors include: Seiji Ikkatai, Satoshi

Konishi, Shiro Saka, Akihisa Mori, Kosuke Mizuno, Haris Gunawan and Yukari
Takamura

Adaptation for environmental change
Contributors include: Hans-Martin Füssel, Susumu Iai and Jiro Akahori

Policy recommendations towards global sustainability
Contributors include: Takamitsu Sawa, Kazuo Matsushita and Seiichiro Hasui

Establishing a Resource-Circulating Society in Asia
Challenges and Opportunities

Edited by Tohru Morioka, Keisuke Hanaki and Yuichi Moriguchi

Sustainability Science

Contents overview:

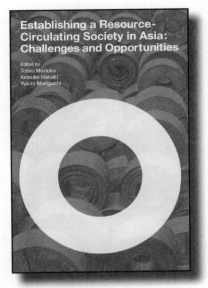

ISBN 978-92-808-1182-7 • paper •
375pp • US$37.00

Introduction: Asian perspectives of resource-circulating society – Sound material metabolism, resource efficiency and lifestyle for sustainable consumption
Tohru Morioka

The Asian approach to a resource-circulating society – Research framework, prospects and networking
Contributors include: Yasushi Umeda, Yusuke Kishita, Tohru Morioka, Terukazu Kumazawa, Takanori Matsui, Riichiro Mizoguchi, Keishiro Hara, Hiroyuki Tada, Helmut Yabar and Haiyan Zhang

Initiatives and practices for a resource-circulating society
Contributors include: Motoyuki Suzuki, Masao Takebayashi, Tsuyoshi Fujita, Rene van Berkel, Yong Geng, Xudong Chen, Kunishige Koizumi, Weisheng Zhou and Yuichi Moriguchi

Characterization and local practices of urban-rural symbiosis
Contributors include: Kazutoshi Tsuda, Toyohiko Nakakubo, Yasushi Umeda, Tohru Morioka, Mitsuru Osaki, Nobuyuki Tsuji, Toshiki Sato, Noriyuki Tanaka, Youji Nitta, Hiroyuki Ohta, Tasuku Kato, Ken'ichi Nakagami, Hironori Hamasaki, Myat Nwe Khin, Ai Hiramatsu, Yuji Hara and Keisuke Hanaki

Biotic resources utilization and technology development
Contributors include: Shinya Yokoyama, Kiyotaka Saga, Toshiaki Iida, Takashi Machimura, Akio Kobayashi, Yoshihisa Nakazawa, Keisuke Hanaki, Noboru Yoshida, Tohru Morioka and Yugo Yamamoto

Exploring opportunities for sustainable city-region design
Contributors include: Tohru Morioka, Shuji Kurimoto and Yugo Yamamoto

Conclusion: Challenges to a resource-circulating society in Asia
Tohru Morioka, Keisuke Hanaki and Yuichi Moriguchi

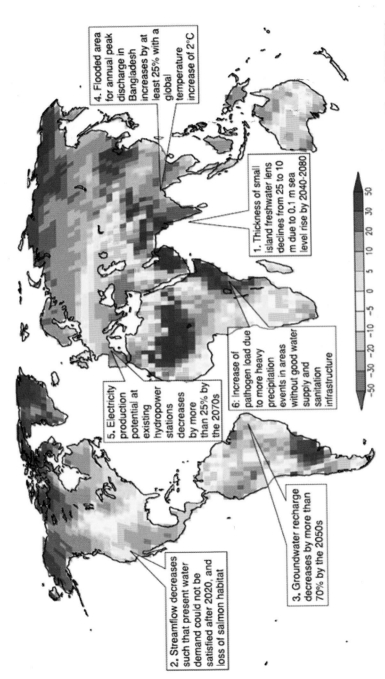

4. Flooded area for annual peak discharge in Bangladesh increases by at least 25% with a global temperature increase of 2°C

1. Thickness of small island freshwater lens declines from 25 to 10 m due to 0.1 m sea level rise by 2040-2080

6: Increase of pathogen load due to more heavy precipitation events in areas without good water supply and sanitation infrastructure

5. Electricity production potential at existing hydropower stations decreases by more than 25% by the 2070s

3. Groundwater recharge decreases by more than 70% by the 2050s

2. Streamflow decreases such that present water demand could not be satisfied after 2020, and loss of salmon habitat

-50 -30 -20 -10 -5 0 5 10 20 30 50

Figure 4.1.1 Illustrative map of combined mean change of annual runoff (%) between the present (1981–2000) and 2081–2100 for the SRES A1B emissions scenario
Source: IPCC (2007c).
Note: Please see page 48 for this figure's placement in the text.

309

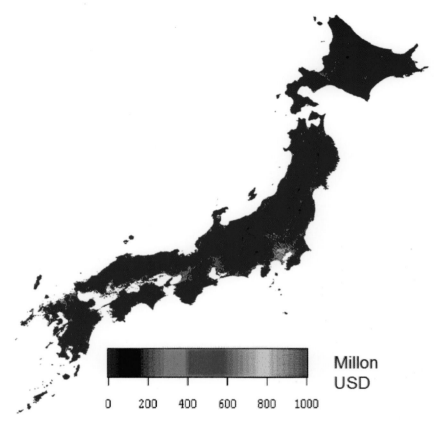

Figure 4.3.1 Distribution of increase in potential damage cost from rainfall with 50- to 100-year return periods
Note: Please see page 74 for this figure's placement in the text.

Figure 4.6.1 Storm surge deviation and potential flooded area
Notes: 1. SLR is 0.51 m. A deviation of 0~2 m is shown in orange, 2~3 m in red, 3 m and above in purple; flooded area in blue; elevation under 20 m in grey.
2. Please see pages 115 and 116 for this figure's placement in the text.

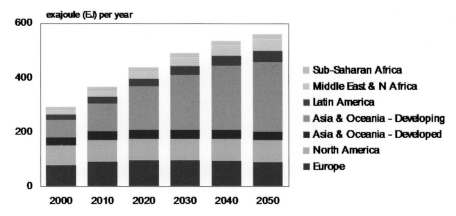

Figure 5.3.1 Final energy consumption by region in Scramble
Note: Please see page 182 for this figure's placement in the text.

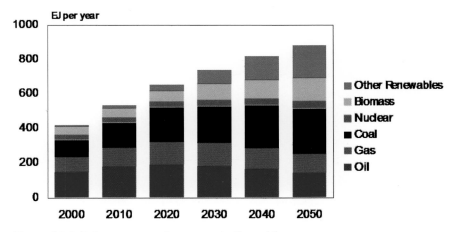

Figure 5.3.2 Primary energy by source in Scramble
Note: Please see page 183 for this figure's placement in the text.

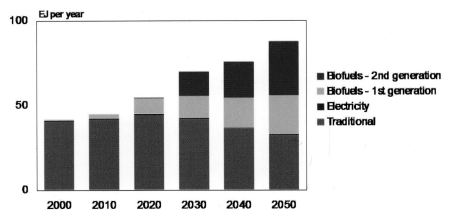

Figure 5.3.3 Final energy consumption of biomass in Scramble
Note: Please see page 184 for this figure's placement in the text.

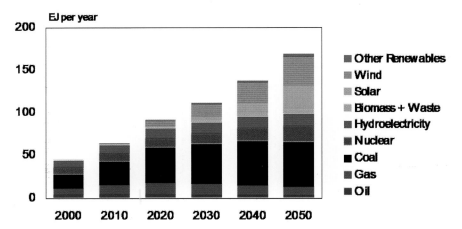

Figure 5.3.4 Final energy consumption of electricity in Blueprints
Note: Please see page 188 for this figure's placement in the text.

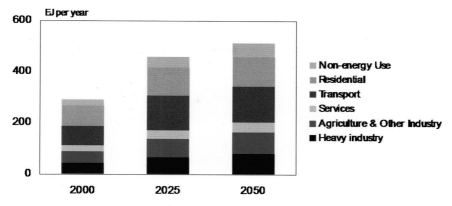

Figure 5.3.5 Final energy consumption by sector in Blueprints
Note: Please see page 190 for this figure's placement in the text.

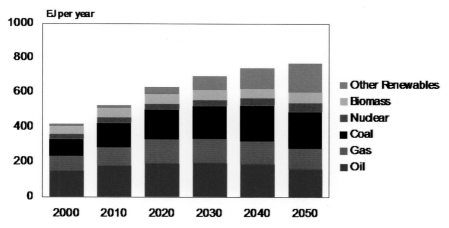

Figure 5.3.6 Primary energy by source in Blueprints
Note: Please see page 191 for this figure's placement in the text.

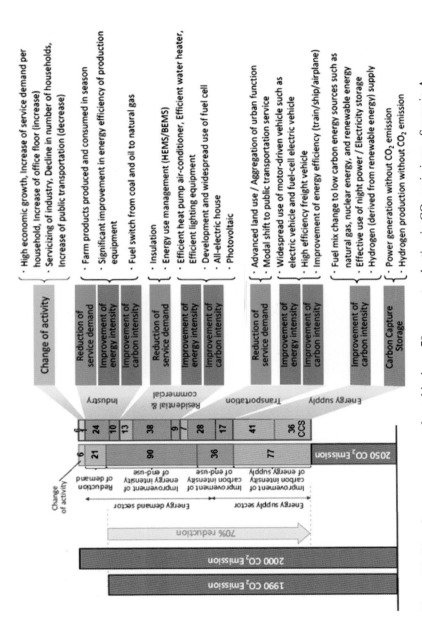

Figure 7.2 List of countermeasures for achieving a 70 per cent reduction in CO_2 emissions—Scenario A

Note: Please see page 268 for this figure's placement in the text.

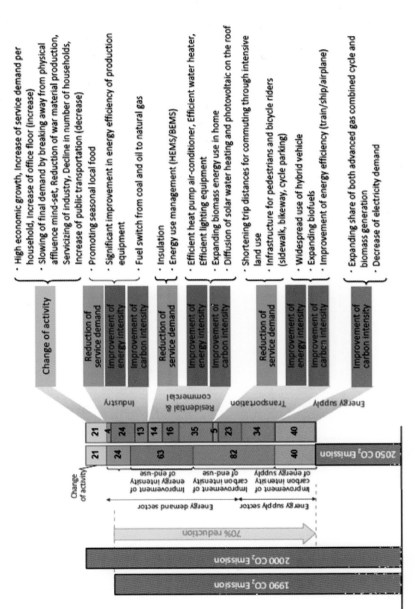

Figure 7.2 List of countermeasures for achieving a 70 per cent reduction in CO_2 emissions—Scenario B
Note: Please see page 269 for this figure's placement in the text.